LECTIONES MEMORABILES

Volume IV

*Selections from Horace,
Livy, Martial, Sallust,
and Vergil*

LECTIONES MEMORABILES

Lectiones Memorabiles, Volume I:
Selections from Catullus, Cicero, Livy, Ovid,
Propertius, Tibullus, and Vergil (2015)

Lectiones Memorabiles, Volume II:
Selections from Horace, Lucretius, Seneca,
Suetonius, and Tacitus (2015)

Lectiones Memorabiles, Volume III:
Selections from Caesar, Catullus, Horace,
Livy, Ovid, and Vergil (2018)

Lectiones Memorabiles, Volume IV:
Selections from Horace, Livy, Martial,
Sallust, and Vergil (2018)

LECTIONES MEMORABILES

Volume IV

Selections from Horace, Livy, Martial, Sallust, and Vergil

Mary Jaeger

Bolchazy-Carducci Publishers, Inc.
Mundelein, Illinois USA

Editor: Laurel Draper
Design & Layout: Adam Phillip Velez
Maps: Mapping Specialists
Cover Graphic: Frieze with acanthus leaves, from the Arch of Titus
 (© 2018 Shutterstock Images LLC)

Lectiones Memorabiles, Volume IV:
Selections from Horace, Livy, Martial, Sallust, and Vergil

Mary Jaeger

© 2018 Bolchazy-Carducci Publishers, Inc.
All rights reserved.

This work has been developed independently from and is not endorsed by the International Baccalaureate (IB).

Bolchazy-Carducci Publishers, Inc.
1570 Baskin Road
Mundelein, Illinois 60060
www.bolchazy.com

Printed in the United States of America
2018
by Seaway Printing Company, Inc.

ISBN 978-0-86516-859-6

Library of Congress Cataloging in Publication Control: 2015010471

Contents

List of Maps and Illustrations vii
Preface ix
List of Abbreviations xv

— Social Criticism —

Introduction to Social Criticism 3
Horace 5
    Introduction to Horace 5
Horace's *Epodes* 7
    Introduction to the *Epodes* 7
    Epodes 7, 16 (SL and HL) 8
Horace's *Satires* 33
    Introduction to the *Satires* 33
    Satire 1.6 (SL and HL) 34
Martial 67
    Introduction to Martial 67
    Epigrams 1.35, 41; 6.64; 10.10, 20; 12.61 (SL and HL) 68
Horace 95
    Introduction to Horace 95
    Horace's *Carmina* 96
    Carmina 1.2 (HL Only) 96
Martial 107
    Introduction to Martial 107
    Epigrams 11.6, 32, 56, 98 (HL Only) 108

— Villains —

Introduction to Villains	125
Vergil	127
Introduction to Vergil	127
Introduction to the *Aeneid*	129
Aeneid 10.689–768 (SL and HL)	132
Livy	153
Introduction to Livy	153
Introduction to *Ab Urbe Condita* 1.57–60	155
Ab Urbe Condita 1.57–60 (SL and HL)	156
Sallust	185
Introduction to Sallust	185
Introduction to *Bellum Catilinae*	187
Bellum Catilinae 1–9 (SL and HL)	188
Livy	229
Introduction to Livy	229
Introduction to *Ab Urbe Condita* 3.44–48	231
Ab Urbe Condita 3.44–48 (HL Only)	232

— ⚜ —

Appendix 1: Historical Timeline	271
Appendix 2: Meter	275
Appendix 3: Glossary of Rhetorical Terms, Figures of Speech, and Metrical Devices	279
Appendix 4: Family Tree of the Tarquins	283
Commentaries for Further Reading	285
Latin-to-English Glossary	287

List of Maps and Illustrations

— Maps —

The Mediterranean. xi
Italy and Sicily. xii
City of Rome xiii
Roman Forum and Capitol. xiv

— Illustrations —

Fresco from the House of Julia Felix. 1
Scenes from the life of Romulus and Remus. 13
Murder of Remus. 19
Mosaic of Orpheus. 23
Mosaic of Theater Scene 53
Apollo with cithara. 63
Relief of a lictor. 83
Thalia. 87
Temple of Vesta. 99
Aeneas and Mezentius 123
Iris and Turnus 133
Shepherd identified as Paris 137
Mosaic of a lion 141
Cloaca Maxima. 157
The Tragedy of Lucretia. 175
The Furies 181

Virtus 191
Achilles Discovered among the Daughters of Lycomedes 195
Cicero Accuses Catiline 207
Sulla 211
Aeneas treated by Iapyx 213
Tarquinius Superbus and the Cumaean Sibyl 219
The trial of Verginia 241
Wedding scene from a sarcophagus 245
Death of Virginia 270

Preface

This volume aims to help students who are preparing for the International Baccalaureate Latin exam as well as other intermediate students—in college as well as in high school—who would like to study a thematically coherent set of Latin passages. In addition to the texts of the passages on the IB syllabus, it contains general introductions to the authors and their works, more specific introductions to sections of text, commentary, vocabulary, a metrical appendix, and a glossary of rhetorical figures and literary terms, as well as maps and a timeline of major events. I have kept ambitious IB high school students in mind throughout the production of this reader, although I hope their teachers will learn from it as well. References to James B. Allen and J. H. Greenough's *New Latin Grammar* (in the public domain) and *The Oxford Latin Dictionary* provide for fuller exploration of matters of syntax and usage than is within the scope of this reader.

Selections from five authors (Sallust, Horace, Livy, Vergil, and Martial) appear in this volume. Sallust and Livy represent history writing, Horace and Vergil the genres of satire, lyric, and epic, all from the tumultuous two and a half decades after the assassination of Julius Caesar (44 BCE); Martial's epigrams and other short poems come from late in the first century CE, when one-man rule had become the norm.

Given the nature of ancient Roman society it is almost inevitable that all our authors are male and connected to the world of wealth and privilege. Sallust's career was mixed: He was kicked out of the Senate at one point, at one point aided by Julius Caesar; and after Caesar's assassination he retired from public life—bitterly, it appears from his own comments. We have no knowledge that Livy ever held any kind of public office or served in the military; but his writing brought him fame and he may have had some contact with Augustus. Of the three poets, we know only that Horace served as a military tribune; but all of them enjoyed support in the most exclusive circles of their time: Vergil and Horace, that of Augustus's friend Maecenas; Martial, that of the emperor Domitian himself. Even though Horace claims to live a simple life, and Martial's poems at times reflect the underbelly of Roman society, all five men were well off enough to live the lives of scholars and writers. Such a life required the leisure afforded by a complex society, one that, we should never forget, exploited the labor of slaves. All of these writers are interested in hierarchy, whether the cosmic hierarchy of gods, humans, and animals, or the social graduation from slave to ex-slave to the highest aristocrat.

Each of these writers, moreover, focused his formidable literary talent on the city Rome, its foundation and history, its greatness and its problems; each created an image of the city as a backdrop and setting, and each made Romans—a rich variety of them, from kings to poor peddlers—the object of commentary and criticism. Horace's *Epodes* 7 and 16 reflect clearly the chaos and violence of the civil wars after Julius Caesar's assassination. The selection from *Satires* 1.6 demonstrates the poet's humorous self-depreciation as well as his keen eye for snobbery in a period of social disruption. Martial's short poems poke fun at pretenders of all types: those who flatter the rich, or think themselves sophisticated, or pretend to be philosophers, or think their own poetry is good.

The villains portrayed here both arise from and explain their times. Sallust represents Catiline as the product of a Rome corrupted by wealth and greed; as leader of a conspiracy to bring down the state, Catiline appeals to the dissolute and desperate. Livy explains historical processes in terms of individuals and their behavior: Sextus Tarquinius and Appius Claudius are driven to crime by desire for a woman. These women's bodies become symbolic of the body politic and their deaths bring political revolution. Vergil's Mezentius embodies conflicted feelings about Rome's past. On the one hand, the Etruscans had, according to tradition, seen to the draining of the forum valley and the construction of the great temple of Jupiter on the Capitoline. (Indeed, Maecenas, patron of Vergil and Horace, was of Etruscan descent.) On the other hand, the last Etruscan king turned into a tyrant and his expulsion was the charter myth for Roman republicanism. A despiser of the gods, and thus the antithesis of *pius* Aeneas (and by extension of the values promoted by Augustus), Mezentius must be destroyed; but he dies trying to avenge his son's death and, unlike Livy's villains, gains some sympathy in the end.

I should like to thank Bolchazy-Carducci Publishers for entrusting me with this volume, and Laurel Draper for her editorial help and patience. Any errors or omissions are my own. For what is worthy in it I owe a debt to the many Latinists who have taught me, both in person and in print, and especially to Patricia Freiert and Will Freiert, who taught me first.

The Mediterranean

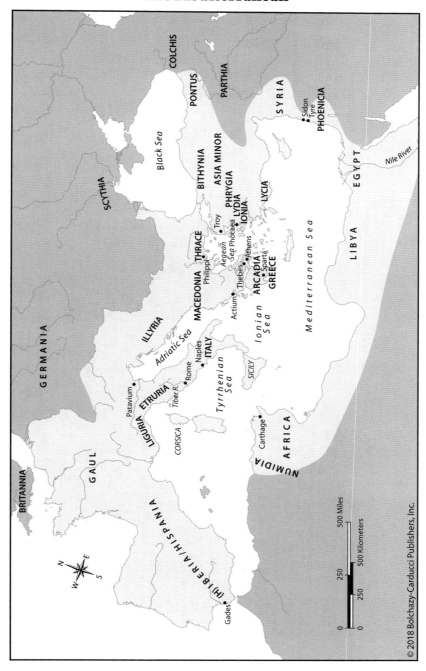

— Italy —

Rome

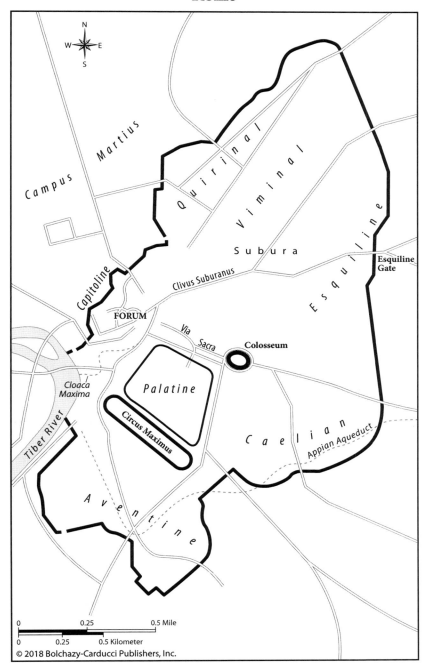

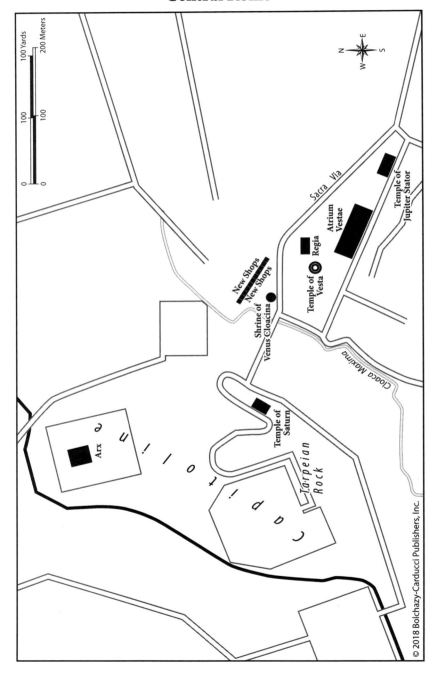

— Central Rome —

Abbreviations

(1) = first conjugation
A&G = Allen and Greenough
abl. = ablative
abl. abs. = ablative absolute
abs. = absolute
adj. = adjective
adv. = adverb
Ap. = Appius, a Roman *praenomen*
C. = Gaius, a Roman *praenomen*
ca. = circa
Cn. = Gnaeus, a Roman *praenomen*
coll. = collective
compar. = comparative
conj. = conjunction
dat. = dative
demon. = demonstrative
encl. = enclitic
esp. = especially
f. = feminine
gen. = genitive
impers. = impersonal
impv. = imperative
ind. = indicative
indecl. = indeclinable
indef. = indefinite
indic. = indicative
inf. = infinitive
interj. = interjection
interr. = interrogative
L. = Lucius, a Roman *praenomen*
M. = Marcus, a Roman *praenomen*
m. = masculine
M' = Manius, a Roman *praenomen*
meton. = metonymy
Mt. = Mount
nom. = nominative
num. = number, numeral
obj. = objective
OLD = Oxford Latin Dictionary
P. = Publius, a Roman *praenomen*
part. = particle
pass. = passive
perf. = perfect
pl. = plural
poet. = poetic
poss. = possessive
pr. = *prologus*
prep. = preposition
pron. = pronoun
rel. = relative
s.v. = *sub vide*, see under
Ser. = Servius, a Roman *praenomen*
Sex. = Sextus, a Roman *praenomen*
sg. = singular
Sp. = Spurius, a Roman *praenomen*
spec. = specifically
subst. = substantive
superl. = superlative
T. = Titus, a Roman *praenomen*

—Social Criticism—

The House of Julia Felix in Pompeii contained frescoes depicting a variety of scenes from local life, such as this stall selling bread. Many of the frescoes, including the one pictured here, are now housed in the Museo Archeologico Nazionale di Napoli (National Archeological Museum in Naples). (Public Domain)

Introduction to Social Criticism

In the poems that appear here under the heading "Social Criticism," Horace and Martial assess and comment upon the behavior of their fellow Romans. It is their social critique that makes these poems markedly Roman, for both Horace and Martial worked within long-standing poetic traditions in meters and genres that were originally Greek: Horace's *Epodes* employ the iambic meters—and emotional vehemence—of the seventh-century Greek poet Archilochus; the meter of *Ode* 1.2 (included here) is named after Sappho of Lesbos; Martial's short poems show him to be a careful student of Greek epigram. Yet for both poets, it is Rome, its political history, social customs, traditional holidays, its topography rich in associations, and its diverse population, that occupies the center. In contrast to these genres, the Romans claimed satire as their own. Although many of satire's literary and philosophical underpinnings, such as its forays into Epicurean philosophy and Stoic argumentation, adapt Greek precedents (as does its meter), the life of satire is in its details, and, as in the case of the epodes and epigrams, these details are Roman and Italian. The poems sketch a portrait of Rome in vignettes of human interaction in the city and its surroundings, on its streets and in its dining rooms. The epicenter of wealth and power, Rome is the point of departure or the point of contrast for each of the individual poems.

Horace

Epodes 7, 16; Satire 1.6
Standard Level and Higher Level

— Introduction to Horace —

An ancient biographer tells us that Horace (Quintus Horatius Flaccus) was born December 8, 65 BCE, in Venusia, a town in Apulia in southeastern Italy. In fact, most of what we know about Horace's life comes either from ancient biographers and commentators or from autobiographical remarks in his own poems, and should not be taken at face value. Horace says that his father was an ex-slave and a money collector at auctions (**coactor**), who nevertheless had the means and ambition to send his son to Rome for his education. He does not mention his mother.

In Athens to continue his education when Julius Caesar was murdered (March 44 BCE), Horace was taken up by Marcus Iunius Brutus, the leader of the assassins, and appointed military tribune. That appointment brought with it membership in the equestrian order (**ordo eques**). Indeed, Horace tells us that he fought at Philippi (42 BCE), when Octavian (the future Augustus) and his forces defeated those of the assassins Brutus and Gaius Cassius Longinus. This defeat ended Horace's military career. He returned to Rome and, although his estate had been confiscated by Octavian's agents, managed to buy his way into a bookkeeping/secretarial position of **scriba quaestorius** and began to write poetry. (The confiscation of property provided funds to pay Octavian's soldiers and land on which to settle them. It had a devastating effect on the dispossessed farmers.) Because of his acquaintance with other poets (one of whom was Vergil), Horace came to know Gaius Maecenas, a wealthy **eques** who was a friend of Augustus and a patron, **patronus**, of poets. Maecenas became Horace's patron, that is, he helped support him financially, possibly with the gift of a farm near modern Tivoli, near Sabine territory. Accordingly, Maecenas is the addressee of Horace's *Satires* and his later *Odes*.

— Introduction to the *Epodes* —

Horace's *Epodes* and first book of *Satires* are from the years 42–31 BCE, a chaotic time of civil war accompanied by proscription (publication of the names of Roman citizens who were declared outlaws) and property confiscation. After Caesar's assassination, several waves of conflict flooded the Roman world: the earliest were between the assassins (who called themselves "liberators") and Caesar's avengers: his surviving co-consul, Mark Antony, his Master of Horse, Lepidus, and his adopted son and heir, Octavian. (This trio, appointed by law as a board of three men with consular power, for the purpose of setting the republic in order, is called the "Second Triumvirate" to distinguish it from an earlier political alliance, that of C. Julius Caesar, M. Licinius Crassus, and Cn. Pompeius Magnus); the last conflict was between the forces of Antony and Octavian. The two had divided the Mediterranean world, with Octavian taking the West and Antony the East. Antony had also married Octavian's sister. The alliance soured as Antony increasingly committed himself to the East, including Egypt and its queen, Cleopatra. The two sides met in a decisive battle in August of 31 BCE on the western coast of Greece, at Actium, where Antony's land forces surrendered to Octavian's and his fleet was destroyed, while Cleopatra, and her fleet, fled to Egypt.

Epodes 7 and 16 reflect the pessimism and strife of that period. They are in iambics, the metrical system used by earlier Greek poets for social attack, and thus particularly suited to poems that present a Roman society at war with itself, divided, enraged, and out of control.

— Meters —

Iambic Strophes (Iambic Trimeter followed by Iambic Dimeter): *Epode* 7
Second Pythiambic (Dactylic Hexameter alternating with Iambic
    Trimeter): *Epode* 16

— *Epode 7* —

We do not know when, exactly, Horace wrote Epode 7; *but the poem refers generally to the civil wars after Caesar's assassination, and perhaps specifically to the naval conflicts of 37 and 36* BCE *involving Pompey the Great's son, Sextus Pompeius, who represented the last of the serious opposition to the Second Triumvirate. The poem traces Rome's current troubles back to the act of fratricide at the city's foundation, that is, Romulus's murder of his twin brother Remus. An unidentified speaker frantically addresses an assembly of citizens whom he cannot control.*

    quo, quo scelesti ruitis? aut cur dexteris
        aptantur enses conditi?
    parumne campis atque Neptuno super
        fusum est Latini sanguinis,
5   non ut superbas invidae Karthaginis
        Romanus arces ureret,

1   **Quo, quo:** interr. adv., "to what place? whither?" The doubled **quo** conveys anger and urgency.

     ruitis: Three short syllables, the first two of which occupy the metrical position of one long syllable, contribute to the sense of haste.

     aut: This conjunction can introduce a question, especially the second of two, and works here in the same way as **et**.

     dexteris: dative with **aptantur** (line 2).

2   **conditi:** here "sheathed"; the idea is probably that the swords were sheathed after the battle of Philippi in 42 BCE, which saw the defeat of Caesar's leading assassins, including Brutus and Cassius.

3–10 **parumne ... dextera:** a long RHETORICAL QUESTION introduced by **-ne**.

3–4   **campis atque Neptuno super/fusum est:** There are two possibilities for case here, depending on whether one reads **superfusum** as a single word (from **superfundo**) pouring over the line ending, or as two words, **fusum** with the adverbial **super**. If one word, then

campis atque Neptuno is dative; if two, with **super** used adverbially, then **campis** and **Neptuno** are ablatives of place where (A&G §429.4). At any rate, the expression **campis atque Neptuno** is a novel way of saying **terra marique**, "on land and sea." (On **Neptuno** see METONYMY.) The polar opposites signify the whole, resulting in an image of the entire world covered over with blood.

Neptuno: possibly an oblique reference to Sextus Pompeius, who after his father's death in 48 BCE carried on the war against Caesar in Africa and Spain. After Caesar's assassination, he used his navy based in Sicily to oppose Antony, Octavian, and Lepidus. He called himself "son of Neptune."

4 **Latini:** SYNECDOCHE for "Roman."

sanguinis: with **Latini,** a partitive genitive (A&G §346.a.4) depending on **parumne** (line 3).

5–10 **non ut ... sed ut:** introduces a series of purpose clauses (**ureret... descenderet... periret**), each of which sets a Roman individual or a place in Rome against an enemy or an enemy place: **Romanus/Karthaginis arces; Sacra Via/Britannus; urbs haec/vota Parthorum**.

invidae Karthaginis: A wealthy North African city founded in the eighth century by Phoenicians, Carthage long dominated the sea trade in the western Mediterranean and fought Rome in three major wars (the Punic Wars) between 264 and 146 BCE. After its defeat in 146 BCE the city was destroyed; but the site was made a Roman colony and became the capital of the province of proconsular Africa.

6 **Romanus:** a collective singular representing the whole people; so too **Britannus** in line 7 (A&G §317.d note 2).

>   intactus aut Britannus ut descenderet
>   Sacra catenatus Via,
>   sed ut secundum vota Parthorum sua
> 10   urbs haec periret dextera?
>   neque hic lupis mos nec fuit leonibus
>   umquam nisi in dispar feris.
>   furorne caecus, an rapit vis acrior,
>   an culpa? responsum date.
> 15   tacent et albus ora pallor inficit
>   mentesque perculsae stupent.

7   **intactus ... Britannus: intactus**, because aside from Caesar's expeditions in 55 and 54 BCE, Britain was relatively untouched by Rome.

8   **Sacra ... Via:** ablative of way by which (A&G §429.4.a). The Sacra Via was Rome's oldest street. Its route, determined by the needs of ritual, was from the **summa Sacrae Viae** in the area of the Temple of Jupiter Stator on the Palatine, to the Capitoline. It was the last stretch for triumphal processions, which traversed the Roman Forum before ascending the Capitoline.

9   **Parthorum:** The Parthians were a semi-nomadic people whose empire occupied what is now northeastern Iran. The Romans tried for years to expand eastward into their territory but were never able to conquer them. Indeed, M. Licinius Crassus and his army suffered a major disaster at their hands in 53 BCE; Caesar was assassinated on the eve of his own Parthian campaign; and after initial success against the Parthians, Antony was forced to retreat in 36 BCE. The Parthians were famous archers, so it is fitting that they do their harm with their **vota**, weapons that, like arrows, are sent from a distance.

9–10   **sua ... dextera:** Note the emphatic HYPERBATON. The repetition **dexteris ... dextera** at the end of lines 1 and 10 brings closure to this half of the poem.

10   **urbs haec:** Note the immediacy: the city *right here* as opposed to the distant Parthians and their prayers.

11 **neque lupis . . . nec leonibus:** possessive datives. The invocation of wolves and lions is a TOPOS. In the view of numerous ancient sources, these proverbially fierce animals do not attack their own kind.

12 **dispar:** neuter as a substantive after **in**.

feris: with **lupis** and **leonibus** (line 11); again, the HYPERBATON is striking.

13 **furorne caecus, an rapit vis acrior:** Latin often portrays violent emotions as controlling the persons who feel them.

responsum date: The imperative captures the urgency of the situation.

15 **tacent . . . inficit:** Switching to the third person, the speaker turns from the Romans he has been addressing to a group of bystanders (as well as the poem's readers), and describes what he observes.

albus . . . pallor: Note the sharp visual contrast to the blood (**sanguinis**, line 4) and gore (**cruor**, line 20) that have stained land and sea.

inficit: Can **pallor** do this? **Inficio** means "to immerse in pigment, dye," or "to darken, stain (with blood)." **Pallor** in the face is caused by blood draining *from* it. The listeners have blanched, gone white in the face, at the poet's rebuke. The METAPHOR is reversed.

16 **mentesque perculsae stupent:** The minds of the guilty are stunned and they have no words with which to answer the speaker.

> sic est: acerba fata Romanos agunt
> > scelusque fraternae necis,
> > ut immerentis fluxit in terram Remi
> > > sacer nepotibus cruor.

20

17 **sic est:** The speaker recognizes that this violence is fated and therefore inevitable.

acerba fata . . . agunt: The **fata** have agency: like the Furies who avenge the killing of relatives, they pursue the Romans.

18 **scelusque fraternae necis: Scelus** recalls **scelesti** from line 1. The repetition helps emphasize how the close of the poem is also paradoxically a beginning, the original crime of fratricide, which is SYNECDOCHE for civil war. The genitive **fraternae necis** is a limiting genitive that defines the **scelus**.

19 **ut:** "since" (A&G §543; *OLD s.v.* **ut** 27).

immerentis . . . Remi: Why does Horace call Remus "blameless"? Other accounts of the fratricide make Remus threaten Romulus's sovereignty. Livy (1.7.2), for example, says that he leapt over Romulus's partially built city walls as an insult and challenge to his brother's rule.

20 **sacer:** + dat., "a curse to" (A&G §384).

nepotibus: "grandchildren," here, "descendants."

cruor: The HYPERBATON, by which the verb **fluxit** (line 19) is separated from the subject, places emphasis on the poem's final word. The final image recalls the image at the beginning of the poem of blood pouring over land and sea (lines 3–4).

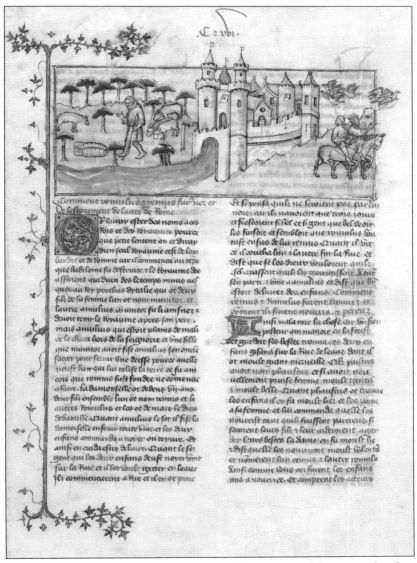

Two scenes from the life of Romulus and Remus illustrate a French history produced ca. 1390–1400. At left, the shepherd Faustulus discovers the twins with the she-wolf. The scene at the right depicts the augury that contributed to the quarrel between Romulus and Remus. Each brother claimed to be the winner, Remus because he was the first to see six auspicious birds, and Romulus because he saw twelve birds. (Getty Museum, California) (Public Domain)

— *Epode* 16 —

Epode *16* has generated a great body of scholarly debate: what time period is represented by **altera . . . aetas** ("another generation")? Does the description of the **beata . . . arva . . . divites insulas** ("happy fields and rich isles") mask a reference to any real place? Is it instead a response to other literary landscapes; or does it picture what Rome was and might be again with the return of peace? Most scholars nevertheless agree that the poem reflects a sense of crisis and feelings of deep pessimism, both of which were understandable in the early 30s BCE, after attempts at peace between Octavian, Antony, and Sextus Pompeius had failed, and Rome found itself facing yet another wave of civil war.

The poem opens by setting out the crisis: Rome is destroying itself in an unceasing series of civil wars. Like Epode 7, it opens with a catalog of external enemies. There are no **Britanni** here, but Gauls and Germans instead; **invida Karthago** reappears by way of the reference to Hannibal.

> altera iam teritur bellis civilibus aetas,
> > suis et ipsa Roma viribus ruit:
> quam neque finitimi valuerunt perdere Marsi
> > minacis aut Etrusca Porsenae manus,

1   **altera . . . aetas:** From its first line the poem's setting is established by its relationship to a previous age. The Latin does not specify whether **aetas** means an "era" or a "generation," that is, the group of people that represent a generation (for example, Octavian and Sextus Pompeius, who are now continuing the conflict of Julius Caesar and Pompey the Great).

   teritur: According to the *OLD*, **tero** means literally "to subject to friction," thus "to wear down," or "destroy by attrition, wear away." It can also be used metaphorically to mean "to use up (time) in an activity (esp. of an ineffectual or frivolous kind)." The metaphor, then, conveys both the futility of civil war and, with **altera . . . aetas**, the speaker's sense of despair at wasteful destruction.

2   **suis . . . viribus:** The idea of Rome's collapsing because of its own strength was a TOPOS. In the preface to his history, Livy refers to Rome growing to such a size that it struggles because of its enormity: **ut iam magnitudine laboret sua**; later Livy places in Hannibal's

mouth the observation that a great **civitas** will, if it has no external enemies, find internal ones, just as bodies that are outstandingly strong are burdened by their own strengths (30.44.8).

ruit: one of several echoes of words and ideas in *Epode* 7: **quo, quo scelesti ruitis?** (line 1).

3–8 **quam . . . Hannibal:** A catalog of Rome's enemies. It begins with peoples of Italy, then moves northwest, north, and south to include Gaul, Germany, and Carthage.

finitimi . . . Marsi: The Marsi were a people of central Italian origin from an area east of Rome, and over the Apennines. The Marsi were leaders in Rome's conflict with its Italian allies (known both as the Social War, from **socius** = "ally," and also as the Marsic War).

valuerunt perdere: instead of **potuerunt perdere**. The use of **valere** places emphasis on physical strength.

4 **minacis . . . Porsenae:** After Rome expelled its kings (see Livy selection), Lars Porsenna, king of the Etruscan city Clusium, attacked Rome. His siege gave rise to well-known stories of heroic Romans: Horatius Cocles, who defended the bridge across the Tiber until it could be destroyed beneath him; Cloelia, a young woman who, handed over to Porsenna as hostage, escaped with a number of other young women by swimming across the Tiber; and Mucius Scaevola, whose attempt to assassinate Lars Porsenna and whose disregard for his own physical safety when he was captured impressed and intimidated the enemy into giving up the siege.

aemula nec virtus Capuae nec Spartacus acer
    novisque rebus infidelis Allobrox,
nec fera caerulea domuit Germania pube
    parentibusque abominatus Hannibal,
impia perdemus devoti sanguinis aetas,
    ferisque rursus occupabitur solum.

5   **aemula ... virtus Capuae:** an instance of HYPALLAGE, where **Capua virtutis aemulae** would be the expected phrasing. Capua was a large and powerful city in the prosperous Campanian plain, famous for its luxury and arrogance. By the time of the Second Punic War (218–201 BCE), it rivaled Rome and Carthage. Cicero said that at that time it was **Roma altera**, "a second Rome" (*Philippics* 12.7.17). Capua's loyalty to Rome was always inconsistent and after the battle of Cannae (216 BCE), it defected to Hannibal; in 211 BCE, Rome recaptured Capua, executed its leading citizens, and confiscated its territory.

Spartacus: Thracian leader of a slave revolt in 73–71 BCE that had its origins in a gladiatorial school in Capua. Spartacus's forces, which may have numbered up to 100,000, defeated several Roman armies, before they were caught by M. Licinius Crassus in southern Italy as they prepared to invade Sicily.

6   **novis rebus:** abl., "by reason of revolution." **Res novae** is the regular Latin idiom for "revolution."

Allobrox: A collective singular (A&G §317.d note 2). The Allobroges were a tribe in Gallia Narbonensis (here a single **Allobrox** may signify all Gauls by SYNECDOCHE). The Allobroges initially conspired with Catiline and his co-revolutionaries in 63 BCE, but ended up providing evidence against the conspirators instead. (See introduction to Sallust.)

7   **nec fera caerulea domuit Germania pube:** Note the SYNCHESIS (interlocking word order): **fera ... Germania / caerulea ... pube.** From a Romanocentric point of view, **Germania** was a wild place toward the edges of the known world, its people savages, primitive drinkers of milk and eaters of meat, not like the Romans, cultivators of the land who drank wine and ate bread. Two Germanic tribes, the Cimbri and Teutoni, invaded Gaul and Italy in the late second

century BCE. The terror this invasion caused led to the extraordinary rise of Gaius Marius, who, reorganizing and improving the Roman army, defeated the invaders in 102 and 101 BCE. In the 80s BCE, however, Marius clashed with his former subordinate, Lucius Cornelius Sulla over the consulship and then over military command of the campaign against Mithridates of Pontus. In the ensuing violence, Sulla marched on Rome and took the city by force (88 BCE); Marius fled but returned the next year and captured Rome. Also Julius Caesar's uncle by marriage, Marius represents doubly another, older, generation of civil war.

caerulea: not blue all over, but "blue-eyed." **Caerulea...pube**, then, means "with its blue-eyed manpower."

8 **parentibusque abominatus Hannibal:** a passive use of the participle of the deponent **abominor**, which means, according to the *OLD*, "to (seek to) avert (an omen or eventuality) by prayer." It also means "to loathe." The adjective, then, alludes to the number of deaths Hannibal caused and the number of parents who lost their sons to him. The dative of agent is common with perfect participles, especially when they are used as adjectives (A&G §375). **Hannibal** is, with **Germania**, subject of the singular **domuit**.

9 **impia...aetas:** compare line 1, **altera...aetas**.

perdemus: repeats **perdere** of line 3. Note that the speaker now includes himself.

devoti sanguinis: a gen. of quality (A&G §345).

10 **ferisque rursus occupabitur solum:** The future dystopic Rome will be a desolate place, inhabited by wild animals. **Feris** recalls the **fera** of line 7 to suggest that Rome will be as savage a place as **Germania**; and **rursus** shows that the city's destruction will be a return to a past primitive condition, when there were no houses, no temples, nothing but bare earth (**solum**), and scorched earth at that (see **cineres**, line 11).

Barbarians will trample the abandoned city and violate its most sacred site. The speaker offers his advice, if his listeners want it: They should leave the city to the wild animals, just as the Phocaeans left their city long ago, and go wherever the winds send them.

> barbarus heu cineres insistet victor et Urbem
> > eques sonante verberabit ungula,
> quaeque carent ventis et solibus ossa Quirini,
> > nefas videre! dissipabit insolens.

11 **barbarus:** another collective singular. To the Greeks, who invented the word, a **barbarus** was a non-Greek speaker, one whose language sounded like "barbar." This, of course, included non-Greek-speaking Italians. To the Romans, **barbari** were those who were neither Greek nor Roman, whether, for example, Germans, Gauls, Carthaginians or, to continue the circuit of the known world, Parthians, Rome's rivals for power in the East.

heu: an interjection, expressing sorrow, and showing the speaker's strong emotions at the thought of the **barbarus** trampling the city.

victor: in apposition (A&G §282) to **barbarus**.

Urbem = Romam.

12 **eques ... ungula:** The image is of a single horseman riding through the burnt shell of a city, with the sound of hoofbeats echoing in a lifeless and desolate landscape.

13 **quaeque carent ventis et solibus:** The relative clause precedes its antecedent.

carent: + abl. It is not that the bones lack something they need, but that they "are free from," that is, "not exposed to," wind and sun. They were safely buried in an ancient tomb.

solibus: the warmth or heat of the sun, or sunlight, often plural.

ossa Quirini: a god worshipped on the Quirinal Hill, and commonly identified with the deified Romulus. To scatter these bones is to destroy the protective presence of the city's founder.

14 **nefas videre = nefas est videre,** the infinitive as the subject (A&G §452.1). Another emotional outburst.

insolens: The adjective brings us back to the **barbarus** of line 11 and concludes this section.

This seventeenth-century Flemish tapestry depicts the fratricide that Horace (in *Epode* 7.17–20) cites as a cause of civil war in his own day. The text at the top of the tapestry reads *Romulus Remum fratrem interficit*. Following Remus's murder, Romulus became king of Rome and was credited with setting the city's boundaries and establishing the Senate, among other accomplishments. The deified Romulus was later worshipped as Quirinus. (Getty Museum, California) (Public Domain)

> 15 forte quid expediat communiter aut melior pars
> malis carere quaeritis laboribus:
> nulla sit hac potior sententia, Phocaeorum
> velut profugit exsecrata civitas
> agros atque Lares patrios habitandaque fana
> 20 apris reliquit et rapacibus lupis,
> ire pedes quocunque ferent, quocunque per undas
> Notus vocabit aut protervus Africus.

15–16 **forte ... quaeritis:** The speaker turns to a group of listeners. **Quaeritis** introduces the indirect question **quid expediat ...**

communiter aut melior pars: Aut joins the adverb and the singular subject (**melior pars**) of the plural verb.

carere: an infinitive expressing purpose with **expediat** (A&G §460), "what is useful for avoiding ..."

malis ... laboribus: abl., with **carere** in its sense of "avoid." **Laboribus** here has less the meaning of "work" and more the meaning of Greek **ponos**, "struggle" or "toil."

17 **sit:** jussive subjunctive (A&G §439).

hac = After the nominative **nulla ... sententia**, add a second, comparative ablative, **sententia** with **hac**. The substance of **hac sententia** is the idea expressed in the phrase, **ire pedes quocunque ferent ...**

17–20 **Phocaeorum ... lupis:** Note the long syllables in the fifth foot, which make this a rare "spondaic" line.

The historian Herodotus (1.165) writes that the Phocaeans were the first of the Ionian Greeks attacked by Cyrus the Great, king of Persia. They were accomplished sailors, who had already sent expeditions far to the west, to Italy and to Spain. Instead of submitting to the Persians, the Phocaeans, men, women, and children, abandoned their city, taking with them their divine images and such temple offerings as were portable, and sailed off, first to Chios, then to Corsica. (Eventually they ended up in Rhegium, at the toe of the Italian boot.) Before setting sail for Corsica, the Phocaeans cursed any of their people who would stay behind; they sank an iron bar into the sea and swore that they would not return to Phocaea until that bar resurfaced. But more than half the citizens were so homesick that they broke their oath. Horace both Romanizes the Phocaeans (the gods they take are **Lares**, Roman household gods) and generalizes the story (rocks will resurface, not a specific bar of iron).

18 **exsecrata:** "having bound themselves with a curse."

19 **Lares patrios:** the Phocaeans' individual household gods, if we follow Herodotus, because they have taken the temple images.

habitandaque fana . . . lupis: The temples are now empty of divine images and dedications; the desolation of the city and its abandonment to wild animals recalls the image of Rome when the **barbarus** rides in.

habitanda: a gerundive expressing purpose after **reliquit** (A&G §500.4, with note 1).

20 **apris . . . rapacibus lupis:** The wolves get the epithet **rapacibus**; but wild boars were famous objects of heroic hunts (*Iliad* 9; *Odyssey* 19; Herodotus 1.34–45) and just as dangerous as wolves. Moreover, domestic swine quickly revert to the feral state and within very few generations their offspring begin to share the phenotype of their wild ancestors.

21 **ire pedes quocunque ferent:** the substance of the **sententia** from line 17.

quocunque: relative adverb, "wherever."

22 **Notus:** the *south* wind, which brings rainstorms.

protervus Africus: a fierce southwest wind. Horace calls it **pestilens** in C. 3.23.5; and Cicero (*De Natura Deorum* 1.101) says that it carried flying snakes out of the desert of Libya.

The poem shifts to a series of ADYNATA, *"impossibilities," or events that defy the laws of nature (rocks floating; rivers flowing backward; predators and prey living in peace and even interbreeding; land animals taking to the sea). The speaker urges his listeners to swear that it shall not be permitted to return until these things happen.*

    sic placet? an melius quis habet suadere? —secunda
        ratem occupare quid moramur alite?
25 sed iuremus in haec: simul imis saxa renarint
        vadis levata, ne redire sit nefas;
    neu conversa domum pigeat dare lintea, quando
        Padus Matina laverit cacumina,

23 **sic placet:** The speaker canvasses the assembly for any better proposals.

melius ... suadere: "to recommend better."

quis: indefinite, "anyone."

habet: habere + inf., *OLD* 12 c, "be in a position (to)."

secunda ... alite: The **ales** here is the source of omens.

24 **ratem:** A raft instead of a ship suggests hasty construction and reinforces the sense of urgency in the RHETORICAL QUESTION **occupare quid moramur?**

25 **sed iuremus in haec:** The speaker turns to urging in the hortatory subjunctive. **In haec** (= **in haec verba**) points ahead to the oath **ne redire sit nefas** (line 26).

25-34 **simul ... aequora:** a series of ADYNATA, "impossibilities."

saxa ... renarint: not the Phocaeans' iron ingot, but more generally available items that produce a more universalizing image.

renarint = renaverint, future perf. ind. with **simul.** The use of the verb with the **re-** prefix presumes that someone has thrown the rocks into the water so that they can return to the surface.

26 **ne redire sit nefas:** LITOTES for "that it *not* be an abomination to return."

27 **domum:** acc. with **conversa**.

dare lintea: "to set sail."

28 **Padus:** the Po river in northern Italy.

Matina . . . cacumina: the peaks of Mt. Matinus, in Apulia, the region of Horace's birth. Not only will the Po be flowing upward if it washes mountain peaks; it will also be running far out of course.

laverit: future perf., like **renarint** (line 25).

The theme of predators and prey living in harmony often occurs as a positive indication of order and peace, as in this mosaic depicting Orpheus using his music to tame wild animals. This mosaic (ca. 200 BCE) was found at the Piazza della Vittoria in Palermo, Sicily, and is now housed in the Regional Archeological Museum Antonio Salinas. (© Marie-Lan Nguyen / Wikimedia Commons / CC-BY 2.5)

> in mare seu celsus procurrerit Appenninus,
> 30 novaque monstra iunxerit libidine
> mirus amor, iuvet ut tigres subsidere cervis,
>   adulteretur et columba miluo,
> credula nec ravos timeant armenta leones,
>   ametque salsa levis hircus aequora.
> 35 haec et quae poterunt reditus abscindere dulcis
>   eamus omnis exsecrata civitas,
> aut pars indocili melior grege; mollis et exspes
>   inominata perprimat cubilia.

29 **procurrerit Appenninus:** not exactly an ADYNATON to the eyes of the modern geologist. The Apennine mountain range, which runs the length of the Italian peninsula from the Ligurian Alps in the northwest, does extend (**procurrerit**) into the sea to form the mountains of northern Sicily.

30 **novaque:** "strange," or "unheard of."

monstra: The word **monstrum** can mean a monstrous or horrible creature; but it can also mean an unnatural thing or event regarded as an omen; a portent, prodigy, or sign.

31 **mirus:** "extraordinary."

31-32 **iuvet ut ... adulteretur et:** The subjunctive clauses express the results of this strange lust and extraordinary love.

subsidere: Used of female animals with the dative, the verb means "adopt a position under" in copulation. While this interspecies mating is in itself impossible, that the predator should take the female—and from the Roman point of view passive—part, is even more impossible.

33 **credula:** As prey animals, herds (**armenta**) of horses and cattle are ready to believe something will harm them; they run first, ask questions later; in this ADYNATON they trust that they will not be attacked.

34 **levis hircus:** The meter tells us that this is **lēvis**, "smooth," not **lĕvis**, "light" or "swift." Goats are usually rough-coated; but this one is slick, either because he is wet or because he is turning into a fish.

35 **quae = illa quae.**

reditus . . . dulcis: The expression recalls the "honey-sweet return" of *Odyssey* 11.100.

36 **exsecrata:** here with **haec et quae** (line 35) as internal accusatives, "having uttered these curses and . . ."

37 **pars . . . melior:** Abandoning the city, then, is the act of the virtuous, an idea that flies in the face of Roman tradition. A good example is the story Livy tells about the proposal made by one of the surviving officers after the Roman defeat at Cannae during the Second Punic War: M. Caecilius Metellus suggests sailing away to take up service with some king (22.53.5, **ut deserta Italia ad regum aliquem transfugiant**) and is stopped only by Scipio's drawing his sword.

indocili grege: abl. of comparison. The **grex** is **indocilis**, presumably because it will not listen to the speaker.

mollis et exspes: To be **mollis** is to be effete and unmanly; to be **exspes** is to be cowardly. Another good example from Livy: after Cannae, when the surviving consul Varro returned to Rome, the entire city came out to meet him and to thank him, "because he had not despaired of the republic" (22.61.15: **quod de re publica non desperasset**).

38 **inominata:** "ill-starred"; a rare adjective, it appears only here.

perprimat: With verbs, the prefix **per-** adds the idea of thoroughness, completion, or an intensive force.

The speaker exhorts his listeners to flee to a better place, the Blessed Fields and Rich Isles, where nature spontaneously produces grain, grapes, olives, figs, milk, and honey. This spontaneous production is also characteristic of a bygone "Golden Age" associated with the Greek god Cronus, who came to be identified with the Italian god Saturnus. Cronus came to power when he overthrew his father, Uranus. Cronus's reign ended, as did the Golden Age, when he was overthrown in turn by his own son Zeus.

> vos, quibus est virtus muliebrem tollite luctum
> 40   Etrusca praeter et volate litora.
> nos manet Oceanus circumvagus: arva, beata
>   petamus arva divites et insulas,
> reddit ubi Cererem tellus inarata quotannis
>   et imputata floret usque vinea,
> 45   germinat et numquam fallentis termes olivae,
>   suamque pulla ficus ornat arborem,
> mella cava manant ex ilice, montibus altis
>   levis crepante lympha desilit pede.
> illic iniussae veniunt ad mulctra capellae,
> 50   refertque tenta grex amicus ubera;

39   **quibus:** dat. of possession (A&G §373) = **qui habetis virtutem.**

    virtus: here manliness, as opposed to **muliebrem ... luctum**. The idea is not to grieve but to act. But shouldn't the opposite of "lie in bed and cry" be "stand and fight"? The speaker continues to turn the Roman tradition of fortitude on its head.

40   **Etrusca ... litora:** acc. because of **praeter**. The speaker expresses a desire to sail northwest from the mouth of the Tiber.

41   **Oceanus circumvagus:** The compound **circumvagus**, "encircling," "moving round," appears first in Horace. The river of Ocean was envisioned as a sea flowing around the known world.

41-42 **arva, beata/ petamus arva:** **Arva beata** or **arva laeta** is the Latin term for the Elysian Fields, the abode of heroes and of the righteous in the far west, by the river of Ocean (*Odyssey* 4.560–565). The focus in the following lines is on the spontaneous production of food, which perhaps explains why **arva** appears twice.

insulas: The Elysian Fields are frequently identified with the Islands of the Blessed. The geography/topography of these places shifts according to each poet's purpose. For Horace's, it seems that the **arva beata** are part of the **insulae divites**.

43 **Cererem:** METONYMY for grain, as Ceres (in Greek mythology, Demeter) was the patroness of this crop.

inarata: first in a series of participles compounded with the negative or privative **in-** prefix. The earth of the Islands of the Blessed does not need to be plowed.

quotannis: "every year." The spontaneous generation of the fruits of the earth is not a fluke. It happens perpetually in the Islands of the Blessed.

44 **imputata = inputata.**

45 **numquam fallentis:** Olive trees normally produce a substantial crop only every other year. Here, they defy nature by producing consistently and thus "never disappointing."

46 **suam ... arborem:** The fig trees are not grafted (normally a requirement to produce more desirable varieties of figs) and therefore another example of natural production.

47 **mella:** honeycombs. Note the ALLITERATION and ASSONANCE (**man-/mon-; ex ilice**) of this line, and how the short vowels in **mellă** and **căva** give way to the long vowels of **cavā** and **mānant** and thus slow the line to the speed of honey dripping.

48 **levis crepante lympha desilit pede:** Note the ONOMATOPOEIA of this line as well as the personification of the water. Note also how the alliteration emphasizes the interlocking word order of the subject and its modifier, **levis ... lympha**, and the ablative absolute **crepante ... pede**.

49 **iniussae ... capellae:** The cooperation of animals is also characteristic of the Golden Age. This is "a land flowing with milk and honey," conventional description for a blessed place in the Western tradition.

Not only are the earth and its plants and animals generous and friendly to mankind, but poisonous and predatory animals are absent, as is disease. Moreover, the Islands of the Blessed are outside of time and thus unaffected by such developments in technology as the sailing vessel.

> nec vespertinus circumgemit ursus ovile,
>   neque intumescit alta viperis humus.
> pluraque felices mirabimur: ut neque largis
>   aquosus Eurus arva radat imbribus,
> 55 pinguia nec siccis urantur semina glebis,
>   utrumque rege temperante caelitum.
> non huc Argoo contendit remige pinus,
>   neque impudica Colchis intulit pedem;
> non huc Sidonii torserunt cornua nautae
> 60   laboriosa nec cohors Ulixei.
> nulla nocent pecori contagia, nullius astri
>   gregem aestuosa torret impotentia.

51-62   **nec ... neque ... ut neque ... nec ... non ... neque ... non ... nec ... nulla ... nullius:** The Golden Age and Islands of the Blessed (conflated here) are characterized as much by what is absent as by what is present. Note the catalog of famous sailors.

51   **ursus:** a natural enemy of the sheep. Note how predator and prey do not get along peacefully as they would in an ADYNATON. In the Islands of the Blessed, threats are simply absent.

    ovile: acc. with **circumgemit**.

52   **intumescit:** Some ancient writers thought that snakes were born from the earth.

    alta ... humus: not the "deep earth," but the depths of the earth.

53   **felices:** The travelers will take on this quality from the place.

54   **aquosus Eurus:** the east or southeast wind, which brings rainstorms along with it.

55 **siccis:** The land is thus neither too wet nor too dry.

pinguia: a TRANSFERRED EPITHET. The attribute properly belongs to **glebis**, if they are not too dry.

56 **utrumque:** either extreme of wet or dry.

caelitum: obj. gen. with **rege** (A&G §347).

57 **non huc Argoo contendit remige pinus:** The sailing of the first ship, the Argo, marked the end of the Golden Age. While time goes on everywhere else, the Islands of the Blessed are untouched by change. The noun **remex** can refer to a single oarsman or collectively to the oarsmen of a ship (*OLD s.v. remex*, b). **Pinus** is SYNECDOCHE for "ship."

58 **impudica Colchis:** a reference to Medea, who deceived her father, the king of Colchis, to help Jason, leader of the Argonauts. When running away with Jason, she killed her brother and threw his body parts in the sea, thus slowing her pursuers, who had to stop and collect the pieces for proper burial.

59 **Sidonii . . . nautae:** Phoenicians, early sailors, from Tyre, Sidon, and, eventually, Carthage.

torserunt cornua: "steered." **Cornua** are yardarms (i.e., the ends of the spars from which the sails are hung).

60 **laboriosa cohors . . . Ulixei:** Ulixes (gen. -is, -i, or -ei), is the Latinized form of "Odysseus." As in **malis laboribus,** line 16, here too the idea of **labor** is that of struggle or travail. The adjective **laboriosus, -a, -um** is here used of the **cohors**, but in *Epode* 17.16 of Ulixes himself, the proverbial man of struggles. The speaker's description of a place that does not know the plow recalls Odysseus's assessment of the island offshore from the Cyclops's cave in *Odyssey* 9.

61 **nulla . . . nullius:** an instance of POLYPTOTON.

nocent: + dative.

astri: The ancients considered the heat of the dog star, Sirius, which rose in late summer, to be harmful to humans and animals.

62 **gregem:** The flock is friendly to mankind (line 50); and in turn, the climate is friendly to it.

The myth of the Ages of Man, finally mentioned explicitly here, recalls **altera iam aetas** at the beginning of the poem. The earliest written version of the myth comes from the Works and Days of the Greek poet Hesiod. The myth lists an age of gold, a silver age, a bronze age, a heroic age, and finally the present age of iron, each of which, with the exception of the heroic, is worse than the one that preceeded it. Hesiod's poem is ostensibly about making a living by farming the hardscrabble ground of Boeotia in mountainous central Greece; it is, however, also about how to live in an iron age world that is far from perfect; in which the gods hold themselves aloof from humankind; one's fellow humans, male and female, are not to be trusted; the land gives up its riches only after hard labor; and survival requires careful planning. Horace clearly has Hesiod's dystopia in mind as he brings the poem to a close.

> Iuppiter illa piae secrevit litora genti,
>   ut inquinavit aere tempus aureum;
> 65 aere, dehinc ferro duravit secula, quorum
>   piis secunda vate me datur fuga.

63   **Iuppiter:** Zeus, whose expulsion of his father Cronus ended the Golden Age of peace and bounty.

illa ... litora: perhaps in contrast to the **Etrusca ... litora** of line 40.

piae ... genti: not "happy," not "blessed," not even heroic, but "dutiful," or "righteous."

64   **inquinavit aere tempus aureum:** The Latin **aes** does not differentiate between copper and bronze. The Golden Age, then, is followed by an age "stained" by **aes**, that is, a copper/gold alloy; an age of pure **aes**; and one of iron. Hesiod (*Works and Days*) includes a silver age between the ages of gold and bronze.

65   **aere:** Some of the heroes, says Hesiod (*Works and Days*), now inhabit the Islands of the Blessed, where the earth gives forth sweet fruit three times a year.

ferro: For centuries of Greek and Latin poets, the iron age is this harsh present. Hesiod wishes that he did not have to live among this generation of men, that he had died before it or were not yet born. It is an age of unceasing work and grief.

duravit: As gold is soft, and the other metals harder, so too the ages become metaphorically harder.

quorum: obj. gen. with **fuga** (line 66).

66 **piis:** The repetition of the adjective **pius** places emphasis on duty and righteousness as qualifications for admission to the Islands of the Blessed, which are now described as **litora** (line 63), perhaps in contrast to the **litora ... Etrusca** of line 40.

secunda ... fuga: Is there a slight OXYMORON here? **Secundus, -a, -um** is the old participial gerundive of **sequor**, so this is not just a "favorable" flight, it is flight that is *pursuing*.

vate me: ablative absolute. Horace takes on the character of seer/prophet in the *Odes* as well.

— Introduction to the *Satires* —

This poem considers family background and class prejudice. Rejecting public life, Horace sets the discrimination that comes from snobbishness and wealth against the discernment that comes from taste and natural modesty. Moving back and forth between "once" (**olim**) and "now" (**nunc**), as he sketches the outlines and important details of his autobiography, Horace contrasts his humble past with his present privileged position in Maecenas's circle of friends. The idea of the Roman census, the sorting of citizens according to both property qualifications and moral rectitude, runs through the poem.

Related to ideas of both property and rectitude are matters of restraint: in speech, in ambition, in appetite and expenditure. Satire is a good vehicle through which to explore such ideas, for the very name of the genre evokes the idea of fullness.

The etymologies for satire, **satura**, given in late antiquity pointed to these connections, first with the adjective **satur, -a, -um**, "full": satire, because one of the hallmarks of satire is variety, and a **lanx satura** was a platter replete with a mixture of foods; satire, because an interest in eating, and indeed in all the appetites—and functions—of the body is central to the genre and **satura** was also the word for an edible stuffing of mixed ingredients; satire, because "What is enough?" is a central question of these poems. Finally (and inaccurately) satire, because the idea of enslavement to appetite that runs throughout the poems recalls the mythological figure of the Satyr—drunk and lusty—who could also (per Plato on Socrates) serve as a trope for perfect beauty within an ugly container.

— Meter —

Dactylic Hexameter

— *Satire* 1.6 —

Horace juxtaposes the distinguished family background of his patron, Maecenas, to his own.

    non quia, Maecenas, Lydorum quidquid Etruscos
    incoluit fines nemo generosior est te,
    nec quod avus tibi maternus fuit atque paternus
    olim qui magnis legionibus imperitarent,
5   ut plerique solent, naso suspendis adunco
    ignotos, ut me libertino patre natum.

1–6   **non quia ... natum:** The first six lines form one long periodic sentence. Note how, after two major subordinate clauses (**non quia ... te** [lines 1–2]; **nec quod ... paternus** [line 3]), each of which either contains or introduces another subordinate clause (**Lydorum quidquid ... incoluit fines** [lines 1–2]; **olim qui ... imperitarent** [line 4]), and another short one (**ut ... solent** [line 5]), the sentence achieves syntactical completion only with the main verb **suspendis** (line 5) and its direct object **ignotos** in line 6. Note also the imbalance in topic: after five lines on Maecenas, Horace begins talking about himself only in line 6, with **ut me ... natum**. Thus asymmetry in the beginning of the poem reflects the contrast in background and social status between the two men.

1–3   **non quia ... nec quod:** The negative expressions are part of the rhetorical figure called ANAIRESIS, "negation": "not this ... nor this ..."

1   **Maecenas:** The first words of Horace's first satire were **qui fit Maecenas, ut nemo, quam sibi sortem / seu ratio dederit seu fors obiecerit, illa / contentus vivat, laudet diversa sequentes?** "How does it come about, Maecenas, that nobody lives content with the lot that either Reason has given him or Chance thrown in his face?" Now, in the poem that begins the second half of the collection, Maecenas returns, in the same metrical position he occupied earlier, and in the same role as addressee, as does **nemo**, "nobody," or perhaps, capitalized, Nobody.

Lydorum quidquid: quidquid with a partitive gen. (A&G §346), "whatever Lydians." According to the historian Herodotus, the Etruscans originated in Lydia, the western part of modern Turkey.

1–2 **Etruscos ... fines:** In the plural, **fines** can mean simply "territory"; but since this is a poem about social boundaries, the word **finis** also resonates thematically.

2 **nemo:** in APPOSITION to **Lydorum quidquid**.

generosior: In the near-contemporary *Georgics*, Vergil uses the adjective to describe a well-bred colt. In the *Odes* Horace again uses the comparative to describe a candidate for office as "of higher birth" (C. 3.1.10–11: **hic generosior / descendat in Campum petitor**).

3–5 **nec ... naso suspendis adunco:** "nor do you look down your hooked nose at." Lit.: "hang from your hooked nose."

4 **imperitarent:** subjunctive in a relative clause of characteristic, "of such a sort to ..." (A&G §535).

6 **ut:** "such as."

libertino patre: ablative of source with **natum** (A&G §403.a). In contrast to Maecenas, whose noble ancestry reaches far back, beyond his grandparents (**avus ... maternus ... atque paternus**), and into Etruscan prehistory, Horace is not even a generation removed from slavery.

Horace gives examples of men in the past who rose above their lowly birth or disgraced their noble origins. Yet the people are captivated by symbols of distinction and value men accordingly.

    cum referre negas quali sit quisque parente
    natus dum ingenuus, persuades hoc tibi vere,
    ante potestatem Tulli atque ignobile regnum
10 multos saepe viros nullis maioribus ortos
    et vixisse probos amplis et honoribus auctos;

7–8   **cum … negas … persuades:** a present more general condition, with **cum** having the meaning "whenever" (A&G §§542, 548).

        referre: "that it matters."

        quali sit … parente / natus: indirect question.

        quali … parente: as in line 6, another abl. of source with **natus**.

        quisque: "each man."

8   **dum ingenuus** = **dum ingenuus** [sit], a **dum** proviso clause (A&G §528), **dum** = "provided that."

        hoc: points ahead to lines 9–15.

9   **Tulli:** Servius Tullius, the sixth king of Rome. Tradition assigned the first census to Servius Tullius, who placed Roman citizens in ranks by property qualifications. Originally the highest property qualification was that of the *equites*, or knights, the **ordo equestris**. By the first century BCE, the highest property qualification was that of the senator.

        ignobile regnum: i.e., that of a man not known.

        nullis maioribus: ablative of source, with **ortos**. In an impassioned speech in Livy (4.3), a plebeian tribune argues against a law preventing plebeians intermarrying with patricians; he also argues that the consulship should be open to plebeian candidates. He introduces examples (see EXEMPLUM) of worthy individuals from early Rome whose ancestry was not patrician, and sometimes not even Roman. He points out that Rome's second king, Numa Pompilius, was not

Roman, but Sabine, and that the first Tarquin was not even Italian but the son of a man from Corinth. Then he goes on: "And after him, Servius Tullius, born from a woman captured at Corniculum; a man of no father, and slave mother, did he not rule by his intellect and excellence?" (**Servium Tullium post hunc, captiva Corniculana natum, patre nullo, matre serva, ingenio, virtute regnum tenuisse?**). Livy presented his own, different opinion in the first book of his history (1.39): He agreed with those who wrote that the elder Servius was the chief man (**princeps**) in Corniculum when it was captured. Livy says that the elder Servius was killed there, but his pregnant wife, on account of her **unicam nobilitatem**, was taken into the royal house at Rome and gave birth there. It was the mother's being a prisoner of war that led to the story of King Servius's being born to a slave woman (**serva natus**).

11 **et:** joins **vixisse** and **auctos** [**esse**]. **Honoribus** here refers to public offices.

contra Laevinum, Valeri genus unde superbus
Tarquinius regno pulsus fugit, unius assis
non unquam pretio pluris licuisse, notante
15   iudice quo nosti populo, qui stultus honores
saepe dat indignis et famae servit ineptus,
qui stupet in titulis et imaginibus. Quid oportet
nos facere a volgo longe longeque remotos?

12   **contra:** "in contrast."

Laevinum: P. Valerius Laevinus. Previous members of this family had distinguished themselves in the war with Pyrrhus and the Second Punic War; one had triumphed over the Ligurians of northwestern Italy in 175 BCE. This Laevinus has degenerated from his noble ancestors.

Valeri: The *gens Valeria* was a very old and prestigious clan. According to tradition, one of the first Roman consuls was Publius Valerius, who helped Brutus expel the Tarquin kings from Rome; a number of Valerii played prominent roles in early Roman politics.

unde = a quo.

12-13   **superbus / Tarquinius: Tarquinius Superbus**, "Tarquin the Proud," was the last of Rome's seven kings. He was extravagant and capricious, as well as arrogant; but it was his son (or grandson) Sextus Tarquin who, according to Livy, attacked Lucretia and thus brought about revolution, including the expulsion of the royal family.

unius assis: a genitive of quality (A&G §345.b) depending on **pretio** in line 14 ("the price of one **as**"). As an indication of small value, this expression has a distinguished pedigree: Catullus (poem 5) tells his beloved Lesbia that they should place precisely this value on the gossip of strict old men who criticize their love.

14-15   **notante iudice ... populo:** abl. abs. The people takes on the role of the censor: **Notare** means to make a mark of disgrace beside the name of a citizen in the senatorial or equestrian rolls and thus remove him from his rank. The census was both a financial and a moral means of organizing the state. It arranged citizens by age and property, but also by merit.

15 **iudice quo nosti: nosti = novisti,** "the judge, what kind, you know." The verb **nosco** is at the root of **ignotos** (line 6), **ignobile** (line 9), and **notante** (line 14). Maecenas, then, can judge the people judging.

16 **famae:** dat. with **servit**.

servit: Horace has avoided using the noun **servus**, "slave," although he has skirted it by referring to his father as a freedman (line 6) and to **Servius** Tullius (line 9). It is the people, **stultus** and **ineptus**, that is in slavery, and not to a person, but to **fama**.

17 **in titulis:** commemorative inscriptions that give details of a person's ancestry or career.

imaginibus: the ancestral portrait masks that were stored in the atrium, the central hall in a Roman house, and brought out to be carried in funeral processions.

17–18 **quid oportet / nos facere ... remotos: Oportet** is impersonal and may take, as here, the accusative and subject infinitive (A&G §565 note 3).

18 **volgo = vulgo.**

longe longeque: The repetition is emphatic.

remotos: a different kind of exclusivity, based on aloofness. To be removed from the senatorial or equestrian rolls is a disgrace; to remove oneself from the crowd is to assert one's superiority to it.

Horace presents a series of alternatives and preferences: Laevinus vs. Decius; obscure vs. high-born; magistrate vs. private citizen. The desire for glory drives everyone, highborn or humble; and no matter a candidate's origins or aspirations, he brings ill-will and jealousy upon himself by entering public life.

    namque esto populus Laevino mallet honorem
20 quam Decio mandare novo, censorque moveret
    Appius ingenuo si non essem patre natus:
    vel merito quoniam in propria non pelle quiessem.
    sed fulgente trahit constrictos Gloria curru
    non minus ignotos generosis. Quo tibi, Tilli,
25 sumere depositum clavum fierique tribuno?
    invidia accrevit privato quae minor esset.

19   **esto:** the future imperative, here third person, used concessively with the subjunctives **mallet** (line 19) and **moveret** (line 20): "let it be that..."

19-20 **Laevino ... / quam Decio ... novo:** datives of the indirect object with **honorem ... mandare.** As in line 11, here too an **honor** is a public office.

20   **Decio ... novo:** P. Decius Mus was a **novus homo,** "a new man," that is, one with no senatorial ancestors. Consul in 340 BCE, he "devoted" himself and the enemy to the gods of the Underworld by riding into the midst of the fighting and saving his army by his own destruction. His son, who was consul four times and censor as well, was also said to have performed a **devotio,** as was his grandson. That all three died in battle is quite possible; scholars are skeptical about three generations of Decii devoting themselves in the same way. Horace's point here is that Decius was the first of a highly distinguished family line.

20-21 **censorque...Appius:** a reference to Appius the censor could point to Appius Claudius Pulcher, who was censor in 50 BCE and struck all sons of freedmen from the Senate; but it also calls to mind Appius Claudius Caecus, the famous censor in 312 BCE, who built the

Appian Way and Appian aqueduct and was known for bringing freedmen *into* the Senate while excluding their social superiors on moral grounds. Once again, Horace brings to the fore the idea of family background: the Claudii were an old and prestigious clan.

moveret = **me moveret**; here, **movere** means to strike from the list of the members of the Senate.

21 **ingenuo ... patre natus:** Appius would strike Horace from the Senate on the grounds that he is the son not of a freeborn man but of an ex-slave.

22 **vel merito:** "or deservedly"; Horace suggests that the second reason why Appius would remove Horace from a hypothetical Senate position (explained by **quoniam ... non ... quiessem**) is more legitimate than the first.

23 **sed fulgente trahit constrictos Gloria curru:** Note the PERSONIFICATION. **Gloria** in her shining chariot drags her captives behind as if celebrating a triumph.

24 **ignotos generosis:** The two categories are now juxtaposed. **Generosis** is ablative of comparison.

quo tibi: "to what end for you?" or "what good is it to you?"

Tilli: Possibly L. Tillius Cimber, who was removed from the Senate by Julius Caesar and became one of his assassins.

25 **sumere ... et fieri:** substantive infinitives after **quo**. "What good is it to?" (*OLD s.v.* **quo** *interr.*): "to what end?" "to what purpose?"

depositum clavum: The **clavus** was the **latus clavus**, the broad purple stripe that distinguished a senator's toga. The stripe was **depositum** presumably because Tillius is returning to office after spending time as a private citizen.

tribuno: dative by attraction to **tibi**, where we would expect a predicate nominative with **fieri**.

25 **privato:** possessive dative with **esset**. The idea is conditional, in a present contrary to fact condition (A&G §514.A.1): **si privatus esses, invidia minor esset.**

Any signs that a man has ambition, whether to be considered handsome or to advance politically, make him the object of scrutiny, in regard to his looks or his background.

> nam ut quisque insanus nigris medium impediit crus
> pellibus et latum demisit pectore clavum,
> audit continuo: "Quis homo hic est? quo patre natus?"
> 30 ut si qui aegrotet quo morbo Barrus, haberi
> ut cupiat formosus, eat quacumque puellis
> iniiciat curam quaerendi singula, quali
> sit facie, sura, quali pede, dente, capillo:
> sic qui promittit cives, urbem sibi curae,
> 35 imperium fore et Italiam, delubra deorum,
> quo patre sit natus, num ignota matre inhonestus,
> omnes mortales curare et quaerere cogit.

27 **ut . . . medium impediit crus:** "as soon as he has bound "his leg up to the middle of his calf" (A&G §543). The dark straps of a senator's red sandals wound up his calves and were tied at the back.

insanus: Horace represents political ambition as a form of insanity.

nigris . . . pellibus: the dark laces that bound sandals to the foot and shin.

28 **continuo:** adv. "immediately."

29 **quis homo hic est? quo patre natus?:** the first quoted direct speech in the poem consists of two short questions. Scan the line. Note that the *h* of **homo** does not make **quis** a long syllable; note also the elision over the *h* of **hic**; note also the interplay of the ictus (stress) on the first part of the metrical foot and the word accent, which puts emphasis on **hic** and **quo** and creates an impression of speed. The questions circulate quickly.

30-31 **aegrotet quo morbo Barrus** = aegrotet illo morbo quo Barrus aegrotat. Political ambition, like the desire to appear attractive, is a metaphorical illness.

HORACE, SATIRE 1.6.27–37

Barrus: The name means "elephant," which meaning lends humor to the idea of discussing the details of his physical beauty.

haberi / ut cupiat formosus: a result clause. **Haberi** with predicate nominative **formosus**, "to be considered handsome."

eat quacumque: jussive subjunctive: "Let him go wherever."

puellis: dat. with **iniciat**.

32   **iniciat:** The apodosis is that of a future less vivid condition (A&G §516.2).

singula: the neuter plural is the direct object of **quaerendi**, in apposition to the indirect questions **quali sit ... quali**.

quaerendi: objective genitive with **curam** (A&G §348).

32–33   **quali / sit facie, sura, quali pede, dente, capillo:** ablatives of quality (A&G §415); **sit** is subjunctive because it is in an indirect question.

34   **sibi curae:** double dative construction, with a dative of purpose and a dative of person (A&G §382.1): **cives, urbem, imperium, Italiam, delubrum** will be a source/cause of **cura** to **sibi**.

35   **fore:** an alternate form of the future infinitive, here (because of the plural subject) = **futura esse**.

36   **quo patre sit natus, num ignota matre inhonestus:** indirect questions depending on **curare** and **quaerere** in the following line. Repeat **sit** with **num ... inhonestus**.

num: expects the answer "no." So the question can be introduced with some such phrase as "surely he isn't?"

37   **curare ... quaerere:** picks up **curam quaerendi** of line 32.

In a short embedded dialogue between two social climbers, both of whom look down on someone else, Horace mimics an example of the snobbery aimed at the sons of ex-slaves.

    "tune Syri, Damae aut Dionysi filius, audes
    deiicere e saxo cives aut tradere Cadmo?"
40   "at Novius collega gradu post me sedet uno;
    namque est ille pater quod erat meus." hoc tibi Paullus
    et Messalla videris? at hic, si plostra ducenta
    concurrantque foro tria funera magna, sonabit
    cornua quod vincatque tubas; saltem tenet hoc nos."

38   **Syri:** a Syrian; also, a slave-name used in Roman comedy.

    Damae aut Dionysi: typical slave-names, both Greek.

    deiicere e saxo cives: Romans punished traitors by throwing them off the Tarpeian Rock, a precipice of the Capitoline Hill. Note the contrast between foreign slaves and Roman citizens.

    tradere Cadmo = tradere eos [cives] Cadmo.

    Cadmo: another Greek name, here that of an executioner.

40   **Novius:** The **-ius** suffix in Latin names originally indicated a patronymic. **Novius**, then, means "son of a new man" (**novus homo**).

    gradu ... uno: ablative of comparison with **post**, "behind me by one seat," or "one seat behind me," that is, a row higher in the theater, a slightly inferior seat.

41   **namque est ille pater quod erat meus:** that is, **ille (Novius)** is a **libertus**.

    hoc: "for this reason."

    Paullus: a member of the old and illustrious family the Aemilii Paulli, who produced one of the consuls who fought at Cannae (216 BCE) as well as the conqueror of Macedonia in 168 BCE.

42 **Messalla:** another old and illustrious cognomen. A number of Valerii Messallae held the consulship during the republic. A Marcus Valerius Messalla Corvinus, whom Horace knew personally, was a literary patron of the poet Tibullus and supporter of Octavian.

hic = Novius.

plostra = plaustra.

tria funera magna: The most detailed description of a Roman funeral is in the sixth book of the *Histories* of Polybius, who tells how, whenever a noble Roman died, a retinue escorted the body of the deceased to the Forum, where he was eulogized before an audience consisting of his living relatives, images of his dead relatives, and the public.

cornua quod vincatque tubas: a relative cause of characteristic (A&G §535). The enclitic **-que** joins **cornua** and **tubas**, the objects of **vincat**.

saltem tenet hoc nos: Novius's one claim to attention is his loud voice. The verb **tenet** here means "he holds our attention" (*OLD, s.v. teneo,* 22 a).

Horace returns to his own lowly background, and to Maecenas as well. The envy aimed at Horace's holding political office now comes from his close friendship with Maecenas.

45 nunc ad me redeo libertino patre natum,
quem rodunt omnes libertino patre natum,
nunc, quia sum tibi, Maecenas, convictor; at olim,
quod mihi pareret legio Romana tribuno.
dissimile hoc illi est; quia non ut forsit honorem
50 iure mihi invideat quivis ita te quoque amicum,
praesertim cautum dignos assumere prava
ambitione procul. Felicem dicere non hoc
me possim casu quod te sortitus amicum;
nulla etenim mihi te fors obtulit: optimus olim
55 Virgilius, post hunc Varius dixere quid essem.

45 **nunc ad me redeo:** Has Horace ever really left himself as the main topic?

libertino patre natum: The repetition within two lines echoes the repetition of this insult. That Horace repeats it, having first brought it up in line 6, suggests that it is eating at him.

46 **rodunt:** to "gnaw," "nibble," "eat away at," a striking METAPHOR for backbiting.

47 **nunc:** The contrast is, again, with **olim**.

sum tibi ... convictor: The dative is possessive; **convictor** is from **convivo** + **tor** and signifies a person who lives on close terms with another, a friend or companion.

Maecenas: Horace has just returned to himself as a topic; now the vocative directs attention to Maecenas as the poem's addressee and gives the impression that Horace is speaking to him face-to-face.

48 **pareret legio Romana:** Horace compares himself to Maecenas, whose ancestors were the sort to command legions: **olim qui magnis legionibus imperitarent** (line 4); but Horace is two generations behind and less exalted in rank. The subjunctive **pareret** gives the alleged grounds of the criticism.

49 **hoc illi: hoc** refers to Horace's friendship with Maecenas; **illi** to his gaining the office of tribune. **Illi** is dat. with **dissimile**. The dative is used with some adjectives of likeness and their opposites (A&G §384).

non: negates the entire construction: "it's not the case that…"

ut … ita: correlative: "just as … so too."

forsit: "perhaps."

iure mihi invideat: "would rightly begrudge me." Repeat this with both **honorem** and **te … amicum** as objects.

cautum: [te] … cautum + infinitive. "Careful to…"

ambitione: The Latin for "ambition" is an abstraction from the verb **ambire**, which can mean simply to go around, but also to canvass for votes in an election. There can be no reason to begrudge Horace Maecenas's friendship, because it lies outside of politics.

procul: adverb used as quasi-preposition with the ablative (A&G §432.c).

felicem: that is, it was not luck that brought Horace and Maecenas together.

hoc: ablative of specification (A&G §418); it looks forward to **casu quod te sortitus [sum] amicum**.

nulla … fors obtulit: Note how Chance is the active agent.

optimus olim / Virgilius: a slightly different use of **olim**, to mean "at some point in the past," "some time ago."

55 **post hunc Varius:** Varius Rufus was an Augustan epic, elegiac, and tragic poet, who, with Plotius Tucca, edited the *Aeneid* after Vergil's death.

dixere quid essem: dixere = **dixerunt quid essem**, an indirect question.

Horace describes his first meeting with Maecenas. He was tongue-tied but responded honestly, if awkwardly, to Maecenas's questions about his background. This pleased Maecenas, who established Horace within the circle of his friends.

> ut veni coram singultim pauca locutus,
> infans namque pudor prohibebat plura profari,
> non ego me claro natum patre, non ego circum
> me Satureiano vectari rura caballo,
> 60   sed quod eram narro. Respondes ut tuus est mos
> pauca: abeo; et revocas nono post mense iubesque
> esse in amicorum numero. magnum hoc ego duco
> quod placui tibi qui turpi secernis honestum,
> non patre praeclaro sed vita et pectore puro.

56   **ut veni: ut** + perfect indicative, "when."

57   **singultim pauca locutus:** Note the ONOMATOPOEIA produced by the gulping sounds of these words as well as the stuttering effect of the ALLITERATION of *p* sounds in **pudor prohibebat plura profari**.

pauca: object of the active **locutus** (from the deponent **loquor**).

58–60   **non . . . non:** more ANAIRESIS. The ANAPHORA of **non ego** also produces the effect of short, stammering sentences. **Non . . . eram** are in indirect speech introduced by the main verb **narro**.

me claro natum patre: the most important thing on Horace's mind, even before his lack of property. Note the repetition of **me . . . natum patre**.

circum . . . vectari: TMESIS for **circumvectari**.

vectari: the passive of **vecto**, thus "to be conveyed" or "to ride."

Satureiano . . . caballo: ablative of means (the horse being considered as an instrument, A&G §405 note 2); the adjective **Satureiano** recalls the idea of fullness, **satur**, associated with Satire.

60 **quod eram:** Subordinate clauses in indirect speech have their verbs in the subjunctive. Note here the use of the indicative to form a simple relative clause expressing reality that is independent of Horace's telling of it (A&G §§583, 583.a).

61 **pauca = pauca verba.** Neither Horace nor Maecenas says much.

post: adv., "afterward."

iubesque: Even in friendship there is a power imbalance.

62 **magnum hoc = magnum hoc esse**, explained by **quod placui tibi**.

duco: here in its sense of "reckon" or "consider."

turpi secernis honestum: Note how the verb literally divides "disgraceful" and "respectable." **Turpi** is ablative of separation.

64 **patre praeclaro:** ablative of cause (A&G §404) explaining **placui**. Horace uses the adjective **praeclarus** sarcastically later (line 110).

vita et pectore puro: another ablative of cause explaining **placui**: moral distinction is more valuable than an illustrious family.

Horace's father deserves credit for his son's character, which is mostly good but marked by a few human foibles. His father sent him to Rome for an upper-class education and supervised it carefully.

> 65 atqui si vitiis mediocribus ac mea paucis
> mendosa est natura alioqui recta, velut si
> egregio inspersos reprehendas corpore naevos;
> si neque avaritiam neque sordes nec mala lustra
> obiiciet vere quisquam mihi, purus et insons
> 70 (ut me collaudem) si et vivo carus amicis;
> causa fuit pater his, qui macro pauper agello
> noluit in Flavi ludum me mittere, magni
> quo pueri magnis e centurionibus orti,
> laevo suspensi loculos tabulamque lacerto,
> 75 ibant octonis referentes idibus aeris:

65–70   **atqui si ... est ... si ... obiiciet ... si et vivo ...:** The ANAPHORA of **si** holds together a triple protasis ("if-clause") in a mixed conditional sentence. The verbs of the protasis are present and future (**est, obiiciet, vivo**), while that of the apodosis is perfect (**fuit**). Horace intends a pointed contrast between his (presumably deceased) father's efforts and the results felt in the present.

65   **vitiis mediocribus ac ... paucis:** causal ablatives. Horace's point is that the flaws in his nature are neither many nor extreme.

66   **alioqui:** adv., "otherwise," "in other respects."

67   **egregio ... naevos:** The word order (a so-called golden line, whose word order is adjective 1-adjective 2-verb-noun 1-noun 2) focuses attention on the adjectives; but the very balance of the line also plays against the physical flaws discussed.

reprehendas: the potential subjunctive in the indefinite second person.

68   **avaritiam:** one of the common vices, according to Horace in *Satire* 1.4.

sordes: both physical dirt and metaphorical meanness of character, stinginess.

mala lustra: dens of iniquity, places of vice.

69 **vere:** People can slander Horace; but the point is, their slander will not be true.

purus et insons: Translate with **carus** as part of the **si**-clause of the following line.

70 **(ut me collaudem):** concessive **ut** + subjunctive.

71 **causa fuit pater his:** the main clause and apodosis of the mixed condition. Note how the long and complicated protasis builds up to this simple statement. The dative **his** is possessive.

macro . . . agello: not just an **ager macer**, "a meager farm," but a diminutive plot of land.

72 **Flavi:** the local schoolmaster.

72–73 **magni . . . magnis:** Note the repetition; the adjective also recalls **magnis legionibus** from the opening lines and Horace's own assertion of his values in line 62: **magnum hoc ego duco.**

74 **laevo . . . lacerto:** abl. of place from which.

suspensi loculos: the perfect passive participle (from **suspendo, -dere, -si, -sum**), here has a middle meaning (A&G §156.a and note): "having hung their writing cases," or "dangling their writing cases."

75 **ibant:** the imperfect here conveys repeated action (A&G §470).

aeris: genitive with ELLIPSIS of the accusative of the specific coinage, either **asses** or **nummos**.

octonis . . . idibus: From this reading, tuition was due on the first of every eighth month. Other texts read **octonos** [sc. **assos** or **nummos**] **referentes idibus aeris**: "each carrying his eight-**as** fee on the first of the month."

sed puerum est ausus Romam portare docendum
artes quas doceat quivis eques atque senator
semet prognatos. Vestem servosque sequentes,
in magno ut populo, si qui vidisset, avita
80 ex re praeberi sumptus mihi crederet illos.

76 **docendum:** gerundive with **puerum**, expressing purpose (A&G §500.4).

77 **artes:** direct object of **docendum**.

quas doceat: rel. clause of characteristic (A&G §535).

78 **semet** = **se**, but intensified by the suffix **-met**.

79 **in magno ut populo:** "as happens in a large crowd."

79-80 **si quid vidisset / . . . crederet:** The tenses in this mixed (past and present contrary-to-fact) condition reflect the sequence of events.

avita / ex re: The noun **res** here has the meaning of "property."

80 **sumptus . . . illos:** the expenditure on clothing and on slaves to follow Horace, protect his morals, and carry his books. The accusatives are subjects of **praeberi**.

mihi: dative of the indirect object, with **praeberi**.

Books, in the form of papyrus rolls, were often kept in a case called a *capsa* or *scrinium* as depicted in the center of the mosaic. A poet, left, holds a scroll, while an actor, right, holds a mask. This third-century CE mosaic is now in the collection of the Sousse Archaeological Museum in Sousse, Tunisia. (© Ad Meskens / Wikimedia Commons)

Horace's father kept a careful eye on his son's schooling and morals. He protected his son's integrity of both body and reputation.

> ipse mihi custos incorruptissimus omnes
> circum doctores aderat. quid multa? pudicum,
> qui primus virtutis honos, servavit ab omni
> non solum facto verum opprobrio quoque turpi;
> 85 nec timuit sibi ne vitio quis verteret olim
> si praeco parvas aut, ut fuit ipse, coactor
> mercedes sequerer; neque ego essem questus: at hoc nunc
> laus illi debetur et a me gratia maior.

81–82 **mihi:** dat. with **aderat**. See A&G §370 for compound verbs with datives of the indirect object.

incorruptissimus: one of the poem's few superlatives (Horace calls Vergil **optimus** in line 55; and **primus**, superlative of **prior**, appears in line 83). Note too that in lines 1–2, Horace talks around a superlative by telling Maecenas **nemo est generosior te** instead of directly calling him **generosissimus**. Here with the superlative and with **omnes . . . doctores**, Horace emphasizes the exceptional and unrelenting nature of his father's care.

quid multa? = quid multa dicam?

pudicum = me pudicum. Horace's father protected the **pudicitia**, the sexual aspect of the **pudor** that so impressed Maecenas (line 57).

83 **qui primus virtutis honos:** All higher steps on the **cursus honorum** of excellence rest on a foundation of **pudicitia** and **pudor**. The term **cursus honorum** refers to the ladder of offices a Roman aristocrat would attempt to climb, those of **quaestor, aedile, praetor, consul,** and **censor**.

omni . . . turpi: The adjectives modify both **facto** and **opprobrio**.

85 **sibi ne vitio quis verteret:** a clause of fearing. **quis = aliquis; vitio vertere:** "to treat as a fault"; **vitio** is a dative of the purpose or end (A&G §382) after **verteret; sibi** is a dative of the person affected (A&G §382); this is sometimes simply called the "double dative" construction.

olim: here "ever," "someday," looking ahead to the future in the clause **si . . . sequerer.**

86-87 **si . . . sequerer:** The condition is subordinate to the verb of fearing. Without subordination, the fear in the head of Horace's father would be a future more vivid condition, for example: **si praeco aut coactor parvas mercedes sequetur, aliquis mihi vitio vertet.**

86 **praeco . . . coactor:** auctioneer and collector (of money or taxes), a pair of modest if not actually seedy occupations.

87 **neque ego essem questus:** past contrary to fact.

at . . . nunc: "but as it is."

hoc: "in this respect." Ablative of specification, with **maior.**

laus . . . gratia: Horace owes both praise and gratitude to his father (**et** joins **laus** and **gratia**); the phrasing, however, suggests that the praise can (and perhaps should) come from other sources as well. For two subjects considered as a single whole, see A&G §317.b.

Horace claims that, unlike the majority of people, he will not feel shame at his humble parentage. Indeed, given the choice, he would choose the same ancestors all over again.

   nil me poeniteat sanum patris huius, eoque
90 non, ut magna dolo factum negat esse suo pars
   quod non ingenuos habeat clarosque parentes,
   sic me defendam. longe mea discrepat istis
   et vox et ratio. nam si natura iuberet
   a certis annis aevum remeare peractum
95 atque alios legere ad fastum quoscunque parentes
   optaret sibi quisque, meis contentus honestos
   fascibus et sellis nollem mihi sumere, demens
   iudicio volgi, sanus fortasse tuo, quod
   nollem onus haud unquam solitus portare molestum.

89 **nil:** with adverbial force: "not at all."

   poeniteat = **paeniteat.** Jussive subjunctive. When this verb is used impersonally, that is, without a subject, it takes an accusative of the person who is affected with regret and a genitive of the thing causing the emotion.

   sanum: "as long as I am sound of mind."

   eoque: "and for that reason."

90-92 **ut ... sic:** "as ... so too," a correlative (A&G §323.g).

90-92 **magna ... pars:** "the majority of people," in contrast with the speaker, subject of **defendam** in line 92.

   dolo ... suo: "by its own stratagem."

   factum esse: here "came about," "was brought about," neuter, in agreement with the clause **quod ... parentes** (line 91). **Habeat** is a subjunctive in a subordinate clause in indirect statement, here introduced by **negat** (A&G §580).

92 **longe:** Note the emphatic position of the adverb.

92-93 **discrepat:** the singular verb with two subjects (**vox, ratio**) considered as a single whole (A&G §317.b).

istis: dative with **discrepat**.

93 **et vox et ratio:** both the expression of the sentiment and the reckoning that went into it.

93-96 **si natura iuberet . . .:** the protasis of a present contrary to fact condition.

iuberet: + infinitives **remeare** and **legere**.

a certis annis: "after a fixed period," or "from a given age," depending on how one takes **remeare** (see next note).

aevum remeare peractum: According to the *OLD*, **remeare** here has the sense of "to come round again" (*OLD s.v.* **remeare** 2.c), with **aevum ... peractum** its subject, so that one's lived-through lifetime recurs; a number of translators and commentators, however, take an implied "us" as the subject of **remeare** in the sense of "return to," or "travel back through," the **aevum ... peractum**, one's lived-through lifetime. It is a nice point; but whatever side of the issue one comes down on, the meaning is clearly along the lines of "if I could relive my life all over again."

95 **alios ... parentes:** object of **legere**. There are two ways to take lines 95-97. One is to take **quoscumque** with **alios legere**, and thus produce a double apodosis: **optaret sibi quisque**, "each might choose for himself," and **meis contentus ... nollem**, "content with my own, I would not wish . . ." In this case the ANTITHESIS of **quisque** and **meis** takes the place of a conjunction. The other is to take **optaret sibi quisque** closely with **quoscumque parentes**: "to select *whichever* other *parents each chose for himself.*"

ad fastum: "to match his pride."

quoscunque: relative pronoun; direct object of **optaret**.

97 **fascibus et sellis:** causal ablatives with **honestos**.

volgi ... tuo: The possessives are parallel and depend on **iudicio**.

98-99 **quod ... molestum:** explains the grounds for Maecenas's judgment.

Horace explains why he would not want to be ambitious. Seeking political office involves increased demands and obligations. He will need more money, have to expend more energy in the ancient equivalent of networking, and take along more of a retinue as well as more baggage, wherever he goes.

100   nam mihi continuo maior quaerenda foret res
    atque salutandi plures, ducendus et unus
    et comes alter uti ne solus rusve peregreve
    exirem; plures calones atque caballi
    pascendi, ducenda petorrita. nunc mihi curto
105 ire licet mulo vel si libet usque Tarentum,
    Mantica cui lumbos onere ulceret atque eques armos.
    obiiciet nemo sordes mihi quas tibi, Tilli,
    cum Tiburte via praetorem quinque sequuntur
    te pueri lasanum portantes oenophorumque.

100   **maior ... res:** the first of several expressions of quantity in this passage (**plures ... unus ... alter ... solus ... plures ... nemo ... quinque**). Note how the hexameter comes to a thumping end with the one-syllable word **res**, "wealth" or "property."

   foret = esset.

100–4   **quaerenda ... salutandi ... ducendus ... pascendi, ducenda:** The series of heavy-sounding gerundives conveys the burden imposed by these obligations.

   salutandi: The institution of the **salutatio** obliged the up-and-coming politician to pay a morning visit to his social and political superiors; likewise, the superiors were obliged to receive those calls.

   uti ne = ne.

   solus: The ability to go about alone is an important part of Horace's freedom.

   rusve peregreve: "into the country or abroad."

103–4   **plures calones atque caballi pascendi:** Note how Horace thinks of both human attendants and horses as a herd that has to be fed.

104   **petorrita:** This Gallic word for a four-wheeled cart appears twice in Horace, and otherwise rarely, except in grammarians and writers commenting on Horace. Perhaps the exotic term helps emphasize the excessiveness of these demands.

nunc: "as it is."

104–5   **curto ... mulo:** a gelded mule, which, given that mules are sterile hybrids, is overstatement. As the sole carrier of both rider and baggage, he is the very antithesis of increase.

105   **Tarentum:** A coastal town about three hundred miles southeast of Rome, in the instep of the Italian "boot." See map.

106   **mantica cui ... ulceret:** a consecutive clause, here, a relative clause of result (A&G §537).

eques: The word means both "knight" and "rider." The narrating Horace pokes fun at himself for having achieved Equestrian status.

107   **obiiciet nemo:** Horace is so solitary that Nobody's criticisms accompany him.

108   **cum ... sequuntur: cum,** "whenever," taking the construction of relative clause in a general condition, A&G §542 and §548.

Tiburte via: the road from Rome to Tibur (modern Tivoli), a very short journey of about eighteen miles. See map. Tibur was a fashionable resort.

praetorem: An etymological joke. **Praetor** is from the verb "to go in front," **praeire**. Horace addresses Tillius (also of line 24) as both officeholder and the one who goes in front of the **pueri**, who follow with the undignified crockery.

109   **lasanum:** a chamber pot.

oenophorumque: In contrast to the monosyllabic **res** that concludes the first line of Horace's explanation, a long Greek word for "wine jug" occupies the last two metrical feet of the final line.

Horace extols the virtues and the freedom of his own simple life. He passes through the center of Rome without taking part in the political life of the great city; and his economical participation is minimal.

110   hoc ego commodius quam tu, praeclare senator,
      milibus atque aliis vivo. quacunque libido est,
      incedo solus; percontor quanti olus ac far;
      fallacem Circum vespertinumque pererro
      saepe Forum; adsisto divinis; inde domum me
115   ad porri et ciceris refero laganique catinum;
      coena ministratur pueris tribus, et lapis albus
      pocula cum cyatho duo sustinet; adstat echinus
      vilis, cum patera guttus, Campana supellex.

110   **hoc:** ablative of specification.

        commodius: the only comparative in this section; not "more" in quantity, like **maior** and **plures**, but "more convenient."

        praeclare: sarcastic.

111   **milibus ... aliis:** Again, Horace separates himself not just from the individual whom he is addressing, but from the crowd. Note that he has switched from a comparative **quam** construction (**ego ... quam tu**) to a comparative ablative.

        libido: Horace's **libido** is less aggressive than the one that *seizes* tyrants (see the Livy selections in this volume).

112   **incedo:** This verb suggests slow and stately going. Horace is in no rush and he is in control of his movements.

        solus: in emphatic contrast to traveler of lines 100–104.

        percontor: Horace asks the price; he does not necessarily buy.

        quanti: a genitive denoting indefinite value (A&G §417).

        olus = holus. Vegetables or potherbs were locally produced and therefore modest foods.

far: emmer wheat, the earliest wheat used by the Romans, often cooked into porridge.

113 **fallacem Circum:** The Circus Maximus was **fallax** because of the astrologers who set up there.

vespertinumque: The adjective modifies **forum** but has adverbial force: "at night."

pererro: In no hurry and with no particular goal, Horace can roam about the place.

114 **Forum:** the heart of the city; the center of Roman politics and finance, both of which Horace avoids, since he is there during the "off" hours.

adsisto divinis: Horace observers the diviners at work. He does not appear to participate.

115 **porri:** leeks, a vegetable easily grown locally, and therefore neither rare nor prestigious.

ciceris: chickpeas (garbanzo beans), another humble food.

laganique: a flat pasta.

catinum: a dish; here a "dish" consisting of the ingredients listed (like the use of "bowl," for example, in "a bowl of rice and beans").

116 **coena = cena.**

pueris tribus: dative of agent, more common in poetry (A&G §375.a). Horace has a very small staff at home.

lapis albus: a piece of marble.

117 **pocula ... duo:** two cups and a ladle: Either Horace has two kinds of wine or he has one companion who is willing to share a modest meal. In either case, the point is that the simplicity of the dinner extends to the utensils.

echinus: perhaps a saltcellar.

118 **guttus:** a narrow-necked vessel, for pouring libations.

Campana supellex: locally manufactured pottery, therefore not luxury goods.

> deinde eo dormitum, non sollicitus mihi quod cras
> 120 surgendum sit mane, obeundus Marsya, qui se
> voltum ferre negat Noviorum posse minoris.

119 **dormitum:** supine after a verb of motion (A&G §509).

cras: a monosyllabic jolt from sound slumber.

120 **surgendum . . . obeundus:** As in lines 100–104 above, the gerundives convey obligation.

sit: The subjunctive shows that **quod . . . surgendum sit** is what would be in Horace's thoughts, troubling him, if he were ambitious.

Marsya: Marsyas was a satyr who challenged Apollo to a flute-playing contest and was defeated. His statue was in the Roman Forum. By using the statue as a meeting point, Horace invokes the painful connotations of Marsyas's name: he was flayed alive as punishment for defeat. (Horace, in contrast, is neither boastful nor ambitious.)

121 **Noviorum:** Although we do not know the specific identity of the **Novii**, we can still note the name's connotations of newness.

ferre: here, "endure," "tolerate," or "bear." When a statue of someone who was flayed alive says he cannot "endure" someone, that someone must be awful.

minoris: "the younger," as opposed to **maioris**, "the elder."

Apollo, here depicted with a cithara and wearing a laurel crown, is the patron god of many realms, including music and the arts. This statue, a Roman copy of a fifth-century BCE Greek original, is housed in the New Wing of the Vatican Museums. (© Creative Commons 3.0/Sailko)

The next day sees Horace equally serene, his life controlled not by the clock, but by the enjoyment of moderate pleasure and the avoidance of discomfort.

>   ad quartam iaceo; post hanc vagor; aut ego, lecto
>   aut scripto quod me tacitum iuvet, ungor olivo,
>   non quo fraudatis immundus Natta lucernis.
> 125 ast ubi me fessum sol acrior ire lavatum
>   admonuit fugio Campum lusumque trigonem.
>   pransus non avide, quantum interpellet inani
>   ventre diem durare, domesticus otior. Haec est
>   vita solutorum misera ambitione gravique;
> 130 his me consolor victurum suavius ac si
>   quaestor avus, pater atque meus patruusque fuisset.

122 **ad quartam = ad quartam horam:** late mid-morning (A&G §221.2.b).

post hanc = post hanc horam.

vagor: Horace's aimless rambling serves no apparent purpose.

122-123 **lecto aut scripto quod ... iuvet:** ablative absolute; the clause **quod ... iuvet** takes the place of the substantive in the ablative (A&G §419.b).

123 **tacitum:** Horace emphasizes the solitary nature of his pleasure.

ungor: I anoint (myself) or "I have myself anointed."

non quo = non [illo olivo] quo ... immundus Natta [unguitur].

fraudatis ... lucernis: ablative absolute. Oil taken from the lamps would be less pure than cosmetic oil. It might also be recycled: At the baths, the oil used for cleaning the body was scraped off and reused.

Natta = Natta unguitur. Natta might refer to Pinarius Natta, brother of Fulvia (wife of Mark Antony) and brother-in-law of Publius Clodius Pulcher. Perhaps Horace means to call to mind the Greek verb *natto*, which means "to cram" or "to stuff." A platter or a sausage stuffed with many ingredients is a metaphor for the variety found in satiric verse.

125 **ast:** an amplified form of **at**, "but."

125-126 **sol acrior ... admonuit:** The perceived intensity of the sun causes Horace to flee, not the length of its shadow, which was, of course, an ancient means of telling the hour of day.

125 **lavatum:** supine, as often, with a verb of motion (A&G §509).

126 **Campum:** the Campus Martius, a floodplain in the Tiber bend north of the city center. Largely undeveloped until Augustus's time, it was the city's exercise field and the place where citizens assembled in arms.

lusumque trigonem: "playing the three-sided [ball] game." We do not know what this game was, or even, in fact, if it included a ball, but infer from its name, **trigon**, that the players stationed themselves at the points of a triangle.

127 **pransus:** perfect participle, in active sense, from **prandeo**.

quantum = tantum, quantum.

127-128 **interpellet:** + inf., "obstruct," or "impede" from doing something.

otior: Yet, while ostensibly at leisure, away from the forum or the courts, Horace is actively studying or writing poetry.

129-130 **haec ... vita ... his:** The demonstratives summarize the activities listed in the previous lines.

ambitione: abl. of separation (A&G §400) with **solutorum**.

130 **consolor:** only mock-seriously: The last half of the poem has argued that a life free from wretched and burdensome (**misera ... gravique**) ambition needs no consolation.

victurum = victurum esse.

ac = comparative **quam**.

131 **quaestor:** Horace ends this "autobiographical" poem with the first step on the Roman **cursus honorum**.

Martial

Epigrams 1.35, 41; 6.64; 10.10, 20; 12.61
Standard Level and Higher Level

— Introduction to Martial —

Almost all we know about Martial comes from his own poems, and is therefore not to be taken completely at face value: even the wife whom he portrays in a hostile manner is quite possibly a poetic construct. The following sketch draws on details that seem reliable: Martial was born in Bilbilis in Spain around 40 CE. After his education in Spain, he came to Rome in 64. He writes of early poverty in cheap urban housing, then the acquisition of a small farm on the edge of Sabine territory, where he found relief from the heat and noise of the city. He was friendly with—or at least he flatters—other literary figures: the satirist Juvenal; the epic poet Silius Italicus; the rhetorician Quintilian; the writer of technical treatises Frontinus; and the provincial governor and author of literary letters and poetry, Pliny the Younger.

Martial's first surviving collection was a set of epigrams on the spectacles that opened the Flavian amphitheater (the Colosseum) in 80 CE. From the years 86 to 98 he issued eleven books of short and witty poems replete with details of urban life and the lives of people of all classes, from the emperor Domitian (whom he praised) to drunken poets, prostitutes, and lowly slaves.

After Domitian's death in 96 CE, Martial left Rome. Pliny the Younger writes (*Ep.*3.21) that he financed Martial's return to Spain, where a patroness gave him a home in the country. Here Martial wrote his final, twelfth, book of epigrams and died a few years later, probably in 104.

— Meters —

Dactylic Hexameter: *Epigram* 6.64
Hendecasyllables: *Epigrams* 1.35, 1.41, 10.20, 12.61

— *Epigram* 1.35 —

Lasciva est nobis pagina, vita proba, "my page is wanton but my life is modest" (Martial 1.4.8). Students who have read Catullus's short poems will recognize echoes of Catullus 1 and 16 in this poem's sentiments, its meter, and the name of its addressee. Martial's Cornelius is obviously not the Cornelius (Nepos) to whom Catullus dedicated his book of poems over a century earlier. Martial's Cornelius is a critic; and his complaints echo those of the critics in Catullus 16. The poem is a literary manifesto; and the address to "Cornelius" is highly ironic if it refers to Gnaeus Cornelius Lentulus Gaeticulus (poet and consul of 26 CE), cited by Martial (Book 1, pr.) as a model for his own obscenity.

> versus scribere me parum severos
> nec quos praelegat in schola magister,
> Corneli, quereris: sed hi libelli,
> tamquam coniugibus suis mariti,
> 5 non possunt sine mentula placere.
> quid si me iubeas thalassionem
> verbis dicere non thalassionis?

1   **versus scribere me:** The word order inverts the general tendency of the subject to come first (**me scribere versus**) and focuses attention on **versus** as the topic of the poem (A&G §598). With **scribere** Martial figures himself as a writer of physical texts, like Catullus, not a singer, like composers of epic or lyric. Moreover, as this poem goes on, we see that Martial's poetry not only is physical writing; it also has a metaphorical body.

         parum severos: Catullus 16 addresses critics who, he says, consider him **parum pudicus**, and his verses **parum pudici**. From the first line, then, it is apparent that Martial is addressing a critic. His friend Pliny the Younger alludes to this poem when he says that he himself writes risqué poems (*Ep.* 5.3.2): **facio non numquam versiculos severos parum**, "I occasionally compose verses that are not serious enough."

         severos: The adjective could recall the old men of Catullus 5, who are **severiores**.

2   **nec quos praelegat in schola magister:** neither poems of educational value, such as, for example, the *Aeneid*, nor poems suitable for children.

praelegat: subjunctive in a rel. clause of characteristic (A&G §534).

schola: This would be a school run by a **grammaticus**, an elementary schoolteacher, or a **ludi magister**, a schoolmaster.

3   **Corneli:** The name **Corneli**, also vocative, appears in the same position in the same line of Catullus 1.

hi libelli: The word **libellus** also recalls the opening of Catullus 1: **cui dono lepidum novum libellum?**

4   **coniugibus suis:** dative with **placere** (A&G §367).

5   **non possunt sine mentula placere:** obviously sexual, but within the bounds of marriage, this is legitimate and appropriate behavior.

mentula: both the male sexual organ and a symbol of obscenity. Some of Catullus's short poems (94, 105, 114, 115) feature a personified **Mentula**.

6   **quid si me iubeas . . .?:** This RHETORICAL QUESTION calls to mind that of the poet Ovid (43 BCE–17 CE) about using the appropriate poetic tools (in his case the appropriate meter) for the job. In *Amores* 1.1, Ovid says that he began to write a military epic, but that Cupid stole a metrical foot from the second line, thus turning the hexameters of epic into the elegiac couplets of love poetry. Ovid asks indignantly: **quid si praeripiat flavae Venus arma Minervae / ventilet accensas flava Minerva faces?** ("What if Venus should snatch up blonde Minerva's weapons, and blonde Minerva brandish kindled wedding torches?").

iubeas: subjunctive in a Future Less Vivid Condition (A&G §516.b), with the ELLIPSIS of the verb in the apodosis: "What [would be the case] if you should order me . . .?"

thalassionem: The Romans cried out "**thalassio**" at weddings. Livy (Book 1) tells the origin story of this custom: When the Romans were kidnapping the daughters of their Sabine neighbors to take as wives, a band of men who were carrying off one conspicuously beautiful young woman cried out repeatedly, "Thalassio!" meaning "[she's] for Thalassius!" The Roman god Talas(s)ius (or Thal-) was the personification of this cry.

7   **thalassionis:** a possessive genitive with **verbis** (see A&G §343 note 1).

quis Floralia vestit et stolatum
permittit meretricibus pudorem?
10　lex haec carminibus data est iocosis,
ne possint, nisi pruriant, iuvare.
quare deposita severitate
parcas lusibus et iocis rogamus,
nec castrare velis meos libellos.
15　Gallo turpius est nihil Priapo.

8　　**quis Floralia vestit?:** a RHETORICAL QUESTION. Flora was the Roman goddess of flowers or the flowering season. Her festival, the **Floralia** (n. pl.), held on April 28, was an occasion of licentiousness. Note Martial's METAPHOR of clothing an abstraction.

8-9　**stolatum . . . / pudorem:** another METAPHOR. The Roman matron, who was ideally modest (**pudica**), wore a **stola**, a long gown that came to be a symbol of respectability (Roman women worshipped a deity of sexual purity called **Pudicitia**). In contrast, prostitutes wore a masculine garment, the toga.

9　　**meretricibus:** dative after **permittit**.

10　**lex haec carminibus data est iocosis:** Here, with **haec**, **lex** means "a particular condition." Roman writers were fond of discussing the "law" of particular crafts, including literary genres and poetic meters. Cicero, for example, talks of the "law" of history writing (which is not to say anything false).

11　**ne possint . . . iuvare:** a substantive clause of purpose, explaining **lex haec** (A&G §563).

　　pruriant: another word from Catullus 16, who says that his verses have wit and charm only if **quod pruriant incitare possunt** ("they can stir up sexual excitement").

12　**quare:** Martial begins to wrap up his epigram with **quare . . .**, just as Catullus did in his first poem (1.8, **quare habe tibi quidquid hoc libelli**).

　　deposita severitate: abl. absolute.

13-14 **parcas ... nec ... velis:** subjunctives without **ut** after **rogamus** (A&G §565.a).

lusibus et iocis: dat. with **parcas**.

14 **castrare:** to make Martial restrain himself would metaphorically mutilate the **mentula** of line 5.

libellos: recalls **quidquid hoc libelli** near the end of Catullus poem 1.

15 **Gallo ... Priapo:** abl. of comparison with **turpius** (A&G §406): "than a Priapus who is a Gallus." Priapus was a god of procreation, whose image, with its conspicuous phallus, was placed in gardens to ward off intruders. A **Gallus** was an emasculated priest of the goddess Cybele. Martial's readers might recollect that Catullus poem 63 is about a priest of Cybele who emasculates himself during the course of the poem.

— *Epigram* 1.41 —

The speaker addresses one Caecilius, who thinks himself a sophisticate but is not. There follows a list of examples of coarseness and vulgarity, which gives a vivid picture of Roman street life, with its food sellers and vendors of other cheap goods, its snake charmers, bad poets, and sexual deviants.

    urbanus tibi, Caecili, videris.
    non es, crede mihi. quid ergo? verna,
    hoc quod Transtiberinus ambulator,
    qui pallentia sulpurata fractis
5   permutat vitreis, quod otiosae
    vendit qui madidum cicer coronae,
    quod custos dominusque viperarum,
    quod viles pueri salariorum,

1   **urbanus:** "of the city," and therefore suave and cultured, elegant, as opposed to **rusticus**, "of the country." The poem leads off with its thematic word, **urbanus**, in the predicate nominative (A&G §283).

    Caecili: vocative. The name of the poem's addressee could be derived from the adjective **caecus**, meaning "blind." The name, then, nicely reflects a lack of self-awareness.

    videris: + dat., "to seem," or "to appear" (A&G §575.b).

2   **mihi:** dat. with **credo** (A&G §362.a).

    quid ergo: "What then [are you]?"

    verna: a common, town-bred person, one of the "locals."

3   **hoc quod:** literally, "[you are] this [thing] which [X is . . .]," but best translated loosely: "the same as" or "exactly like." Note how in the following lines the **quod** is picked up and repeated to form a long list of the disreputable characters Caecilius resembles. What is funny is that they are **urbici**, or even **urbani**, "urban," in that they are city dwellers making their way in Rome. But they are not **urbani**,

"urbane," in the sense of line 1, that is, they do not have the sophistication and polish, refinement and elegance (a quality the Romans called **urbanitas**), that Caecilius thinks he has.

Transtiberinus: The less desirable part of Rome was across the Tiber from the Capitoline and Palatine, the Forum, the Subura, and the Esquiline.

4   **pallentia sulpurata:** probably sulphured sticks, fire starters that resembled large matches but were lit by contact with another flame rather than by striking.

5   **fractis ... vitreis:** Broken glass (called "cullet") aids in the making of new glass both by reducing the need to use new resources and by facilitating the melting process. The "match" sellers, who took broken glass in exchange for their fire starters, were among the recyclers of ancient Rome.

5–6   **otiosae ... / coronae:** dat. with **vendit**. The **corona** was a circle of bystanders, especially in the law courts. That it is **otiosae**, "idle," makes it appear disreputable.

qui: The relative pronoun **qui** is the subject of the verb **vendit**, although here it follows the verb. The fully expanded expression would be **tu es hoc quod ille [ambulator (?)] est qui vendit ...**

6   **madidum cicer:** boiled chickpeas, a humble street food.

7   **viperarum:** an objective genitive with **custos dominusque** (A&G §348). **Viperae** are not just any snakes: these are poisonous.

8   **salariorum:** a dealer in salted fish. The fish that were salted were usually the small and cheap ones. The dealer, then, was himself probably a poor man.

quod fumantia qui tomacla raucus
10 circumfert tepidis cocus popinis,
quod non optimus urbicus poeta,
quod de Gadibus inprobus magister,
quod bucca est vetuli dicax cinaedi.
quare desine iam tibi videri,
15 quod soli tibi, Caecili, videris,
qui Gabbam salibus tuis et ipsum
posses vincere Tettium Caballum.
non cuicumque datum est habere nasum:
ludit qui stolida procacitate,
20 non est Tettius ille, sed caballus.

9 **fumantia ... raucus:** Note the adjectives. The attack on the senses continues with an assault on the ears and nose.

fumantia ... tomacla: sausages, like the chickpeas, a humble street food.

9–10 **raucus / ... cocus:** A cook vending sausages is the stuff of the urban environment; but his hoarse and noisy shouting is neither refined nor elegant.

10 **tepidis ... popinis:** an ablative of place where (A&G §426) or a dative with **circumfert** (A&G §370). Many poorer Romans would not have had the facilities to do much of their own cooking. Cheap restaurants serving cooked food were economical of both fuel and space.

11 **non optimus:** either "second rate," or LITOTES for "worst."

urbicus poeta: note that the **poeta** is **urbicus**, not **urbanus**, urban, that is, not urbane.

12 **de Gadibus:** Gades (Cádiz) a place at the western extreme of the known world—so not a likely source of **urbanitas**.

inprobus magister: The "rascally" **magister** is probably the manager of a troupe of entertainers, such as dancing girls or gladiators.

13	**bucca ... dicax:** A **bucca** is properly a cheek; but here probably indicates the mouth. Martial draws attention to the noise that comes from it.
	vetuli ... cinaedi: a catamite or effeminate man, whose beauty, of body and voice, was slipping away with age.
14-15	**quare ... videris:** The epigram begins to close in on its point.
16	**Gabbam:** Gabba was a court fool of Augustus.
	salibus tuis: "your witticisms." **Sal**, "salt," was the Roman metaphor for wit.
17	**Tettium Caballum:** most likely another comedian. We know of him only from Martial.
18	**cuicumque:** "to just anyone."
	habere nasum: another metaphor for having wit, "to have a sharp wit." The infinitive with its object is the subject of **datum est** (A&G §452).
19-20	**qui ...:** an inversion of the expected order: **ille, qui ludit ... , non est Tettius ...**
20	**caballus:** The point of the epigram lies in the double meaning of **Caballus** as both cognomen of the witty Tettius and the word for a nag or a hack, that is, an undistinguished horse.

— *Epigram 6.64* —

An address to a literary competitor, whom Martial does not dignify with a name. Martial attacks his target's ancestry, his masculinity, and most of all, his talents as critic and poet. This inferior poet, he asserts, should take care: Once provoked, Martial will respond as dangerously as an angry bear.

cum sis nec rigida Fabiorum gente creatus
nec qualem Curio, dum prandia portat aranti,
hirsuta peperit deprensa sub ilice coniunx,
sed patris ad speculum tonsi matrisque togatae
5   filius, et possit sponsam te sponsa vocare:
emendare meos, quos novit fama, libellos
et tibi permittis felicis carpere nugas,
has, inquam, nugas, quibus aurem advertere totam
non aspernantur proceres urbisque forique,

1-15   **cum ... Caesar:** one long periodic sentence, whose main verb, **permittis**, appears in the middle (line 7); and which is, in fact, syntactically complete at the end of line 7, until **has, inquam, nugas** (line 8) repeats the direct object of **carpere**, and the subsequent relative clauses expand upon it.

1-5   **cum sis ... sed [sis] ... et possit:** a long triple concessive **cum**-clause, leading to the main point (**permittis ...**) in lines 6 and 7 (A&G §549).

1   **rigida Fabiorum gente:** The **gens Fabia** was one of Rome's oldest and most prestigious. **Rigida** can mean "stern" and "upright" as well as "rugged" or "primitive."

2   **qualem:** direct object of **peperit**.

Curio: a representative of another ancient clan. M' (Manius) Curius Dentatus was a famous general and model of antique severity in the early third century BCE.

Martial, Epigram 6.64.1–9

dum prandia portat aranti: When the main verb is perfect, as it is here (**peperit**), translate **dum** + present as an imperfect (A&G §556). The plowing husband with wife who fetches and carries is a TOPOS in discussions of both crude rusticity and pristine virtue. See, for example, Livy's story of Cincinnatus in Book 3.27.

3   **hirsuta ... sub ilice:** The shagginess, here transferred to the tree, suggests old-fashioned rusticity.

deprensa: "seized" by labor pains.

4-5   **sed ... vocare:** Martial questions the masculinity of both his critic and his critic's father; he questions the chastity of his critic's mother.

patris ad speculum tonsi: The father's use of mirror suggests that he is too careful about his appearance. His shaving contrasts with the shagginess of olden times.

matrisque togatae: Prostitutes wore the toga instead of the **stola matronalis**. See note on *Epigram* 1.35, lines 8–9.

5   **et possit sponsam te sponsa vocare:** If the addressee's bride can call him a bride, he is very effeminate.

6-7   **emendare ... carpere:** infinitives with **permittis** (A&G §563.c).

meos, quos novit fama, libellos: Unlike the addressee, Martial's poems have a good reputation.

7   **tibi:** dat. with **permittis** (A&G §368.3).

nugas: the usual name for light verse, poetic "trifles."

8   **has, inquam, nugas:** Note how the repetition of **nugas**, made emphatic by both **has** and **inquam**, links the first part of this long sentence to the second and changes its focus to set the quality of Martial's poetry against the quality of the addressee.

9   **proceres urbisque forique:** Lines 10–11 give an example of each.

> 10 quas et perpetui dignantur scrinia Sili
> et repetit totiens facundo Regulus ore,
> quique videt propius magni certamina Circi
> laudat Aventinae vicinus Sura Dianae,
> ipse etiam tanto dominus sub pondere rerum
> 15 non dedignatur bis terque revolvere Caesar.
> sed tibi plus mentis, tibi cor limante Minerva
> acrius et tenues finxerunt pectus Athenae.
> ne valeam, si non multo sapit altius illud,
> quod cum panticibus laxis et cum pede grandi
> 20 et rubro pulmone vetus nasisque timendum
> omnia crudelis lanius per compita portat.

10   **perpetui ... Sili:** Silius Italicus, the author of an epic on the Punic Wars.

dignantur: This deponent verb has **scrinia** as its subject and **quas** as its object.

scrinia: Note the personification.

11   **Regulus:** a famous advocate, that is, someone who represents others in court.

12   **quique videt ... Sura:** The relative clause (line 12) is placed before the antecedent clause (line 13). **Sura (Syra)** means a Syrian. It was a slave name (see Horace, *Satire* 1.6.38 in this volume). Both those at the center of culture and those looking in from the periphery approve of Martial's **nugae**.

13   **Aventinae ... Dianae:** dat. with **vicinus** (A&G §384). The temple of Diana on the Aventine, which overlooked the Circus Maximus.

14   **ipse etiam:** Martial adds the clincher that proves his case.

15   **non dedignatur:** LITOTES. Note also the repetition of a **dign-** verb (cf. **dignantur** in line 10). Martial is defending his **dignitas**, an aristocratic Roman value.

bis terque: "again and again."

Caesar: The HYPERBATON places **Caesar** (the emperor Domitian) in the emphatic, final position.

16–17 **tibi ... tibi:** possessive datives (A&G §373).

mentis ... cor ... / ... pectus: all considered as seats of intellect.

limante Minerva: ablative absolute. Minerva was the Roman correspondent to Athena, goddess of wisdom and the arts.

17 **tenues ... Athenae:** Martial's addressee has studied abroad, in "refined" Athens. The adjective **tenuis** became an important term in Roman poetics particularly in the Augustan period. It referred to a refined and subtle style. There is, then, some sarcasm here as Martial suggests this study has not done his victim any good.

finxerunt: "shaped."

18 **ne valeam, si non ... sapit:** a mixed condition (for examples, see A&G §515).

multo: abl. of degree of difference with the adverb **altius**.

sapit: Martial plays with the literal and metaphorical meanings of "having better taste."

illud = illud cor/pectus; the heart/breast now meant literally, as a body part.

19 **cum panticibus laxis:** "with innards spilling out." **Cum** + abl. (A&G §221.9).

pede grandi: possibly another pun on poetics, because the expression can refer to both a heavy animal foot (like the ox hoof that one of the suitors heaved at the disguised Odysseus in the *Odyssey*) and a lofty or weighty rhythm or meter.

20 **rubro:** "bloody."

vetus nasisque timendum: The meat has gone off. Gerundive with dative of agent (A&G §374).

21 **crudelis:** The adjective **crudelis** is related to **crudus**, "uncooked," and **cruor**, "blood fresh from a wound." It thus helps to convey an image of the butcher with blood on his hands.

omnia ... per compita portat: Note the ALLITERATION that brings the description to its conclusion.

audes praeterea, quos nullus noverit, in me
scribere versiculos miseras et perdere chartas.
at si quid nostrae tibi bilis inusserit ardor,
25 vivet et haerebit totaque legetur in urbe,
stigmata nec vafra delebit Cinnamus arte.
sed miserere tui, rabido nec perditus ore
fumantem nasum vivi temptaveris ursi.
sit placidus licet et lambat digitosque manusque,
30 si dolor et bilis, si iusta coegerit ira,
ursus erit: vacua dentes in pelle fatiges
et tacitam quaeras, quam possis rodere, carnem.

22-23 **praeterea ... versiculos:** Aside from "correcting" Martial's verses, this man has the nerve to write verses of his own attacking Martial.

quos nullos noverit: another relative clause preceding its antecedent. **Noverit** is future perfect form with future meaning (A&G §205).

in me: "against me" (A&G §221.12.1.c).

23 **miseras ... chartas:** The adjective is PROLEPTIC, because the **chartae** are wretched only when the bad poet ruins them.

24 **quid** = **aliquid**, direct object of **inusserit**, which is a future perfect in a Future More Vivid condition (A&G §514.B.1.b).

nostrae bilis: partitive genitive (A&G §346.a.3). "Bile" is a METAPHOR for Martial's poetic attack.

tibi: dat. with **inusserit** (A&G §361).

25 **vivet et haerebit totaque legetur in urbe:** Note the structure, an ASCENDING TRICOLON, that is, three parallel clauses, phrases, or words, each of which is longer than the one before. Here the last clause, **totaque ... urbe,** takes up the entire half-line after the third-foot caesura.

26 **Cinnamus:** a barber.

27 **miserere:** imperative; the bad poet should pity himself, if not his wretched pages.

tui: objective genitive with **miserere** (A&G §354.a).

rabido ... ore: a metaphor for raving poetry.

28 **fumantem nasum:** a fire-breathing animal!

temptaveris: hortatory (jussive) subjunctive (A&G §439), with **nec** (line 27) taking the place of the more usual **ne** (A&G §439 note 3).

29 **sit placidus licet et lambat digitosque manusque:** Both subjunctives are concessive with **licet** (A&G §527.b).

30 **si dolor et bilis, si iusta coegerit ira:** Note the ANAPHORA of **si**, and the ASYNDETON, as the language becomes more vehement.

31 **ursus erit:** The creature is already a bear; this means that he will fulfill his bearish nature.

vacua ... in pelle: a bearskin, not a bear.

31–32 **fatiges ... / quaeras:** hortatory (jussive) subjunctives.

32 **quam possis rodere:** a relative clause of characteristic (A&G §534).

rodere: The word also has a metaphorical meaning, "to slander," "carp at." See on Horace, *Satire* 1.6, line 46, in this volume.

carnem: While Martial's bile will burn his victim's flesh, his own, he asserts, is well-defended.

— *Epigram* 10.10 —

If a great man has to bow and scrape to his superiors, what is a poor poet to do? The speaker compares his own sucking up to the social elite to that of Paulus, who is himself a consul.

This poem comments on the Roman social phenomenon of patronage, by which people of lesser wealth and influence were dependent on those of greater wealth and influence. The person of lesser influence was called a **cliens***, a word whose meaning has little relationship to that of the modern English "client." The person of greater influence was called a* **patronus***. Aspects of the relationship, including the morning visit, or* **salutatio***, were gratifying to the* **patronus** *but humiliating to the* **cliens***.*

cum tu, laurigeris annum qui fascibus intras,
    mane salutator limina mille teras,
hic ego quid faciam? quid nobis, Paule, relinquis,
    qui de plebe Numae densaque turba sumus?

1–2   **cum . . . teras: cum** causal or concessive (A&G §549).

1   **laurigeris . . . fascibus:** The fasces were the insignia, carried by lictors, of higher magistrates. They symbolized a magistrate's power over other citizens and were decorated with laurel (bay) branches for ceremonial use.

     annum qui . . . intras: Consuls took office at the beginning of the year.

2   **mane salutator:** The morning **salutatio** was a formal morning call paid by a client on his patron.

     limina mille: an exaggeration. Martial wants to emphasize how enthusiastic Paulus is in seeking the small gift, **sportula**, that patrons gave clients who visited them for the **salutatio**.

3   **hic:** the adverb, meaning, "in the present case or circumstances," "in the circumstances just indicated."

     ego: Note the ANTITHESIS with **tu** in line 1.

     quid faciam: deliberative subjunctive (A&G §443–444).

MARTIAL, EPIGRAM 10.10.1–4

Paule: Martial addresses Paulus in a number of epigrams. He is apparently a rich acquaintance. Martial complains in 5.22 of going to considerable trouble to visit *him* on a morning **salutatio** but finding him not at home.

4   **de plebe Numae:** Numa was the second king of Rome; this is, then, a way of saying "from the ancient plebeian stock."

A lictor holds fasces over his shoulder and a single rod in his right hand. The number of lictors who accompanied a magistrate varied depending on the rank of the magistrate's office. The relief is in the collection of the Archaeological Museum in Verona, Italy. (© Creative Commons 4.0/José Luiz Bernardes Ribeiro)

⁵ qui me respiciet dominum regemque vocabo?
  hoc tu (sed quanto blandius!) ipse facis.
lecticam sellamve sequar? nec ferre recusas,
  per medium pugnas et prior ire lutum.
saepius adsurgam recitanti carmina? tu stas
¹⁰ et pariter geminas tendis in ora manus.
quid faciet pauper cui non licet esse clienti?
  dimisit nostras purpura vestra togas.

5 **qui me respiciet:** The relative clause is conditional (A&G §519), and the pronoun is indefinite in meaning "if anyone."

6 **quanto blandius!:** an ablative of degree of difference with a comparative adverb (A&G §414).

7 **lecticam sellamve sequar?:** The size of a man's retinue enhanced his reputation. **Sequar** is either a future indicative, parallel in thought with the future **respiciet** (line 5), or a present (deliberative) subjunctive.

nec ferre recusas: Paulus goes Martial one better by insisting on helping to carry the litter or sedan chair.

8 **per medium . . . lutum:** Note the word order, which surrounds the rest of the line with mud.

pugnas et prior ire: pugnas + inf., "to strive (to) in the face of physical opposition," "to struggle (to)." Poets of the Augustan era and later (i.e., 27 BCE and on) often postpone **et** to second place in its clause, as here.

9 **adsurgam recitanti: adsurgo** + dat. (A&G §366), "to rise to one's feet (as a sign of respect) in response to."

tu stas: "You are standing," that is, *already* standing.

10 **pariter geminas tendis in ora manus:** as a gesture of applause.

11 **cui non licet esse clienti:** Instead of the predicate nominative **cliens** (A&G §283, 284), **clienti** has been attracted into the dative case of **cui**. The speaker concludes by pointing out that he cannot even be a client because the rich Paulus is taking up his space.

12 **dimisit nostras purpura vestra togas:** Note the PERSONIFICATION of the color purple. Here it refers to the purple-bordered toga worn by curule magistrates, that is, consuls, praetors, and curule aediles.

— *Epigram* 10.20 —

In the last letter of Book 3 of his Epistulae, *Pliny the Younger mourns the death of Martial. He says that he gave Martial money with which to return to Spain, partly because of their friendship, and partly in gratitude for verses,* **versiculi**. *Pliny then quotes the last ten lines of this poem, in which Martial tells his Muse to approach Pliny in his home on the Esquiline, and to do it with deference, because the man is hard at work. The travel money was not excessive recompense; for what greater gift, asks Pliny, is there than glory, praise, and immortality? Martial's poems may not last forever, Pliny concludes, but Martial wrote as if they would.*

> nec doctum satis et parum severum,
> sed non rusticulum tamen libellum
> facundo mea Plinio Thalia
> i perfer: brevis est labor peractae
> 5 altum vincere tramitem Suburae.

1   **nec ... et = neque ... et:** "while not ... (yet) ... at the same time."

   nec doctum satis: a sly opening move on Martial's part. By including **satis** he leaves room for this poem, which is, after all, part of the book, to show some learning.

   parum severum: an echo of 1.35.1, **parum severos**.

2   **sed non rusticulum tamen libellum:** The diminutive is sly. The poet calls his book "somewhat uncouth." But the very act of imitating the diminutive-rich language of Catullus shows how the **libellus** *is* **doctus**, even if not **doctus** enough.

3   **facundo ... Plinio:** As well as being the author of the literary letters that survive, Pliny was a student of the famous rhetorician Quintilian and a successful advocate (one who represents others in court), prosecutor, and provincial administrator.

   mea ... Thalia: Muse of comedy and light verse, who is to deliver the poet's gift. Note how Martial juxtaposes the names and adjectives.

4   **i perfer:** two commands in the imperative (A&G §448), each an independent statement. **i** = present impv. of **eo**.

brevis est labor: possibly also a metaphor contrasting Martial's poetic "trifles" with Pliny's hard work.

4–5 **peractae / altum vincere tramitem Suburae:** for the infinitive with **brevis est labor**, see A&G §452.

The **Subura** was the valley between the southern end of the Viminal Hill and the western slope of the Esquiline Hill. But the word perhaps also referred to the traffic-packed artery connected to the Forum Romanum, that ran through the **Subura** east to the Esquiline gate. The idea is that the going is easy, once one has battled through the crowds of the **Subura** (note the perfect tense of the participle **peractae**) and come out onto the Esquiline via the **clivus Suburanus**.

Thalia holds a shepherd's crook (*pedum*), symbolizing her role as the muse of pastoral poetry, and a *tympanum*. The mask highlights her role as muse of comedy. This second-century CE statue belongs to a group of muses now in the Vatican's Pio Clementino Museum. (Public Domain)

illic Orphea protinus videbis
udi vertice lubricum theatri
mirantisque feras avemque regis,
raptum quae Phryga pertulit Tonanti;
10 illic parva tui domus Pedonis
caelata est aquilae minore pinna.
sed ne tempore non tuo disertam
pulses ebria ianuam, videto:

6   **illic Orphea protinus videbis:** The beginning of an *ekphrasis* or literary description of a work of art. This structure, the **lacus Orphei**, was on the Esquiline at the head of the **clivus Suburanus**. It was in the shape of a theater. It had at its top a figure of Orpheus, the legendary singer from Thrace, portrayed in the act of astounding wild beasts with his music, including even the eagle that stole Ganymede for Zeus. **Orphea** is the usual accusative for this Greek name.

7   **udi ... theatri:** Perhaps the water cascaded down the seating area.

vertice: ablative of place where (A&G §421).

lubricum: an interesting choice of adjective. It can mean "slippery" (presumably because wet) and even "hazardous." It may call to mind the fate of Orpheus's wife, Eurydice, who stepped on a poisonous snake, was bitten, died, and went to Hades. Orpheus was given the chance to bring her back to the world above, on condition that he not look back at her as he led her to the upper world. Just as they approached the upper world, however, he did look back, and Eurydice vanished back into the world of the dead. Vergil (*Georgics* 4.491–492) says **ibi omnis effusus labor**; as the Sybil says to Aeneas in *Aeneid* 6.126, the path down to the underworld is easy, but the return is hard (6.129): **hoc opus hic labor est**. Ovid (*Metamorphoses* 10.51–52) says that Orpheus is told not to look back at Eurydice **donec Avernas / exierit valles** and describes their journey upward (53–54): **carpitur adclivis per muta silentia trames, / arduus, obscurus, caligine densus opaca.** When Orpheus looks at Eurydice, she slips back immediately (57): **et protinus illa relapsa est**. Note the verbal echoes of these passages in Martial's poem. If Martial's references to **labor**, a **trames**, and a hazardous Orpheus bring about INTERTEXTUAL ALLUSIONS to the earlier versions of the story, then they help portray the Subura, which Martial complains about elsewhere (e.g., 2.17, 5.22, 6.66), as the (hateful) underworld.

8 **mirantisque feras:** Orpheus tamed wild beasts with his songs.

avemque regis: the eagle.

9 **raptum . . . Phryga:** The Phrygians were Trojan allies, and for the poets the name came to mean "Trojan." Martial refers here to Ganymede, the son of Tros (eponymous founder of Troy), who became Zeus's (Jupiter's) cupbearer. Juno's jealousy of Ganymede was one of the causes cited by Vergil at the beginning of the *Aeneid* for her hostility to the Trojans.

quae . . . pertulit: The repetition of the verb **perferre**, from line 4, draws a parallel between Thalia's task and the eagle's, and thus a connection between Pliny and Jupiter.

Tonanti: Jupiter. Dative with **pertulit** (A&G §362).

10 **illic parva tui domus Pedonis:** Albinovanus Pedo was an Augustan poet, whose lost works included both epic and epigram. Pliny has apparently moved into his house.

11 **caelata est aquilae minore pinna:** The decoration again connects Pliny to Jupiter but the "smaller wing" keeps him firmly in the lesser world of mortals.

12-13 **ne . . . / pulses . . . videto: Pulses** is a jussive (hortatory) subjunctive with **videto** (A&G §439 note 2).

tempore non tuo: "a moment that is not opportune" (abl. of time when; A&G §423.1)

12-13 **disertam / . . . ianuam:** The epithet, which properly belongs to Pliny himself, personifies the door.

13 **ebria:** as might be expected of the muse of light and comic verse.

totos dat tetricae dies Minervae,
15 dum centum studet auribus virorum
hoc quod saecula posterique possint
Arpinis quoque conparare chartis.
seras tutior ibis ad lucernas:
haec hora est tua, cum furit Lyaeus,
20 cum regnat rosa, cum madent capilli:
tunc me vel rigidi legant Catones.

14 **totos ... dies:** "entire days" (acc. of extent of time; A&G §423.2).

tetricae ... Minervae: As the goddess of the arts, Minerva is a stern taskmistress, especially in contrast to the drunken Thalia.

15 **centum ... virorum: Centum** is indeclinable; the **centumviri** (actually a board of 105 men, three from each Roman tribe), was a court at Rome that settled civil cases such as those concerning inheritance. There were similar courts in the provinces.

16 **saecula posterique:** Martial implies that Pliny's writings will last more than a generation.

17 **Arpinis quoque conparare chartis:** Cicero is the famous writer from Arpinum; to compare Pliny's writings to his is a high compliment indeed.

18 **seras:** with temporal force, "late in the day."

Tutior has the force of an adverb.

19 **haec hora est tua:** as opposed to **tempore non tuo** (line 12).

19–20 **cum ... cum:** These introduce temporal clauses with the verbs (**regnat, madent**) in the present indicative. They define **haec hora** (A&G §547).

Lyaeus: a cult title of Dionysus (Bacchus), "the one who sets free."

20 **regnat rosa:** the flowers that formed garlands for drinkers at a banquet.

madent capilli: hair wet, presumably, with perfumes.

21　**rigidi ... Catones:** The name **Cato**, which recalls the severe statesman and farmer of the second century BCE as well as Julius Caesar's stern opponent, is Martial's figure for a hostile reader.

— *Epigram* 12.61 —

Another poem about poems juxtaposes Martial's own verses to other forms of writing: graffiti on the walls of a latrine and punitive initials tattooed or branded onto the face of a criminal or slave. The poem gives a vivid impression of life in Rome's stinking and disreputable side streets.

    versus et breve vividumque carmen
    in te ne faciam times, Ligurra,
    et dignus cupis hoc metu videri.
    sed frustra metuis cupisque frustra.
5   in tauros Libyci ruunt leones,
    non sunt papilionibus molesti.
    quaeras censeo, si legi laboras,
    nigri fornicis ebrium poetam,
    qui carbone rudi putrique creta
10 scribit carmina quae legunt cacantes.
    frons haec stigmate non meo notanda est.

1   **versus et ... carmen:** The poet both announces that the subject of his poem will be poetry itself and guides us in interpreting the lines that follow: These **versus** will form a **breve vividumque carmen**.

2–3 **times ... et ... cupis:** The two second-person verbs capture Ligurra's dilemma.

      in te: "against you" (A&G §221.12.1.c).

      ne faciam: clause of fearing after **times** (A&G §564).

      Ligurra: a man's name, which appears only here.

3   **dignus:** predicate adjective in the nominative with **videri** (A&G §283).

      hoc metu: abl. with **dignus**, an ablative of specification (A&G §418.b).

      videri: here as often, translate actively as "to seem," "to appear."

4 **frustra metuis cupisque frustra:** The CHIASTIC word order draws attention to Ligurra's conflicting emotions.

5-6 **in tauros ... molesti:** an extended metaphor for poetic attack. The position of the phrase **in tauros** before subject and verb makes it emphatic: "It's against *bulls* ..."

6 **papilionibus:** dat. with **molesti** (A&G §384). **Papilio** means "moth" or "butterfly"; it is also a word for the soul, or *psyche*, of a dead person. The point is the insubstantiality—of either living insect or *psyche*.

7 **quaeras:** subjunctive without **ut**, after **censeo**.

legi: "to be read of."

8 **fornicis:** A **fornix** is an archway: but the word can also indicate a place of ill repute, a cellar or similar space used for prostitution, hence the English "fornication."

9 **carbone rudi putrique creta:** Note again the CHIASTIC word order, which helps to contrast Martial's verbal artistry with the rough and crumbling implements of the **ebrius poeta**. Note also the ALLITERATION of the letter *c* in this line and the following.

10 **carmina:** Grammatically speaking, the only modifier of **carmina** is the relative clause **quae legunt cacantes**. But the atmosphere created by the other adjectives (**nigri, ebrium, rudi, putri**) suggests the quality of the poems that might take Ligurra as their topic.

cacantes: The participle is here used as a noun. From the Greek **kakkaō**, the verb **cacare** enters into extant Latin by way of "low" literature, that is, mime and farce; Catullus used it in two poems (23 and 36), Horace in one of his *Satires* (1.8.38). So many of his epigrams being abusive, Martial uses it more frequently.

11 **frons haec:** Ligurra's forehead.

non ... notanda est: a gerundive expressing necessity (A&G §194.b), but without a dative of agent.

stigmate ... meo: ablative of means. Whether **stigma** here indicates a brand or tattoo is open to debate; in either case, it is a mark made for the purpose of humiliation and punishment.

Horace

Carmina 1.2
Higher Level Only

— Introduction to Horace —

Information on the life and works of Horace may be found in the introduction to the Standard Level and Higher Level section (page 5).

— Meter —

Sapphic Strophes

— *Carmina* 1.2 —

Horace's first collection of lyric poems (Odes 1–3) appeared probably in 23 BCE; the earliest datable poem in the collection (1.37) refers to Cleopatra's death in 30 BCE. The first nine poems of Book 1 are sometimes called "The Parade Odes," because Horace uses them to display his mastery of nine different lyric meters adopted from Greek. (Catullus had written Sapphic strophes, and there are fragments from the works of other Latin poets in other lyric meters adopted from Greek; but Horace is the first Roman poet fully to exploit their potential in Latin.) Horace's lyrics reflect the variety of the Greek lyric tradition, which included both songs about love, friendship, and the material elements of the symposium (wine, perfumes, garlands) to be sung at private parties, and poems of public prayer and praise. A number of Horace's lyric poems, including this one, reflect the political situation at Rome, which was still unsettled for some years after the battle of Actium in 31 BCE.

Extreme weather events (snow, hail, lightning storms, flooding) all show that Jupiter is angry. He has destroyed mankind before by flooding the earth; recent Tiber floods suggest that he may do so again. To save their city Romans need to reset their relationship with the divine. Prayer to some intermediary may help, as will the leadership—moral as much as military—of Caesar, that is, Augustus. The poem also speaks of the need for expiation and for vengeance: The noun **ultor** *appears twice, the participle* **inultos***, once. Other important ideas come through in the repetition of words or related words: "enough" as opposed to excess (***satis/satiate; nimium/nimis***); the idea of moral failing (***vitio/vitiis***); prayer (***prece/precamur***); the continuity of generations (***pater/pater; parentum; filius; genus/genus; iuventus/iuvenem***).*

    iam satis terris nivis atque dirae
    grandinis misit Pater, et rubente
    dextera sacras iaculatus arces
        terruit Urbem,

5   terruit gentes, grave ne rediret
    seculum Pyrrhae nova monstra questae,
    omne cum Proteus pecus egit altos
        visere montes,

1   **iam satis ...:** weary impatience, "enough already!"

2-3   **terris:** dat. with **misit** (A&G §363.2).

       nivis ... dirae / grandinis: partitive genitives with **satis** (A&G §346). The adjective **dirae**, "ominous" or "portentous," modifies both **nivis** and **grandinis**.

2-3   **Pater:** The angry father is Jupiter.

       rubente / dextera: abl. abs. (A&G §419); participles in **-ns** regularly use **-e** in the abl. abs. (A&G §121.a.2). Jupiter's right hand is glowing red because of the thunderbolts he hurls.

3   **sacras ... arces:** possibly a poetic plural referring to the **arx** on the Capitoline; but also, given that the poem began with the plural **terris** and has not yet focused on Rome, potentially indicating other cities' **arces** as well.

       iaculatus: here transitive.

4-5   **terruit Urbem / terruit gentes: Urbem = Romam.** Note the ANAPHORA of **terruit**, which heightens emotions as it describes fear moving out from the city to the peoples of the world.

5-6   **grave ... / seculum:** an age both "painful" and "dangerous."

       ne rediret: a clause of fearing after **terruit** (A&G §564). Both **urbs** and **gentes** fear the return of the **grave ... seculum**.

6   **Pyrrhae ... questae:** Pyrrha and her husband Deucalion were the two humans left alive after the flood sent by Jupiter to destroy wicked mankind (See Ovid, *Metamorphoses* 1.260–380).

       nova monstra: in the sense of portents that were "strange," because "never before seen."

7   **omne ... pecus:** The metaphor domesticates the seals.

       cum ... egit ... haesit ... natarunt: The **cum**-clause with the perfect indicative defining a point in time (A&G §545).

       Proteus: the Old Man of the Sea, and Neptune's "sealherd."

7-8   **altos / ... montes:** The adjective **altus**, which can denote either depth or height, is particularly apt here.

       visere: an infinitive expressing purpose, which is both archaic and poetic (A&G §460.c).

piscium et summa genus haesit ulmo
10   nota quae sedes fuerat columbis,
et superiecto pavidae natarunt
     aequore damae.

vidimus flavum Tiberim retortis
littore Etrusco violenter undis
15   ire deiectum monumenta regis
     templaque Vestae;

9   **piscium:** genitive of material with **genus** (A&G §344).

summa ... haesit ulmo: a collective singular. The leaves and branches at the top of the tree act as a net.

10   **columbis:** dat. with **nota** (A&G §384).

11–12   **pavidae ... damae:** The adjective adds a note of pathos. A flood expands the habitat for seals and fish, but not for deer.

natarunt = nataverunt.

13   **vidimus:** Note the emphasis on eyewitness. We are jolted back to recent historical events.

flavum Tiberim: The first word after **vidimus** is a strikingly visual one, an adjective often translated as "yellow," but one that also has connotations of shimmering. Whereas Pyrrha saw the world flooded, Romans have seen Tiber floods. Until the river was canalized in the early twentieth century, the Tiber flooded frequently (visitors to the Campus Martius can see plaques indicating high water marks, for example, near the church of S. Maria sopra Minerva, about a half mile from the river). The most serious twentieth-century flood was in 1937 (images of Romans boating on the Via Portuense, a block away from the river, can be found online). A 2008 flood did not overtop the embankment walls. We have to ask ourselves what effect Horace achieves by linking, if not equating, a *relatively* common occurrence with a mythological catastrophe.

13–14   **retortis / littore Etrusco violenter undis:** Horace describes the water as turned back on itself, from the right bank into the heart of the ancient city.

15   **ire deiectum:** supine expressing purpose after a verb of motion (A&G §509), with **monumenta** as its object.

monumenta regis: buildings attributed to Numa, second king of Rome, including the *regia*, the temple of Vesta, and the *Atrium Vestae*, where the Vestal Virgins lived. The temple of Vesta housed Rome's sacred fire, with the result that the river's attack becomes a battle of the elements, like that of the Xanthos (Greek for **flavus**)/Skamandros against the fires of Hephaistos in *Iliad* 21.

16   **templaque Vestae:** a poetic plural for a single building. Horace singles out one of the **monumenta regis**, the one whose destruction jeopardizes the very existence of the city.

The temple of Vesta was once a round structure that stood in the Roman Forum. The temple was destroyed and rebuilt many times. It was entirely stripped of its marble in the sixteenth century CE and was partially reconstructed in the 1930s under the dictator Benito Mussolini, who sought to connect his rule to the Roman Empire. (© Creative Commons 3.0/Wknight94)

Iliae dum se nimium querenti
iactat ultorem, vagus et sinistra
labitur ripa Iove non probante u-
20   xorius amnis.

audiet cives acuisse ferrum
quo graves Persae melius perirent;
audiet pugnas vitio parentum
        rara iuventus.

25 quem vocet divum populus ruentis
imperi rebus? prece qua fatigent
virgines sanctae minus audientem
        carmina Vestam?

17–18 **Iliae ... nimium querenti:** dat. with **se ... iactat ultorem**. The Tiber parades himself *before* or shows off *to* Ilia. **Ultorem** is predicate accusative (A&G §§392, 393). Note that Ilia is, like Pyrrha, another complaining mythical woman.

nimium: properly modifies **querenti**; but the Tiber's boasting and the action that accompanies it appear excessive too.

dum se nimium ... / iactat ultorem: The Tiber is avenging a very old wrong. After Mars raped the Vestal Virgin Ilia (Rhea Silvia in some sources, e.g., *Aeneid* 7.659), and after she gave birth to Romulus and Remus, she was, according to one tradition, drowned in the Tiber, which was said to have "married" her. Another possibility is that he is avenging the assassination of her distant descendant Julius Caesar. But then how could she be complaining "too much" about the death of Augustus's adoptive father?

18–19 **vagus et sinistra / labitur ripa:** oddly gentle language for a river in flood; but it calls to mind the gentle flooding of the left bank that left the basket carrying Romulus and Remus near the base of the Palatine.

Iove non probante: abl. abs. Horace looks at Tiber's personal vengeance from Jupiter's point of view. Jupiter's attitude here (**non probante** is LITOTES) is in marked contrast to Zeus's in *Iliad* 21, where he is amused by watching the gods fighting.

19-20 **u-/ xorius amnis:** The word overruns the line ending as the river overruns its banks. Is it Jupiter's thought—and reason for his disapproval, or is it the speaker's opinion that the Tiber is excessively fond of his wife?

21-23 **audiet ... audiet:** Note the ANAPHORA, which echoes that of **terruit** in lines 4–5. Note also the contrast with the perfect **vidimus**.

cives acuisse ferrum: ferrum as METONYMY for war.

22 **quo ... melius perirent:** The adverb modifies the whole relative clause: "by which it were better ..."

graves Persae: in contrast to **cives**. The "formidable" **Persae** are the Parthians who defeated Crassus in 53 BCE and were the object of Antony's disastrous expedition and his retreat in 36 BCE.

23 **pugnas:** that is, stories of the **pugnae**.

24 **rara iuventus:** The citizenry is engaged in self-destruction, with the result that there are few young men left of military age. Although the civil wars have not destroyed all mortals except two, as did the flood of Pyrrha and Deucalion, the civil wars have been effective at both killing off a generation of young men and reducing the birthrate. Note the HYPERBATON of the subject of **audiet ... audiet**. The second half of the poem maintains the shift to the future by beginning with a series of questions.

25 **quem ... prece qua ... cui:** a series of questions, with the interrogative in three different cases, a figure called POLYPTOTON.

divum: probably genitive plural.

27 **virgines sanctae:** the Vestal Virgins, whose prayers upheld the safety of Rome.

minus audientem: "not listening," "unheeding."

28 **carmina:** direct object of **audientem**.

cui dabit partes scelus expiandi
30 Iuppiter? Tandem venias precamur
nube candentes humeros amictus
    augur Apollo;

sive tu mavis, Erycina ridens,
quam Iocus circum volat et Cupido;
35 sive neglectum genus et nepotes
    respicis auctor,

heu nimis longo satiate ludo,
quem iuvat clamor galeaeque leves
acer et Mauri peditis cruentum
40   voltus in hostem;

29 **partes:** the "office," or "role."

scelus expiandi: a gerund with a direct object, **scelus**, which here means "guilt." (The genitive of the gerund sometimes takes a direct object; see A&G §504.a.)

30 **Iuppiter:** The poem's third reference to Jupiter.

venias: subjunctive without **ut** after **precamur** (for the construction of **precor** with **ut**, see A&G §563; for the subjunctive without **ut** after verbs of commanding see A&G §565.a). In this case the subjunctive is a hortatory subjunctive expressing a command in indirect speech.

precamur: The poem becomes a prayer, an answer to the previous questions.

31 **nube candentes humeros amictus:** after all the bad weather, finally a cloud that does some good!

candentes humeros: Greek accusative (that is, the accusative indicating the part affected) with **amictus** (A&G §397.b).

32 **augur Apollo:** Augustus's patron deity, who helped him at Actium, and to whom Augustus dedicated a temple next to his house on the Palatine.

33 **Erycina ridens:** Venus, called **Erycina** after her temple on Mt. Eryx in Sicily. As the Romans' distant ancestress, she should be interested in the wellbeing of her offspring.

34 **quam:** acc. with **circum volat.**

Iocus ... et Cupido: Jest and Cupid, the one a suitable satellite for "laughing" Venus, the other, her troublemaking son. Both are subjects of the singular verb **volat** (A&G §317.b).

35-36 **sive neglectum genus et nepotes / respicis auctor:** an apt transition to Mars, father of Romulus and Remus, therefore the **auctor** of the Romans, because he is also Venus's lover and subject to her power when they meet.

37 **nimis longo ... ludo:** The expression shows us the civil wars from two points of view: there has been too much war for humans; at the same time, it is a game for gods.

satiate: vocative, "once you are sated."

38 **iuvat:** This singular verb has two closely linked subjects **clamor galeaeque,** and then a third, **voltus,** in line 40 (A&G §317.b).

clamor galeaeque leves: the sounds and sights of fighting (helmets are **leves** because of polishing, and polished helmets gleam).

39-40 **acer ... voltus:** "a look that is fierce."

Mauri peditis: The Moors, who are usually on horseback, have been unhorsed.

40 **cruentum:** "covered in blood."

sive mutata iuvenem figura
ales in terris imitaris, almae
filius Maiae, patiens vocari
    Caesaris ultor:

45 serus in caelum redeas diuque
laetus intersis populo Quirini;
neve te nostris vitiis iniquum
    ocior aura

tollat: hic magnos potius triumphos,
50 hic ames dici pater atque princeps,
neu sinas Medos equitare inultos
    te duce, Caesar.

41   **mutata ... figura:** abl. abs.

    iuvenem ... imitaris: a god portrayed as young takes on the form of a youth.

42   **ales:** "a winged creature," nominative, agreeing with the subject of **imitaris**. Winged boots and a winged hat are part of Hermes/Mercury's iconography.

    in terris: "on earth."

43   **filius Maiae:** that is, Hermes/Mercury, son of Jupiter by Maia. Scholars suggest that Horace is improvising here, because the identification of Mercury and Augustus is unexpected and unusual.

44   **Caesaris ultor:** Octavian presented himself as Julius Caesar's avenger in the civil wars that followed 44 BCE. He also vowed a temple to Mars Ultor (Mars the Avenger) before the battle of Philippi in 42 BCE, and dedicated it in 2 BCE. The building of the Forum Augustum and the temple, which was inside it, was taking place during the time when Horace composed this poem.

45   **redeas:** the first of five jussive (hortatory) subjunctives (**redeas, intersis, tollat, ames, sinas**).

| 46 | **populo:** dat. with the compound **intersis**.

Quirini: voc. **Quirinus** is the name for the deified Romulus.
| 47 | **nostris vitiis:** causal ablative.
| 48 | **ocior aura:** a breeze that is *too* swift.
| 49-50 | **hic:** "here," "among us." Note the ANAPHORA of **hic**..., which, like the repetition of **terruit** at the beginning (lines 4–5), conveys heightened emotion.

magnos potius triumphos: Ames is construed with both **magnos ... triumphos** and **dici**.

potius: "instead."
| 50 | **hic ames dici: amo** + infinitive "to be accustomed to" (*OLD s.v.* **amo** 12).

pater atque princeps: in place of the avenging **Pater** (Jupiter) of line 2. Augustus was given the title **pater patriae** by the Senate in 2 BCE.

princeps: Augustus's preferred title. "First citizen" had no regal connotations.
| 51 | **Medos ... inultos:** another name for Parthians. Note yet another reference to vengeance.
| 52 | **te duce:** abl. abs., referring, as it should *not* if it were grammatically correct, to the subject of the sentence. Horace can get away with this, whereas the novice Latin student cannot.

Caesar: Consider the effect of ending the poem with this name. Does the name **Caesar** sound more military than "Augustus," because it invokes the memory of Augustus's adoptive father Julius Caesar, or does it remind us that Augustus, as Caesar's son, is *divi filius*? Or does Horace use the name simply for metrical reasons?

Martial

***Epigrams* 11.6, 32, 56, 98**
Higher Level Only

— Introduction to Martial —

Information on the life and works of Martial may be found in the introduction to the Standard Level and Higher Level section (page 67).

— Meters —

Elegiac Couplets: 11.32, 11.56
Hendecasyllables: 11.6
Limping Iambics: 11.98

— *Epigram* 11.6 —

The occasion for this poem is the Saturnalia, the festival for the ancient Roman god **Saturn**, who became identified with the Greek Cronus, the son of Uranus and Gaia (Heaven and Earth). Cronus separated his constantly copulating parents by castrating his father with his sickle. The separation of heaven and earth allowed for the movement of the workings of the great clock that is the cosmos. Cronus, then, is responsible for time, in Greek chronos (the two were equated as early as Aristotle in the fourth century BCE). Cronus fled after his own son, Zeus, deposed him and took his place as king of gods. At Rome, Jupiter, assimilated to Zeus, was the chief deity as well, and worshiped on the Capitoline with Juno (assimilated to Hera) and Minerva (assimilated to Athena). Saturn was a very old, possibly Etruscan god, who was thought to have ruled during a "golden age," before private property, slavery, and trade. The story also went that after Cronus fled, he hid in Italy, which was how Latium got its name (from **lateo**, "go into hiding"). Assimilated, Cronus/Saturn is, then, a god of a previous time; he is present but either in hiding or imprisoned: Saturn's cult statue was in his temple in the Roman Forum; its feet were bound with woolen bonds, except during the festival of the Saturnalia. During that limited period of time, he was unbound and allowed to reign again. Masters served their slaves; there was feasting and an exchange of gifts.

A number of Martial's epigrams are presented as labels that are supposed to be fastened to gifts for the Saturnalia. Although not a typical epigram, this poem promises a Saturnalian present to the boy Dindymus.

    unctis falciferi senis diebus,
    regnator quibus inperat fritillus,
    versu ludere non laborioso
    permittis, puto, pilleata Roma.
5   risisti; licet ergo, non vetamur.
    pallentes procul hinc abite curae;

1-4   **unctis ... diebus:** an ablative of time when (A&G §423). The reference is to the Saturnalia, which took place around the time of the winter solstice. **Unctis** here is transferred to the days from the food.

falciferi: an epithet of the god Saturn, who gave his name to the holiday.

2   **regnator quibus inperat fritillus:** Gambling, otherwise forbidden at Rome, was allowed during the Saturnalia. That the dicebox is **regnator** and gives orders reflects the inversion of power sanctioned by the holiday.

   quibus = **quibus diebus**, ablative of time when.

3   **versu ludere non laborioso:** Play, and the absence of labor, even extending to poetry, mark the holiday. It is a conceit shared with other writers of short verse, such as Catullus, that these carefully written works are trifles (**nugae**) tossed off spontaneously. Note the ALLITERATION in this and the following line.

4   **permittis:** an appropriate verb for the Saturnalia. Take **permittis** with the infinitive **ludere** and supply the dative **nobis**.

   puto: The parenthetical **puto** contributes to the ALLITERATION within the line.

   pilleata Roma: vocative. Rome, the poem's addressee in lines 1–5, wears the liberty cap, **pilleus** (or **pilleum**), of a slave freed, if only temporarily by the holiday.

5   **risisti:** Laughter is also part of the Saturnalia; moreover, since Martial's urban audience has already shown it enjoys his work, he is thus free to continue. Note that this line contains three independent clauses.

   licet: a second expression for permission.

   non vetamur: a third expression for permission.

6   **curae:** A second addressee, the personified **curae**, are ordered away, as if shooed from participating in a ritual.

quidquid venerit obvium loquamur
morosa sine cogitatione.
misce dimidios, puer, trientes,
10 quales Pythagoras dabat Neroni,
misce, Dindyme, sed frequentiores:
possum nil ego sobrius; bibenti
succurrent mihi quindecim poetae.
da nunc basia, sed Catulliana:
15 quae si tot fuerint quot ille dixit,
donabo tibi Passerem Catulli.

7 **quidquid venerit obvium loquamur:** Yet another way of pointing out the lack of constraint as well as any lack of effort. **Loquamur** is a hortatory subjunctive. **Quidquid venerit** works like the protasis of a future more vivid clause (compare **si quid venerit**). See A&G §516.a.

8 **morosa sine cogitatione:** The verse will come both without labor and without thought.

9 **dimidios:** half, that is, half wine and half water.

trientes: A **triens** was a drinking vessel that held a third of a **sextarius**, which equalled approximately four **cyathi**, or ladlesful. Not large drinks, then, but if they are to be mixed **frequentiores**, it is a good idea that the wine is mixed half and half with water.

10 **quales Pythagoras dabat Neroni:** Pythagoras was Nero's cup-bearer, with whom he underwent a mock marriage that scandalized observers. The imperfect here denotes a repeated action, "used to give" (A&G §470).

11 **misce, Dindyme, sed frequentiores:** Martial writes of kissing the downy cheeks of Dindymus in 10.42. Note how **misce Dindyme** picks up the sound of **misce dimidios** from the previous line; and note how the two of **dimidios** becomes the three of **trientes**; and note how that multiplication is multiplied further and indefinitely

(someone is getting too drunk to be accurate or to care) by **sed frequentiores**. These are marks of a Catullan way of playing with size and numbers.

12-13 **sobrius; bibenti:** The juxtaposition of the antonyms **sobrius** and **bibenti** sharpens the ANTITHESIS. Translate **bibenti** with a clause, "but when I am drinking..." (A&G §496).

nil ... quindecim: The leap from nothing to a (relatively) large number, a move characteristic of Catullus, anticipates the Catullan references in lines 14–15.

13 **succurrent mihi:** "run to my aid."

14 **da nunc basia, sed Catulliana:** invokes Catullus's address to Lesbia in poem 5.7–9: **da mi basia mille, deinde centum / dein mille altera, dein secunda centum, deinde usque altera mille, deinde centum.**

15-16 **quae si tot fuerint quot ille dixit:** an economical way of summing up Catullus's large and ultimately innumerable numbers (**dein, cum milia multa fecerimus...**).

si tot fuerint ... donabo: a future more vivid construction (A&G §516.b).

16 **donabo tibi:** a reference to the customary exchange of gifts on the Saturnalia.

Passerem Catulli: possibly the name given to the first part of the Catullan corpus, which includes the two poems (2 and 3), describing Catullus's lover Lesbia's delight in her pet bird (**passer**) and then her sorrow at its death, as well as the "kiss" poems 5 and 7. Martial leaves it unclear whether he is going to give Dindymus a book of poetry by Catullus or his own version of Catullus's **passer** poems.

— *Epigram* 11.32 —

A poem addressed to one Nestor, who, according to Martial, cannot be poor, because that means one has something. *The list of what Nestor does not have echoes Catullus's shorter list in poem 23.1–2.*

    nec toga nec focus est nec tritus cimice lectus
        nec tibi de bibula sarta palude teges,
    nec puer aut senior, nulla est ancilla nec infans,
        nec sera nec clavis nec canis atque calix.
5   tu tamen adfectas, Nestor, dici atque videri
        pauper, et in populo quaeris habere locum.
    mentiris vanoque tibi blandiris honore.
        non est paupertas, Nestor, habere nihil.

1–4   **nec . . . nec . . . nec / nec . . . / nec . . . nulla . . . nec / nec . . . nec . . . nec:** The repeated negatives set up the expectation—unfulfilled in the poem—of ANAIRESIS, "not this, nor this . . . but *this.*"

1   **toga . . . focus . . . lectus:** Nestor lacks the basics in clothing and shelter.

   tritus cimice lectus: The bed would be very small and rickety if a bug could trample it.

2   **tibi:** possessive dative (A&G §373).

   de bibula sarta palude teges: Note how the entries in the list of what Nestor does not have are becoming more elaborate. The **lectus** received a participle, itself modified by an ablative noun; the **teges** receives a participle (**sarta**) modified by a prepositional phrase that includes both noun and adjective.

3   **nec puer aut senior, nulla est ancilla nec infans:** no slave, old or young, of either gender.

4 **nec canis atque calix:** Either the list is becoming completely random or, perhaps, we are to think of the mosaic figures of dogs (**cave canem**) in Roman houses and associated with literary scenes of dining such as Trimalchio's dinner party in the *Satyricon*. Or perhaps the reference to the dog calls to mind the Cynic ("Doggy") philosopher, who owned only a cup and threw that away when he saw someone drinking from his hands.

5 **adfectas:** + inf. **dici atque videri**, "to aspire to be called and to seem."

Nestor: The addressee shares his name with the elderly and loquacious king in the Homeric epics, who is also rich in wealth and family.

6 **pauper:** a predicate nominative with **dici** and **videri** (A&G §§283, 284).

7 **tibi:** dative with **blandiris**.

8 **non est paupertas, Nestor, habere nihil:** The addressee would have to have *something* in order to achieve even poverty. Yet the repetition of **Nestor** points out that the addressee does have *something*, if only a name that he has to share with a famous figure from Homeric epic. For the infinitive in apposition to the subject, see A&G §452.2.

— *Epigram* 11.56 —

According to the tenets of Stoic philosophy, the wise man aims at living in harmony with Nature, whose guiding principle was logos *(reason). Whoever lives in accordance with reason possesses the highest good and, therefore, cannot be harmed by pain, sickness, or death. In Book 1, Martial cast aspersions on such famous Stoics who died by suicide as Cato Uticensis and Thrasea Paetus, saying, "I want the man who can be praised without dying for it" (1.8.4,* **hunc volo, laudari qui sine morte potest**). *Here he pokes fun at Chaeremon for going beyond Stoic indifference to death and praising it excessively. The metaphor of the wise man departing from life as if leaving a banquet when he has had enough never surfaces in the poem but runs through it as an undercurrent.*

quod nimium mortem, Chaeremon Stoice, laudas,
    vis animum mirer suspiciamque tuum?
hanc tibi virtutem fracta facit urceus ansa,
    et tristis nullo qui tepet igne focus,
5 et teges et cimex et nudi sponda grabati,
    et brevis atque eadem nocte dieque toga.
o quam magnus homo es qui faece rubentis aceti
    et stipula et nigro pane carere potes!

1   **quod ... mortem ... laudas: quod** + ind., "because" (A&G §§539, 540).

Chaeremon Stoice: Who is Chaeremon the Stoic? He appears only here, and his name has its origins in the Greek verb meaning "to rejoice" (*chairō*). Martial may have made him up for the occasion.

2   **animum:** here, "courage."

mirer suspiciamque: hortatory subjs. after the verb **vis** (A&G §565).

suspiciam: literally, "to look at from below," figuratively, "to look up to." The verb only rarely (and almost always in the perfect participle) means "to be suspicious of."

3–8   **hanc ... potes:** Chaeremon has only the barest necessities of food, clothing, and shelter.

3   **fracta ... ansa:** descriptive ablative or ablative of quality (A&G §415.a). The language makes a comic plunge from the abstract and lofty (**animum; virtutem**, lines 2 and 3) to the humble and concrete.

4   **et tristis nullo qui tepet igne focus:** Note the HYPERBATON delaying the humble noun **focus**.

5   **et ... et ... et:** The sources of Chaeremon's "courage" come thick and fast. These three together suggest that he is probably not getting a good night's sleep.

teges: a piece of matting made of rushes and used for lying upon.

cimex: a bedbug.

nudi ... grabati: a camp bed or pallet. That this lowly piece of furniture is also bare makes the situation even more wretched.

sponda: bed frame.

6   **et brevis atque eadem nocte dieque toga:** Chaeremon has not even a change of his skimpy clothes.

7–8 **o ... potes!** The first half of the poem concludes with an exclamation juxtaposing the great (**quam magnus homo es**) and the humble. Color terms add vivid emphasis to the concrete nouns denoting humble items.

quam: exclamatory, "how!"

7   **faece rubentis aceti:** not wine, but vinegar, including the sediment from the bottom of the amphora.

8   **stipula:** straw (as bedding).

nigro pane: abl. of separation with **carere** (A&G §§400, 401). The lighter bread was in antiquity, and the more closely sieved the flour, the more prestigious it was (even though it was probably less nutritious and the flour could have been adulterated with chalk).

    Leuconicis agedum tumeat tibi culcita lanis
10   constringatque tuos purpura pexa toros,
    dormiat et tecum modo qui dum Caecuba miscet
       convivas roseo torserat ore puer:
    o quam tu cupies ter vivere Nestoris annos
       et nihil ex ulla perdere luce voles!
15   rebus in angustis facile est contemnere vitam:
       fortiter ille facit qui miser esse potest.

9–16   **Leuconis … potest:** The second half of the poem veers abruptly to items of luxury in bedding, clothing, wine, and even sex. These are the attributes of the symposium.

9   **Leuconicis … lanis:** wool from sheep raised by a Gallic tribe, the **Leucones**, in other words, imported wool. For Roman writers, place-names giving the origins of luxury products performed the function of brand names.

9–11   **tumeat … constringatque … dormiat:** jussive subjunctives.

10   **tuos … toros:** The word **torus** can mean several things that do not appear at first glance to have much to do with one another: a muscle, for example; a convex molding on the base of a column; a pillow or bed. What these things have in common is that they are swellings or protuberances (think of the flexed muscle, or the pillow or bed stuffed with wool).

    purpura pexa: a rich color as opposed to the drab color of the bedding above.

11–12   **dormiat et tecum … puer:** a pleasant alternative to the **cimex** of line 5.

    Caecuba: the wine of Caecubum, a district in the south of Latium. Caecuban wine was considered the finest.

    modo: adv., "recently." Chaeremon's change of fortune has been abrupt.

12   **convivas roseo torserat ore puer:** Note the boy's **os roseum** in contrast to the **acetum rubens** of line 7. Instead of the **cimex** causing the sleeper anguish, the beautiful boy "tortures" the guests at the banquet. The use of **torserat** here is another jab at Chaeremon's Stoic ethics, which allowed for suicide as a means of avoiding torture.

13   **o quam:** an exclamatory sentence with **quam** (A&G §269.c).

    Nestoris: the loquacious elder statesman of both the *Iliad* and the *Odyssey*, who is always talking about the greatness of his generation. To outlive him is to have a long life indeed.

14   **ulla … luce = ulla die.**

15   **rebus in angustis:** The poem plays a bit on the ambiguity of **res angustae**, which can mean both "straitened circumstances," that is, "poverty," and "dire straits," that is, "a tight spot." Horace's *Ode* 2.10.21 urges its addressee to "show yourself courageous and strong in dire straits" (**rebus angustis animosus atque fortis adpare**).

    facile est contemnere vitam: This has the ring of a Stoic **sententia**, a gnomic saying conveying a nugget of the philosophical system's wisdom. For the infinitive as subject, see A&G §452.1.

16   **fortiter ille facit qui miser esse potest:** With its alliteration, this line too has the ring of a **sententia**.

— *Epigram* 11.98 —

Everyone has taken up the Catullan practice of demanding kisses: **da mi basia mille** *(poem 5). Neither physical blemishes (and without modern hygiene or medical practices there would have been many) nor the barriers of social class and high political office can fend off their assaults.*

    effugere non est, Flacce, basiatores.
    instant, morantur; persecuntur, occurrunt
    et hinc et illinc, usquequaque, quacumque.
    non ulcus acre pusulaeve lucentes,
5   nec triste mentum sordidique lichenes,
    nec labra pingui delibuta cerato,
    nec congelati gutta proderit nasi.
    et aestuantem basiant et algentem,
    et nuptiale basium reservantem.

1   **effugere non est:** "There is no fleeing." Note the word order. In its substantive use ("there is," A&G §284.b), **est** would normally come first, but here the first thought in the speaker's head is flight; then comes the impossibility of it.

    Flacce: a native of **Patavium** (modern Padua) and the addressee of many poems.

    basiatores: Martial announces his new word and the topic of the poem. Catullus is the first Latin writer to use **basium, basiatio,** and **basiare** for kisses and kissing. Martial is the first and only classical Latin writer to use the word **basiator**; he uses it only here, but four times in this poem. The implication is that, just as the practice of kissing has run rampant, so too the vocabulary of kissing has taken on a life of its own.

2 **instant, morantur; persecuntur, occurrunt:** Note the ASYNDETON in this list of verbs conveying the relentlessness of the **basiatores**. Note also the CHIASTIC arrangement of the regular verbs and deponents, and that **occurrunt** takes up the three long final syllables of the "limping" iambic line, with the result that the verb for "running" brings the line to a slow halt.

3 **et hinc et illinc, usquequaque, quacumque:** Three expressions, overlapping to some degree, and together meaning "everywhere," emphasize the ubiquity of the **basiatores**.

4-15 **non ... nec ... nec ... nec ... non ... nec ... nec ... non ... nec:** The long list of negatives underscores the impossibility of escape.

4 **lucentes:** "inflamed."

5 **triste mentum:** a reference to the skin condition known in ancient Rome as **mentagra**, which involved inflammation of the hair follicles of the beard area and was thought to be transmitted by kissing.

lichenes: skin diseases; possibilities include ringworm, eczema, herpes, and psoriasis.

6 **pingui ... cerato:** An ointment made by mixing wax and oil of itself might not have been offensive; but **pinguis**, which can have the positive sense of being fat or sleek, can also have the negative one of being greasy or oily, especially since **delibuta** means *thickly* smeared.

7 **congelati gutta ... nasi:** The list of offending features moves upward from chin to lips to nose.

proderit: from **prosum**, "to be of aid to." Not even the offending pimples and pustules can defend their owner.

8 **et ... et ...:** "both ... and ..."

et aestuantem basiant et algentem: Using polar opposites is a way of making a universal claim, as if saying "no matter what a man's condition, hot, cold, or anywhere in between." The terms also appear in medical contexts to suggest a harmful deviation from a normal temperature, that is, "feverish" or "chilled."

9 **et nuptiale basium reservantem:** The **basiator** transgresses even the limits set by marriage.

10   non te cucullis adseret caput tectum,
     lectica nec te tuta pelle veloque,
     nec vindicabit sella saepius clusa:
     rimas per omnis basiator intrabit.
     non consulatus ipse, non tribunatus
15   senive fasces nec superba clamosi
     lictoris abiget virga basiatorem:
     sedeas in alto tu licet tribunali
     et e curuli iura gentibus reddas,
     ascendet illa basiator atque illa.
20   febricitantem basiabit et flentem,
     dabit oscitanti basium natantique,
     dabit cacanti. remedium mali solum est,
     facias amicum basiare quem nolis.

10   **cucullis:** a Gallic term for a hood.

     tectum: the participle, from **tego, -gere, -xi, -ctum**.

     adseret: Part of the humor is the juxtaposition of the humble **cucullus** with its foreign name and the verb **adserere**, which can mean "to defend" but also has a Roman technical meaning of "laying claim to a person" (as free or as a slave). See, for example, the several uses of the verb and the related noun **adsertor/assertor** in the selection from Livy, Book 3, in this volume.

11   **lectica:** a litter.

     pelle veloque: The skin was presumably used as awning; and **velum** here means "curtain."

12   **vindicabit:** another potentially legal term. An **assertor** can perform the act **vindicare in libertatem** and thus claim as free.

     sella: a form of conveyance consisting of a chair (enclosed or not) carried by means of poles, like the sedan chairs of the seventeenth and eighteenth centuries.

13 **rimas per omnis basiator intrabit:** The statement sums up the first half of the poem. Note the word order of **rimas per omnis**. It is not uncommon for monosyllabic prepositions to come between an adjective and a noun (see also **rebus in angustis** in 11.56.15, above).

14–16 **non ... basiatorem:** High office cannot save you; not the consulate, nor the tribunate, nor the praetorship.

15 **senive fasces:** The praetor had the privilege of six lictors carrying bundles of rods (**fasces**).

15–16 **superba ... virga:** a TRANSFERRED EPITHET. A stick, even one used as an instrument of corporal punishment, cannot itself be "arrogant."

17 **sedeas:** subj. with impersonal **licet**, meaning "although" (A&G §527.b).

tribunali: a dais or platform from which a Roman magistrate pronounced official judgments.

18 **e curuli** = **e curuli sella.** The curule chair was reserved for upper magistrates: consuls, praetors, and curule aediles.

19 **illa ... atque illa:** adverbial, "by one way or another."

20 **febricitantem:** Note the ALLITERATION with **flentem**.

21 **oscitanti ... natantique:** a pair of activities chosen to give an impression of randomness: any activity will do; any participle that fits the meter could go here.

22 **dabit cacanti:** The extreme case. The determined **basiator** has no sense of disgust.

remedium: Ancient medicine did not know about germs; but the poem conveys a basic understanding, deduced from empirical observation, of contagion.

mali: objective genitive (A&G §348).

23 **facias amicum basiare quem nolis:** How is this a **remedium**? Does Martial mean that if the person is a friend he will not assault Flaccus with kisses? Or does he mean "friend" in the more erotic sense, so that Flaccus won't mind but will welcome the kisses?

facias = **ut facias,** a substantive clause, "that you make," in apposition to **remedium** in line 22 (A&G §570).

quem nolis: a rel. clause of characteristic, with an undefined antecedent (A&G §535).

—Villains—

Aeneas (right) fights Mezentius (left) and his son Lausus (center). Aeneas bears armor and weapons made by Vulcan and brought to him by his mother Venus (*Aeneid* 8.370–453, 608–731). Wenceslaus Hollar (1607–1677), a Czech artist best known for his etchings, produced a series of illustrations for John Ogilby's 1654 translation into English of Vergil's works. (Courtesy of the Thomas Fisher Rare Book Library, University of Toronto)

Introduction to Villains

The following passages were written between Julius Caesar's death in 44 BCE and Vergil's in 19 BCE, twenty-five years that saw wave after wave of civil war before the establishment of peace and stability under Augustus. Although dominating politics as "first citizen," *princeps*, Augustus claimed to have restored the political structure of the Republic by handing back its traditional powers to the Senate. With this restoration went attempts to restore Roman morality—and the population of the nobility—by means of legislation encouraging marriage, fidelity within marriage, and the production of children. To set an example of *pietas* and thus to encourage it in his fellow citizens, Augustus also built and restored numerous shrines and temples within the city.

As figures exemplifying moral corruption and the abuse of power, the villains who stalk the following pages need to be seen in the context of a Rome in crisis then undergoing moral and political restoration. These figures are all, to greater and lesser degrees, their authors' creations. Although dealing with a historical figure and recent events, Sallust makes L. Sergius Catilina a man of extraordinary appetite, for sex as well as power. Sallust's history (together with Cicero's famous speeches) casts Catiline as corrupt, a threat to Rome's very existence, and a byword for conspiracy. Sallust's Catiline, however, has his heroic side and dies on the field of battle.

In contrast to Sallust, who dealt with a documented historical figure, Vergil, and Livy in these passages from his early books, deal with what is largely historical myth: Vergil's Mezentius has no existence outside of legend; Livy's Sextus Tarquinius, son (or grandson) of the last Etruscan king, is as legendary as Mezentius; even with Livy's second villain, Appius, an early member of the old and accomplished *gens Appia*, we are on only somewhat firmer ground.

What this relative lack of factual information means is that Vergil and Livy were free to create characters that were useful to them: Vergil needed to explain the Etruscan presence in Latium and Etruscan opposition to Aeneas, even while making the Etruscans as a people—and contributors to Rome's early progress—still somewhat sympathetic. (Vergil's patron, Maecenas, was of Etruscan descent.) So Mezentius, Etruscan king and *contemptor deorum,* "scorner" or "reviler of the gods," is a king in exile because of his tyrannical behavior; but even he receives some sympathy at his end: His son dies trying to defend him; he himself fights as fiercely and brilliantly as a Homeric hero; and he apparently loves his horse. Likewise, Livy's story of Lucretia uses the crimes of the Etruscan royal house to explain the expulsion of kings from Rome and the founding of the Republic. His villain, Sextus Tarquinius, displays the lust and lack of self-control that are part of the stereotype of a tyrant. So too, in the story of Verginia, Appius's sexual appetite brings about further change in the structure of government and illustrates perceived injustices in Rome's legal system. Both accounts demonstrate Livy's interest in explaining constitutional change via drama rather than historical or legal analysis.

Vergil

Aeneid 10.689–768
Standard Level and Higher Level

— Introduction to Vergil —

Publius Vergilius Maro was born in northern Italy, near Mantua, in 70 BCE, according to tradition. He is said to have received his early education in northern Italy and then to have moved to Rome and Naples for further study. At some point after the battle of Philippi, and at some point after completing his first collection of poems, Vergil joined the circle of poets supported by Maecenas; he also became a friend of Horace (indeed some of their early works seem to engage in poetic dialogue with one another).

The first works securely attributed to Vergil were the ten *Eclogues* (ca. 42–39/38 BCE), pastoral poems that gave a poignant view of the Italian countryside disturbed by civil war, its displaced farmers mingling with goatherds and shepherdesses of distinguished literary pedigree. Next came the *Georgics*, four books nominally about farming, but which also meditate on society, animal as well as human, and humanity's position in the cosmos. The *Georgics* were completed probably around the time of Octavian's return to Italy in 29 BCE. Work on the *Aeneid* occupied the next ten years, that is, the rest of Vergil's life. According to his ancient biographer, the *Aeneid* remained incomplete at Vergil's death in 19 BCE and Vergil left instructions that the manuscript of the poem be destroyed. Augustus refused to honor those wishes and saw to the editing and publication of what quickly became Rome's national epic.

The International Baccalaureate prescribes *Aeneid* 10.689–746 for the Villains option. This reader also provides lines 747–768 for additional context.

— Introduction to the *Aeneid* —

The events of the *Aeneid* lie between the fall of one great city, Troy, and the foundation of another, Rome. The epic tells of the travels of a survivor of the Trojan War, Aeneas, and his struggles as a refugee to make it to a new home in an area of Italy called Latium, a land he has never seen, and whose people are not all welcoming.

Vergil was a scholarly poet. The *Aeneid* drew upon the *Iliad* and *Odyssey*, Apollonius of Rhodes's *Argonautica*, and other Greek epics that are lost to us. It drew upon Greek tragedy and philosophy as well. Moreover, two centuries of Latin poetry preceded and informed Vergil's work, from Livius Adronicus's translation of the *Odyssey* in the mid-third century BCE—the first purely literary translation in the Western world—and Ennius's second-century Roman historical epic, the *Annales* (both now lost), through works that survive, such as Lucretius's *De Rerum Natura*, and Catullus's mini-epic on the marriage of Peleus and Thetis.

The Homeric influence is most immediately obvious. The first two words of the poem, **arma virumque**, encompass both Homeric epics by calling to mind, on the one hand, the fighting that occupies so much of the *Iliad*, and on the other, the man who is the topic of the *Odyssey*. Whereas ancient editors divided the texts of the *Iliad* and *Odyssey* into twenty-four books each, Vergil, as if producing a concentrated version of both epics, wrote the *Aeneid* in twelve carefully arranged and structured books.

The first half of the *Aeneid* tells of the wanderings of Aeneas and his companions as they make their way from fallen Troy to Italy. At times they follow in Odysseus's wake, even rescuing one of his companions whom Odysseus had abandoned on the island of the Cyclops. Like Odysseus, Aeneas suffers a shipwreck and is rescued by a sympathetic woman, and like Odysseus, he tells the story of his wanderings to an entranced audience at a feast. Aeneas's narrative, itself divided like the poem into Iliadic and Odyssean halves, recounts the fall of Troy (Book 2) and the Trojan refugees' subsequent wanderings (Book 3). Like the *Odyssey*, the first half of the *Aeneid* also includes a visit to the dwelling of the dead (Book 6).

The second half of the *Aeneid* recapitulates some main points of the *Iliad*: battles between a force invading by sea and the defending army; famous scenes of single combat; the deaths of heroes, the extended description of a hero's shield. Moreover, as in the *Iliad*, the proximate cause of the fighting is the contested possession of a woman. In the *Aeneid*, the woman is Lavinia, daughter of the Italian king, Latinus. Influenced by prophecy, Latinus promises Lavinia in marriage to the newcomer, Aeneas. But Juno, always hostile to the Trojans, is outraged at the prospect of an alliance that will make Aeneas's settlement easy. She sends a Fury to inflame Lavinia's mother, Amata, who wants her daughter to marry Turnus, king of the Rutulians. War flares up between Turnus's Italian forces and Aeneas's Trojans, the latter aided by allies from Pallanteum, Evander's settlement on the site of the future Rome.

Aeneas takes on Achilles's role from the *Iliad* as best fighter among the invaders and their allies, and Turnus takes on Hector's as best fighter among the defenders. As Hector killed Achilles's friend Patroclus and stripped him of his arms, so too Turnus kills Aeneas's protégé Pallas and strips him of his. With Pallas dead, Turnus's fate is as sealed as that of Hector: Aeneas will kill him in revenge; it is only a matter of when.

As in the *Iliad* and *Odyssey*, in the *Aeneid* the gods make decisions and agreements that affect the lives of humans. Juno's rage caused the Trojan shipwreck, delayed Aeneas's arrival in Italy, and threw up obstacles to his union with Lavinia. At the end of the epic, however, Juno sets her anger aside and agrees to a settlement with Jupiter, on condition that the Trojan refugees give up their old language and customs and become Italians, men of Latium.

Right before the passage included here, Juno, as Turnus's divine champion, has delayed his defeat and death by whisking him away. His departure leaves the battlefield free for other warriors to display their courage and prowess in battle. One of them is the Etruscan king, Mezentius. The passage included here is part of his *aristeia* or "display of excellence" in the Homeric tradition. Indeed, this passage contains marked Homeric features: extended similes; allusions to characters and events mentioned in the *Iliad*; and even Latin versions of a number of Homeric phrases.

Mezentius is a striking figure in the *Aeneid*. Vergil says that he was a cruel tyrant, exiled for his atrocities, who has taken refuge with Turnus and the Rutulians, a tribe of central Italy. Vergil also calls Mezentius **contemptor deorum**, "scorner of the gods," the very antithesis of Aeneas, who is **insignis pietate**, "marked by his sense of duty" (to gods, family, and his people). Among Mezentius's atrocities: binding the bodies of living prisoners to corpses, so that the dead infect the living and kill them slowly. After Mezentius's *aristeia*, he is wounded, and then killed by Aeneas. He goes to his death willingly, because Aeneas has just killed his son.

— Meter —

Dactylic Hexameter

— *Aeneid* 10.689–768 —

The poet compares Mezentius, as he confronts his opponents, to a cliff bearing the force of the wind and waves. Mezentius kills three Trojans and, in Homeric fashion, takes their armor as spoil.

    at Iovis interea monitis Mezentius ardens
690 succedit pugnae Teucrosque invadit ovantis.
    concurrunt Tyrrhenae acies atque omnibus uni,
    uni odiisque viro telisque frequentibus instant.

689   **monitis:** causal abl. with **succedit** (line 690). Even though Mezentius was introduced as one who scorns the gods, he still acts in response to Jupiter's promptings.

690   **succedit:** with **pugnae**, dat., "enters into battle in place of," that is, in place of Turnus. The almost completely spondaic meter adds solemnity to his entrance.

        Teucrosque ... ovantis: The **Teucri** (Trojans) are rejoicing at Turnus's apparent retreat.

691   **Tyrrhenae:** Etruscan. The other Etruscans hate Mezentius because of his cruelty, egregious even for a tyrant.

691-92   **omnibus uni, / uni odiisque viro telisque frequentibus:** The juxtaposition of **omnibus** and **uni** and the repetition (ANADIPLOSIS) of **uni / uni** across the line break together emphasize that the hatred of all is focused on one man alone. Note also the SYLLEPSIS of abstract "all ... hatreds" and concrete "weapons" that surround **uni ... viro**. The **fr-** of **frequentibus**, being a combination of a mute (*f*) and a liquid (*r*) consonant, does not lengthen the **-que** of **telisque**.

        -que ... -que: "both ... and ...," a poetic usage.

A scene illustrating Book 9 of the *Aeneid* depicts the goddess Iris exhorting Turnus to attack the Trojan refugees. Wenceslaus Hollar (1607–1677), a Czech artist best known for his etchings, produced a series of illustrations for John Ogilby's 1654 English translation of Vergil's works. (Courtesy of the Thomas Fisher Rare Book Library, University of Toronto)

ille velut rupes, vastum quae prodit in aequor,
obvia ventorum furiis expostaque ponto,
695 vim cunctam atque minas perfert caelique marisque,
ipsa immota manens, prolem Dolichaonis Hebrum
sternit humi, cum quo Latagum Palmumque fugacem,
sed Latagum saxo atque ingenti fragmine montis
occupat os faciemque adversam, poplite Palmum
700 succiso volvi segnem sinit, armaque Lauso
donat habere umeris et vertice figere cristas.

693   **ille velut rupes:** the first SIMILE of several that contribute to this passage's marked Homeric quality.

693–695   **aequor ... ponto ... marisque:** Note that the words for the sea are at the ends of their lines, and thus opposed spatially to the **rupes**.

696   **ipsa immota manens:** This phrase describing the cliff occupies the same position in the line as **ille velut rupes** (line 693). The **rupes**, therefore, literally remains unmoved.

       prolem Dolichaonis: proles in the sense of **filius**, a more elevated expression suitable to the dignity of epic. Dolichaon is mentioned only here in the *Aeneid*.

       Hebrum: also the name of a river in Thrace; this is the *Aeneid*'s only reference to him.

697   **Latagum Palmumque:** Like Hebrus, these two receive mention only when killed. A catalog of victims is typically part of a hero's *aristeia*.

698–99   **sed Latagum ... occupat os faciemque adversam:** where we might expect **Latagi** (genitive) **... occupat os faciemque adversam**. But here **Latagum** is the direct object and **os faciemque adversam** is in the "Greek" accusative, of the part affected (see A&G §397.b). The adjective **adversam** ("facing him" or "turned toward him") makes it clear that, unlike the fleeing Palmus, Latagus stands up to Mezentius and meets death with heroic courage. The conjunction **-que** "combines the two words into one connected whole" (A&G §324.a).

698 **saxo ... ingenti fragmine:** abl. of means. Note how the simple **saxo** is expanded to the **ingenti fragmine montis**, the kind of massive object only an epic hero can lift.

699 **poplite Palmum:** Note the ALLITERATION.

700 **succiso volvi segnem sinit:** Note the sequence of seven long syllables (three spondees and the long syllable of the fourth foot), which give the impression of Palmus's slowing in his flight after Mezentius hamstrings him, and then collapsing. The verb **volvo** appears here in the middle sense of the passive, "to fall headlong."

700-701 **armaque ... cristas:** Spoils are dangerous in both the *Iliad* and the *Aeneid*: In the *Iliad* it is to Hector's misfortune that he strips Patroclus of Achilles's weapons and wears them; and it is to Turnus's misfortune that he wears spoils stripped from Evander's son, Pallas. Moreover, what happens to Acron later in this passage (lines 719–31) shows that conspicuous armor attracts the eye of the enemy.

Lauso: Mezentius's son. Lausus's death later in Book 10, Mezentius's mourning and attempt to avenge him, and Mezentius's own death at the end of Book 10 make these Etruscan opponents more sympathetic figures.

701 **habere ... figere:** The infinitive expressing purpose appears in early authors and in poetry (A&G §460.c).

Mezentius's aristeia *continues with additional victims and an extended simile that compares him to a cornered wild boar, and his opponents to fearful hunters.*

    nec non Euanthen Phrygium Paridisque Mimanta
    aequalem comitemque, una quem nocte Theano
    in lucem genitori Amyco dedit et face praegnas
705 Cisseis regina Parim: Paris urbe paterna
    occubat, ignarum Laurens habet ora Mimanta.

702   **nec non:** "also," "furthermore."

      Euanthen ... Mimanta: Greek names, with the accusative in **-en** and **-nta**. Euanthes and Mimas are mentioned only here. Mimas's identity is elaborated at the moment of his death. This is a typical Homeric practice.

      Paridis: a Greek genitive form for the name Paris. This is the Trojan prince, son of Priam and Hecuba.

703-704 **quem ... Theano ... Amyco / face ... Cisseis ... Parim:** Note the CHIASTIC order: child, mother, father/father, mother, child.

703   **Theano:** nominative. A Trojan woman, she is mentioned only here.

704   **in lucem ... dedit:** an elevated METAPHOR for "giving birth."

      genitori Amyco: Amycus appears in Book 5.373 as king of the Bebryces, a people of Bithynia.

      face praegnas: "made pregnant by a firebrand," a portent predicting that the child thus conceived will grow up to cause destruction.

705   **Cisseis:** nominative, "daughter of Cisseus" (a king of Thrace). This is Hecuba, wife of the Trojan king Priam, and mother of both Paris and Hector.

      Parim: Paris: Repeating a word that ends a clause at the beginning of another is ANADIPLOSIS. Repeating it in a different form is POLYPTOTON. Note also the CHIASTIC effect: Mimas's birth, Paris's birth / Paris's death, Mimas's death.

706   **ignarum:** Mimas can be **ignarus,** "unknown," "unfamiliar," from the point of view of the **Laurens ... ora** because he is a stranger to it, or **ignarus,** "unaware," because he is dead.

A shepherd wearing a "Trojan cap," identified as the Trojan prince Paris, holds a shepherd's crook (*pedum*) and the golden apple that Eris used to sow discord at the wedding of Peleus and Thetis. The statue, ca. 100–200 CE, was reworked in the eighteenth century and may not have originally depicted Paris. (Getty Museum, California) (Public Domain)

ac velut ille canum morsu de montibus altis
actus aper, multos Vesulus quem pinifer annos
defendit multosque palus Laurentia, silva
710 pastus harundinea, postquam inter retia ventum est,
substitit infremuitque ferox et inhorruit armos,
nec cuiquam irasci propiusve accedere virtus,
sed iaculis tutisque procul clamoribus instant,
haud aliter, iustae quibus est Mezentius irae,
715 non ulli est animus stricto concurrere ferro;
missilibus longe et vasto clamore lacessunt.
ille autem impavidus partis cunctatur in omnis,
dentibus infrendens, et tergo decutit hastas.

707–18 **ac velut . . . hastas:** The second SIMILE of the passage, and an extended one. It begins by comparing Mezentius to a wild boar; then it compares the men he is fighting to hunters.

708 **aper:** an animal hunted by Homeric heroes (see note on *Epode* 16.20).

multos . . . annos: accusative of extent of time.

Vesulus: a mountain in Liguria, a region on the northwestern coast of the Italian peninsula.

709 **multosque = multosque annos.**

palus Laurentia = palus Laurentia defendit.

710 **pastus:** passive, with abl., "to grow rich or fat upon."

ventum est: an impersonal use (A&G §208.d).

711 **substitit infremuitque . . . et inhorruit:** The prefix **in-** here adds intensive force.

armos: "Greek" acc. of the part affected, with **inhorruit**.

712 **cuiquam:** dat. of possession: **nec est virtus cuique.** The boar is fearsome; but Vergil makes it clear that the hunters lack courage, **virtus**, and **animus** (line 715).

713 **iaculis:** from **iacio**, that is, weapons that are thrown, which like **tutis ... clamoribus** do not require close contact with the deadly animal.

714 **iustae quibus est Mezentius irae:** double dative construction (see A&G §382.1 note 1).

715 **ulli:** dat. of possession with **est animus** + inf., "none has the courage to ..." The construction of **est animus** with the infinitive (**concurrere**) is rare. On the similar use of the infinitive with an *adjective*, a Greek idiom, see A&G §461, under the heading "Peculiar Infinitives."

716 **missilibus longe:** Vergil repeats his point: the men fight the boar at a distance; note also the repetition of **clamor**.

717 **partis ... in omnis:** "in all directions."

718 **infrendens:** The participle recalls the **in-** verbs (**infremuit ... inhorruit**) of line 711 and helps to bring closure to the simile. The phrase **dentibus infrendens** appeared in Book 3 describing Polyphemus, the Cyclops, after his blinding by Odysseus. The INTRATEXTUAL ALLUSION emphasizes Mezentius's fury and monstrosity.

decutit: The spears are just irritants to the boar/Mezentius. He shakes them off as a dog shakes off water.

Another victim is singled out and described; a third simile compares Mezentius to a hungry lion.

      venerat antiquis Corythi de finibus Acron,
720 Graius homo, infectos linquens profugus hymenaeos:
      hunc ubi miscentem longe media agmina vidit,
      purpureum pinnis et pactae coniugis ostro,
      impastus stabula alta leo ceu saepe peragrans,

719   **Corythi:** a town in Etruria.

      Acron: mentioned only here in the *Aeneid*.

720   **Graius homo . . . hymenaeos:** The letter *h* does not function as a consonant (for example, the dactyl **Graĭŭs ho-**); but to make this line scan, we must take the last syllable of **profugŭs** as a long one: **profugūs hymenaeos**.

      infectos: "not brought to completion," "unfinished," that is, "unconsummated," like the marriage of Laudamia and Protesilaus, who, newly married, was killed at Troy as he leapt from his ship (*Iliad* 2.700–701), described in Latin in Catullus 68.74–75: on her wedding, Laudamia entered a **domum / inceptam frustra**, "a household begun in vain."

      profugus: We do not know why Acron is an exile or refugee; but that identity, which he shares, of course, with Aeneas, makes his death more pathetic.

721   **miscentem:** "throwing into confusion."

      vidit = Mezentius vidit.

722   **purpureum pinnis et . . . ostro:** either a dyed crest on his helmet or naturally red feathers and a dyed cloak as well. The tragic turn is that it is the gifts of his bride that make Acron conspicuous and therefore Mezentius's next victim.

      pinnis: on the crest of the helmet.

723   **impastus:** Note how Vergil aims for variety in the similes: the boar in lines 707–28 was **pastus**; the lion in contrast is hungry.

alta: possibly, "situated on high ground," but Vergil has elsewhere used the phrase to mean the "deep lairs." Compare *Aeneid* 6.179, **itur in antiquam silvam, stabula alta ferarum**, "they go into the ancient forest, the deep lairs of wild beasts."

ceu: Here followed by **sic** in line 729, **ceu** introduces the simile.

This third-century CE mosaic depicting a lion is in the collection of the Bardo National Museum in Tunis, Tunisia. The inscription addresses the lion: *O leo, praesumsisti, expedisti, dedicasti.* (© Creative Commons 4.0/Sinda BF)

(suadet enim vesana fames) si forte fugacem
725 conspexit capream aut surgentem in cornua cervum,
gaudet, hians immane comasque arrexit et haeret
visceribus super incumbens, lavit improba taeter
ora cruor:
sic ruit in densos alacer Mezentius hostis.
730 sternitur infelix Acron et calcibus atram
tundit humum exspirans infractaque tela cruentat.

724 **(suadet enim vesana fames)**: **Suadet** seems an understatement. Homer uses a stronger verb (*keletai* = "command," "urge on," "exhort") when comparing Odysseus to a hungry lion in *Odyssey* 6.133.

725 **conspexit capream aut surgentem in cornua cervum:** Like Acron's purple crest, the stag's horns make their bearer conspicuous.

726 **immane:** adverbial accusative with **hians**.

727 **visceribus:** dat. with **haeret**.

super incumbens: can be spelled as one word or two. As one word, **superincumbo** means "to lean over." Either gives a clear image of the big cat crouching over the viscera.

lavit: The verb **lavo** can be either first or, as here, third conjugation. At *Georgics* 3.221, Vergil uses a similar expression to describe fighting bulls: **lavit ater corpora sanguis**, "the black blood bathes their bodies."

improba: a poetic use of an adjective that regularly means "morally unsound" or "shameless."

taeter: The first meaning of this adjective is "physically offensive" or "foul." Vergil uses it elsewhere only of the Harpies' abominable smell (*Aeneid* 3.228). Used of persons, **taeter** means "morally offensive" or "vile." Given Mezentius's abominable cruelty, **taeter**, like **improba**, is a good adjective to use as the simile comes to its point of comparison.

728 **ora cruor:** There are over fifty such incomplete lines in the *Aeneid*. They have been taken as evidence of the poem's incomplete nature. (There are no such lines in the *Eclogues* or *Georgics*.) Some of them, however, have the obvious rhetorical effect of making the reader pause before continuing.

ora: plural for singular, as often in poetry.

729 **sic ruit in densos alacer Mezentius hostis:** After the delays caused by the long and syntactically complicated simile, the narrative continues in a rush. Note how the word order reflects Mezentius's location.

730 **sternitur infelix Acron:** Another short independent clause moves the narrative swiftly along.

730-31 **calcibus atram / tundit humum:** Such physically detailed death throes are yet another Homeric touch.

731 **infracta:** "shattered," not "unbroken." The prefix **in-** is intensive.

Like Palmus, Orodes flees; but Mezentius circles him and runs to meet him face-to-face. This passage is the most highly elaborated of Mezentius's kills, and it involves an exchange of words (another Homeric touch) with the dying Orodes.

    atque idem fugientem haud est dignatus Oroden
    sternere nec iacta caecum dare cuspide vulnus;
    obvius adversoque occurrit seque viro vir
735 contulit, haud furto melior sed fortibus armis.
    tum super abiectum posito pede nixus et hasta:
    "pars belli haud temnenda, viri, iacet altus Orodes."
    conclamant socii laetum paeana secuti.
    ille autem exspirans: "non me, quicumque es, inulto,
740 victor, nec longum laetabere; te quoque fata
    prospectant paria atque eadem mox arva tenebis."
    ad quem subridens mixta Mezentius ira:
    "nunc morere. ast de me divum pater atque hominum rex
    viderit." hoc dicens eduxit corpore telum.
745 olli dura quies oculos et ferreus urget
    somnus, in aeternam clauduntur lumina noctem.

732 **idem:** here showing that the same subject (Mezentius) is involved: "likewise."

      haud est dignatus: LITOTES for "he scorned."

      Oroden: Orodes appears only here in the *Aeneid*.

733 **caecum:** The wound is **caecum** either because it would not be evident who was responsible for it or because it would be in the back, and Orodes could not see it.

734 **obvius adversoque occurrit seque viro vir:** By juxtaposing the words describing the opponents—**obvius** and **adverso**, **viro** and **vir**—the language reflects the direct nature of the clash.

735 **haud furto melior sed fortibus armis:** ablatives of specification. The particle **haud** negates **furto**, which here means "a military stratagem." Note the TRANSFERRED EPITHET **fortibus**.

736 **abiectum = eum abiectum.**

posito pede nixus et hasta: Take **nixus** with both ablatives.

737 **pars belli haud temnenda:** another use of **haud** in LITOTES.

iacet altus Orodes: Mezentius points out the irony: He who was high (**altus**) has been brought low.

738 **laetum paeana:** dir. obj. of **conclamant**. **Paeana** is the accusative of this Greek borrowing (**paean, -is/-os**).

739 **ille autem:** marks a change of both subject and point of view.

quicumque es: Mezentius honored Orodes in killing him by saying his name and pronouncing him **pars belli haud temnenda** (line 737). But Orodes either does not know or does not acknowledge Mezentius's identity, and thus denies him the glory of the kill.

740 **victor:** Orodes does grant Mezentius this much.

laetabere = laetaberis.

longum = diu.

741 **prospectant:** a poetic use of a verb that means "look intently at." The more common expression would be **manent**, "await."

741 **eadem ... arva:** Mezentius too will die here.

743 **nunc morere:** an INTERTEXTUAL as well as INTRATEXTUAL ALLUSION: Mezentius "quotes" the words spoken in Book 2 by Achilles's son, Pyrrhus, during the sack of Troy, when he kills Priam, who has taken refuge at his household altar. The command also translates Achilles's command to Hector at *Iliad* 22.365.

744 **viderit:** the hortatory/jussive subjunctive, which rarely occurs in the perfect except in prohibitions. See A&G §439 and Livy 1.58 in this volume.

745 **olli:** archaic spelling for **illi**, a dative in the sense of a genitive.

745-46 **dura quies ... ferreus ... / somnus ... aeternam ... noctem:** The increasing distance between adjectives and nouns slows the movement of the line as Orodes dies.

Vergil presents another catalog of deaths as the view of the fighting becomes general. The catalog is Homeric in style, but not so much in vocabulary: Vergil's original audience would have noticed immediately that the names, most of which appear only here in the Aeneid, are a mixture of Latin for the Italians and Greek for the Trojans and allies from Evander's Pallanteum, who were originally from Arcadia in Greece.

For the forms of the Greek names, consult the glossary.

> Caedicus Alcathoum obtruncat, Sacrator Hydaspen,
> partheniumque Rapo et praedurum viribus Orsen,
> Messapus Cloniumque Lycaoniumque Ericaeten,
> 750 illum infrenis equi lapsu tellure iacentem,
> hunc peditem. pedes et Lycius processerat Agis;
> quem tamen haud expers Valerus virtutis avitae
> deicit; at Thronium Salius, Saliumque Nealces
> insignis iaculo et longe fallente sagitta.

747-51 **Caedicus:** another **Caedicus** appears in Book 9.362. The **Caedicii** were an Italian tribe.

obtruncat: One main verb serves this part of the catalog. An ARCHAISM, **obtruncare** originally meant "to lop off the head of," then takes on the general meaning of "to slaughter."

Alcathoum: only here in Vergil; other mythological figures of this name were killed at Thebes or in the Trojan War; the name, then, had strong heroic connotations.

Sacrator: only here in Vergil; from the verb **sacro**, the name means "one who sanctifies," or more fittingly here, "one who devotes to destruction."

Hydaspen: also the name of the Jhelum, a tributary of the river Indus; he appears only here in the *Aeneid*.

748 **parthenium:** "having to do with Parthenius" (a mountain in Arcadia). The adjective occurs only here in the *Aeneid*.

Rapo: only here in Vergil.

Orsen: only here in Vergil.

749 **Messapus Cloniumque:** Messapus is one of Mezentius's **primi ductores** (8.6). He is a son of Neptune and cannot be laid low by fire or iron (7.691–92). This particular Clonius appears only here; Turnus killed a different Clonius at 9.574.

Lycaoniumque Ericaeten: Ericaetes is possibly descended from the famous Arcadian king Lycaon, who tried to feed Zeus human flesh and as punishment was turned into a wolf.

750–51 **illum . . . hunc:** When **ille** and **hic** are used together to refer to a previously mentioned pair, **ille** usually means "the former," and **hic** "the latter." See A&G §297.a, b.

infrenis: The horse is "not reined" because his rider dropped the reins in falling.

751 **Lycius . . . Agis:** The Lycians were Trojan allies. Agis appears only here.

752 **haud expers Valerus virtutis avitae:** another example of LITOTES with **haud**. Valerus is presented here as an ancestor of the illustrious *gens Valeria*. The repetition of sounds (**va- vi- avi-**) ties together tightly the name **Valerus** (related to **valeo**), the idea of manly courage, and the idea of ancestry.

753 **Thronium:** only here in Vergil.

Salius, Saliumque: The ANADIPLOSIS and POLYPTOTON, juxtaposing Salius as killer and Salius as killed, emphasize the speed of events in the battle.

Nealces: only here in Vergil.

754 **longe fallente sagitta:** The arrow "escapes notice."

The gods watch the fighting and pity both sides; indeed, their pity grows to embrace mortals in general. As Mezentius charges about the battlefield, Vergil compares him to the hunter Orion.

755   iam gravis aequabat luctus et mutua Mavors
       funera; caedebant pariter pariterque ruebant
       victores victique, neque his fuga nota neque illis.
       di Iovis in tectis iram miserantur inanem
       amborum et tantos mortalibus esse labores:
760   hinc Venus, hinc contra spectat Saturnia Iuno;
       pallida Tisiphone media inter milia saevit.
       at vero ingentem quatiens Mezentius hastam
       turbidus ingreditur campo. quam magnus Orion,

755-56   **aequabat luctus et mutua / ... funera:** The METAPHOR is of weighing out with a set of scales.

755   **Mavors:** Mars, METONYMY for fighting.

756-57   **caedebant pariter pariterque ruebant:** The chiastic arrangement of words and the ANADIPLOSIS of **pariter** reinforce the balance of the fighting, as does the JUXTAPOSITION of **victores victique** and the balance and repetition in **neque his fuga nota neque illis**.

his ... illis: dative with **nota** [est].

758   **Iovis in tectis:** The gods watch from Mt. Olympus. The transition to the perspective of the gods is another Homeric touch.

iram ... inanem: The gods pity the futility of mortal wrath; and Vergil works in another INTERTEXTUAL ALLUSION to the *Iliad*, whose declared topic was the anger of Achilles, and whose first word was "wrath."

759   **amborum:** The balance of the fighting makes the gods pity both sides.

et tantos mortalibus esse labores: The verb **miserantur** (line 758) first took a simple direct object **iram ... inanem**; now it introduces an indirect statement: the gods do not feel pity for any particular **tantos labores**. Rather, they feel pity at the fact that humans *have* **tantos labores**.

760 **hinc Venus, hinc contra spectat Saturnia Iuno:** The two opposing goddesses watch as the two sides fight evenly.

761 **Tisiphone:** one of the Furies.

762 **ingentem ... hastam:** It is as if the great spear of Mezentius is being thrown onto the scales to sway the course of the battle.

763 **turbidus:** "wild" "turbulent"; used of the sea and storms, and also of the winds and constellations associated with such weather.

763–68 **quam magnus Orion ... talis:** The simile compares Mezentius to Orion, a giant, a hunter, and identical with the constellation. Homer in *Iliad* 18 places the constellation on Achilles's shield and in *Odyssey* 11, Odysseus sees the shade of the hunter Orion in the Underworld, where he (Orion) is carrying a brazen club and rounding up the shades of the wild animals he killed in the mountains. Vergil mentions Orion at four other points in the *Aeneid*: 1.535, as a bringer of storms; 3.517, where the helmsman Palinurus sees "Orion armed with gold" along with other constellations in the clear night sky; and 4.52, **aquosus Orion**, and 7.719, **saevus Orion**, both as a bringer of storms.

cum pedes incedit medii per maxima Nerei
765 stagna viam scindens, umero supereminet undas,
aut summis referens annosam montibus ornum,
ingrediturque solo et caput inter nubila condit:
talis se vastis infert Mezentius armis.

764-65 **pedes ... umero:** Orion's brightest stars form his shoulders, belt, and feet, so **pedes** "foot-man" or "man on foot" is particularly apt as is the reference to the shoulder, visible above water, as the constellation appears to rise from the horizon.

764 **medii ... Nerei:** METONYMY for the sea.

766 **referens:** This can be taken figuratively to mean "resembling," or it can be taken literally to mean "carrying back." Does Orion resemble the mighty old tree, or is he carrying a tree down from the mountains?

767 **ingrediturque solo et caput inter nubila condit:** The description draws the mind's eye upward from the ground (**solo**), to the clouds where Orion's head is hidden. Note the ALLITERATION in the second half of the line.

768 **talis:** As **sic** does elsewhere, here **talis** introduces the point of the comparison.

se ... infert = ingreditur.

vastis ... armis: Note the RING COMPOSITION (an ordering of a description, speech, or narrative that follows an extendable ABA pattern) with **ingentem ... hastam** in line 762. Mezentius's enormous weapons help portray him as a monstrous giant.

Book 10 of the *Aeneid* closes with a fight in which Aeneas kills Lausus, the son of Mezentius, and then Mezentius himself. Mezentius's *vasta arma* are here displayed as a trophy, which memorialized a victory and often included a dedication to a god. Wenceslaus Hollar (1607–1677), a Czech artist best known for his etchings, produced a series of illustrations for John Ogilby's 1654 translation into English of Vergil's works. (Courtesy of the Thomas Fisher Rare Book Library, University of Toronto)

LIVY

Ab Urbe Condita 1.57–60
Standard Level and Higher Level

— Introduction to Livy —

The authorities disagree on whether Livy (Titus Livius) was born in 64 or 59 BCE; he was, then, either twenty or fifteen when Julius Caesar was assassinated, old enough in either case to be aware of events during the tumultuous years of civil war that followed. Livy came from Patavium (now Padua), a prosperous city in the Po valley with a reputation for old-fashioned moral virtue. The city supported the Senate against Antony and his forces during the civil war campaigns of the late 40s in Italy. We do not know when Livy came to Rome; but he probably spent considerable time there. He had some contact with Augustus, how directly is uncertain, as well as with the young future emperor Claudius, whom he encouraged to write history.

Livy's major work is his great history of Rome, *Ab Urbe Condita Libri*, "Books from the Founding of the City" (= *AUC*). In 142 books the *AUC* covered Rome's history from its beginnings to 9 BCE (the year of the death of Tiberius's brother Drusus). Of the 142 books, books 1–10 and 21–45 survive (we have summaries of the others). We do not know when Livy began writing his history; but internal evidence shows that he completed books 1–5 between 27 and 25 BCE, and it is safe to say that his outlook was strongly influenced by the decade and a half of civil war that ended with Octavian's (i.e., Augustus's) defeat of the forces of Antony and Cleopatra at Actium in 31 BCE.

Livy's education would have involved the study of literature, rhetoric, and philosophy. (He wrote philosophical dialogues before embarking on his history.) There is no evidence that he either held public office or served in the army. He has been faulted as a historian for relying almost exclusively on his literary predecessors rather than official records and the autopsy of sites. Livy is, however, a sophisticated prose stylist and a superb storyteller who weaves his political theories into his compelling narratives.

— Introduction to *Ab Urbe Condita* 1.57–60 —

According to tradition, Rome at first was ruled by kings; monarchy, however, deteriorated into tyranny and, in 510 BCE, the Romans expelled their last king, the Etruscan Tarquinius Superbus (Tarquin the Proud). They then formed a republic characterized by the rule of annually elected magistrates. The impetus for this transition—again, according to tradition—was the rape of a woman named Lucretia, who was connected to the royal house through her husband, Collatinus.

By presenting an attack on a married woman—and thus on the sanctity of marriage—as the immediate cause of revolution, Livy uses Lucretia's story to bring Rome's political transformation into the personal realm. Such a manner of explanation was not new: Helen's defection from her husband brought down Troy; and the fifth century Greek historian Herodotus explained dynastic changes in Lydia through the story of Gyges's appropriation of both Candaules's wife and Candaules's throne (*Histories* 1.7–13).

On the one hand, Lucretia seems pitiable and helpless, victim of both Sextus's crime and her own rigid concept of chastity; on the other, she is a formidable figure, one staunchly determined to politicize her rape and control how her story is used. Her truest precedent, perhaps, is neither Helen nor Candaules's wife, both of whom survive the transfer of power and change of husbands, but Iphigenia at Aulis, who at the end of Euripides's play sees clearly her role in the larger picture of the expedition against Troy, anticipates a glorious reputation, and acquiesces in her own sacrifice. It is not by chance that Livy presents the events of Lucretia's story as scenes in a tragedy.

The events of Lucretia's story take place in three locations: Rome; Ardea, about twenty-two miles south of Rome and two miles from the sea; and Collatia, about ten miles east-northeast of Rome, along the Via Collatina.

— *Ab Urbe Condita* 1.57–60 —

*As it sets out the background for unrest (**motus**) and revolution, the first part of the narrative draws a sharp contrast between the work demanded of the common people and the consumption—of time and resources—by the royal family. The king has a double motive for attacking the town of Ardea: to enrich himself through plunder; but also to soothe the minds of a people that feels enslaved. The opening scene also establishes the physical setting of events, first generally, in the Roman camp outside Ardea, then more specifically, in the quarters of Sextus Tarquinius.*

[57] Ardeam Rutuli habebant, gens ut in ea regione atque in ea aetate divitiis praepollens. eaque ipsa causa belli fuit, quod rex Romanus cum ipse ditari, exhaustus magnificentia publicorum operum, tum praeda delenire popularium
5 animos studebat, praeter aliam superbiam regno infestos etiam quod se in fabrorum ministeriis ac servili tam diu habitos opere ab rege indignabantur.

1 **Ardeam:** the chief city of the **Rutuli**, a people of Latium (led by Turnus in the *Aeneid*). Normal word order would be **Rutuli Ardeam habebant**, but Livy is focusing the reader's attention on the setting of events.

ut in ea regione: concessive use of **ut**, "for that area."

2 **divitiis:** ablative of specification with **praepollens** (A&G §418).

praepollens: a rare adjective, meaning "predominant," "outstanding."

eaque ipsa causa belli: "and that itself was the cause of war," further explained by **quod . . . studebat** (lines 3–5).

3–12 **rex Romanus . . . regno . . . ab rege . . . regii . . . iuvenes:** Livy makes it clear that the royal family is responsible for discontent and revolution.

3–4 **cum . . . tum . . . :** The adverbs are used correlatively, "both . . . and . . ." (A&G §323.g and §549.b). Take **studebat** (line 5) with both **ditari** and **delenire**.

4 **publicorum operum:** The two major public works of Tarquinius Superbus's reign were the temple of Juppiter Optimus Maximus on the Capitoline and the Cloaca Maxima, the sewer that drained the Forum valley.

4-5 **popularium animos ... infestos:** Although **animos ... infestos** is the object of **delenire**, the idea of **populares** (here simply "citizens") predominates in **quod se ... habitos ... indignabantur** (lines 6-7).

5 **aliam:** "every other." It anticipates the specific reason given in **quod ... indignabantur** (lines 6-7).

regno: dative with **infestos**. The dative is used with some adjectives to denote that to which a quality of the adjective is directed (A&G §383 and §384).

6 **in fabrorum ministeriis:** "in artisans' tasks."

The Cloaca Maxima, whose construction was attributed to Tarquinius Superbus, carried stormwater and waste from the center of Rome and drained into the Tiber. During the reign of Augustus, Marcus Agrippa oversaw an expansion that channeled the flow of water from eleven aqueducts through the Cloaca Maxima to prevent blockages in the sewer system. Portions of the system are still visible today. (© Creative Commons 4.0/Chris 73)

temptata res est si primo impetu capi Ardea posset. ubi id parum processit, obsidione munitionibusque coepti
10 premi hostes. in his stativis, ut fit longo magis quam acri bello, satis liberi commeatus erant, primoribus tamen magis quam militibus; regii quidem iuvenes interdum otium conviviis comisationibusque inter se terebant. forte potantibus his apud Sex. Tarquinium, ubi et Collatinus
15 cenabat Tarquinius Egerii filius, incidit de uxoribus mentio; suam quisque laudare miris modis.

8   **si ... posset:** an indirect question depending on **temptata res est**. Translate **si** as "to see if" (A&G §576.a).

       ubi: "when."

       id: Here the pronoun has no specific neuter antecedent, but refers to the siege generally.

9   **coepti = coepti sunt.**

10   **premi:** complementary infinitive with **coepti**.

       ut fit: "as happens."

11   **commeatus:** nominative plural of the fourth declension. **Commeatus** is a technical term for a "furlough" or "leave of absence."

12   **regii quidem iuvenes: Quidem** throws emphasis on **regii**, thus singling out the young men of the royal house from the rest of the privileged **primores**.

       otium: a culturally loaded word. The elder Cato, statesman and author, wrote that prominent men were as responsible for their use of their leisure, **otium**, as their business, **negotium**. Note how the details of the rest of this passage draw attention to the irresponsible behavior of the royal youth. **Otium ... terebant** (lines 12–13) is a striking expression.

14–15   **Collatinus ... Tarquinius Egeri filius:** Demaratus of Corinth, who came to Etruria as a refugee, had two sons, Arruns and Lucumo. Arruns predeceased Demaratus by a short period of time; moreover, shortly after Arruns died a son was born to him. But, because

Demaratus too died before that child, his grandson, was born, he made no provision for him in his will. Thus, says Livy earlier in Book 1, that grandson was named Egerius, "Needy" (a pun on the verb **egeo**, "to need"). Demaratus's other son, Lucumo, sole heir to his father's wealth, became the first Tarquin king at Rome (Tarquinius Priscus). He was the father of Tarquinius Superbus and grandfather of Sextus Tarquinius, the villains of this episode. Collatinus, then, is the nephew of Tarquinius Superbus and second cousin of Sextus; and these events take place within the extended royal family. See Appendix 4.

14 **ubi et Collatinus:** "where Collatinus *too* . . ."

15 **incidit . . . mentio:** The verb **incidit**, meaning "to present itself in conversation," or "to crop up," reflects the idle nature of the talk.

16 **suam = suam uxorem.**

laudare: historical infinitive, here standing in for the imperfect indicative (A&G §463).

miris modis: "in a remarkable manner," "amazingly" (A&G §412).

The debate as to womanly excellence heats up. Any such contest should make readers uneasy: In Greco-Roman mythology and historiography, such competitions are deadly (e.g., the competition as to beauty among Hera, Athene, and Aphrodite, which led to the Judgment of Paris and the Trojan War; or Candaules's insistence on the surpassing beauty of his wife in Herodotus, Histories I, and his insistence that Gyges should see it for himself. In this section, Livy emphasizes both the idleness of the young royals and the hastiness and thoughtlessness of youth.

inde certamine accenso Collatinus negat verbis opus esse, paucis id quidem horis posse sciri, quantum ceteris praestet Lucretia sua. "quin, si vigor iuventae inest, conscendimus equos invisimusque praesentes nostrarum ingenia? id cuique spectatissimum sit quod necopinato viri adventu occurrerit oculis." incaluerant vino; "age sane!" omnes; citatis equis avolant Romam.

17 **certamine accenso:** ablative absolute. The metaphor of "kindling" or "igniting" suggests that, like a fire, a competition can get out of control.

negat: the historical present, used in lively narrative, here introducing indirect speech.

verbis: ablative with **opus esse**.

18 **id:** anticipates the indirect question **quantum ceteris praestet Lucretia sua**.

quidem: emphasizes **id**, and thus draws a contrast between the speed with which the princes can judge the contest of wives and the lack of progress in the siege.

19 **"quin, si vigor iuventae inest . . .":** The transition to direct speech brings the scene fully to life. The young royals expend effort and energy on frivolities that would be better directed at winning the war. That Lucretia's own husband Collatinus makes the fatal proposition contributes to the tragic structure of the story.

quin: "why not?" used here with the indicative **conscendimus** to add force to a proposition in a situation of heightened emotion. The effect is that of a command (A&G §449.2.b).

iuventae: "youth," as in the time of life.

20   **nostrarum:** Note the feminine gender. **Nostrarum = uxorum nostrarum.**

20-22   **id ... spectatissimum sit quod ... occurrerit oculis:** The appeal to sight recalls Herodotus's story of Candaules who, boasting to Gyges about his wife's beauty, told him essentially that "seeing is believing."

cuique: dat. with **spectatissimum**.

21   **sit:** a jussive subjunctive.

22   **oculis:** dat. with **occurrerit** (line 21). Note also the ALLITERATION of the two words.

incaluerant vino: the first of a series of short sentences that convey the speed of events. The pluperfect gives the fact explaining the young men's impulsiveness.

age sane: a colloquial expression as a summons to action: "come on!"

omnes = omnes aiunt.

22-23   **citatis equis avolant Romam:** A sentence of only four words encompassing over twenty miles of hard riding draws attention to the speed with which the royal youths can act when motivated. The accusative **Romam** indicates the end point of their motion (A&G §427).

quo cum primis se intendentibus tenebris pervenissent,
25 pergunt inde Collatiam, ubi Lucretiam haudquaquam ut regias nurus, quas in convivio luxuque cum aequalibus viderant tempus terentes, sed nocte sera deditam lanae inter lucubrantes ancillas in medio aedium sedentem inveniunt. muliebris certaminis laus penes Lucretiam fuit.
30 adveniens vir Tarquiniique excepti benigne; victor maritus comiter invitat regios iuvenes. ibi Sex. Tarquinium mala libido Lucretiae per vim stuprandae capit; cum forma tum spectata castitas incitat. et tum quidem ab nocturno iuvenali ludo in castra redeunt.

24 **quo:** connective relative: "and to this place." A relative pronoun or adverb often stands at the beginning of an independent sentence or clause (in this case a sentence) and serves to connect it to the preceding sentence or clause (A&G §308.f).

primis se intendentibus tenebris: an ablative absolute serving as a temporal clause. The visual detail describing early evening helps suggest that the royal wives are *already* banqueting.

25 **pergunt inde Collatiam:** another expression emphasizing speed.

25-27 **Lucretiam haudquaquam ... nocte sera:** The temporal contrast between **primis ... tenebris** (line 24) and the expression of time **nocte sera** makes Lucretia's excellence stand out in sharp contrast to the other royal wives' behavior.

26 **regias nurus:** The adjective again emphasizes that it is the royal family that is corrupt.

26-27 **convivio luxuque cum aequalibus ... tempus terentes:** The royal wives' activity recalls the earlier expression, **otium ... terebant** (lines 12–13), describing the **regii iuvenes** at Ardea.

27 **deditam lanae:** Spinning and weaving were tasks expected of Roman women of all statuses. Augustus himself ostentatiously wore clothes produced by his wife and daughter. The words **lanam fecit** were high praise on a Roman wife's tombstone. **Lanae** is dative with **deditam**.

29 **penes:** prep. + accusative, "in the hands of."

30 **vir Tarquiniique:** Livy's distinguishing Collatinus as husband, **vir**, obscures for the moment the fact that he too is a Tarquin.

victor maritus: These are two nouns in apposition (A&G §282), so that the idea is not "the married victor," but "the husband, [who was] the victor." The military metaphor draws attention to the misplaced effort.

31 **invitat:** Note the shift back to the historical present of lively narrative.

regios iuvenes: Again, Livy distinguishes between Collatinus and the other youths.

32 **stuprandae:** objective genitive after **libido**.

33 **spectata castitas:** "chastity that was proven."

et tum quidem: Made emphatic by **quidem, tum** raises expectation of what follows.

33-34 **iuvenali ludo:** The adjective is ironic: What began as a youthful prank ends in rape, death, and revolution.

The chilling description of the rape of Lucretia. Sextus's physical threats do not persuade Lucretia; but his threatening her reputation does. She gives in so that she can survive in order to bear witness to his crime and her own resistance.

[58] paucis interiectis diebus Sex. Tarquinius inscio Collatino cum comite uno Collatiam venit. ubi exceptus benigne ab ignaris consilii cum post cenam in hospitale cubiculum deductus esset, amore ardens, postquam satis tuta circa
5   sopitique omnes videbantur, stricto gladio ad dormientem Lucretiam venit sinistraque manu mulieris pectore oppresso "tace, Lucretia" inquit; "Sex. Tarquinius sum; ferrum in manu est; moriere, si emiseris vocem."

1–2   **paucis interiectis diebus Sex. Tarquinius ... Collatiam venit:** A sentence that is relatively simple, even with two ablative absolutes, introduces the next act in the drama.

2   **cum comite uno:** Why Sextus brings one, unnamed, companion becomes clear later.

2–8   **ubi ... vocem:** This complex sentence is a good example of Livy's ability to pack a great deal of information into few words, particularly through the use of participles. It is also a good example of his changing, as it were, his camera angles, from panorama to close-up, by altering sentence length, adding physical details, and moving from narrative to direct speech. We can break the sentence down as follows, with the subject, its modifiers, and the main clauses, at the far left-hand margin, and subordinated material indented:

ubi exceptus benigne ab ignaris consilii
   cum post cenam in hospitale cubiculum deductus esset,
amore ardens,
   postquam satis tuta circa sopitique omnes videbantur,
   stricto gladio
ad dormientem Lucretiam venit
   sinistraque manu mulieris pectore oppresso
"tace, Lucretia"
inquit;

> "Sex. Tarquinius sum;
> ferrum in manu est;
> moriere,
>   si emiseris vocem."

ubi: a connective relative introducing a new sentence: "And in this place (i.e., Collatia)."

exceptus benigne: repeats **excepti benigne** of the first visit (57.30) and thus reinforces the sense of consistently hospitable behavior in Collatinus's household.

2–3   **ab ignaris** = **ab eis qui ignari erant.**

3   **consilii:** objective gen. with **ignaris**.

4   **amore ardens:** A frequent metaphor in Latin love poetry, it continues the fire metaphor introduced earlier with the expression **certamine accenso** (57.17).

4–5   **satis tuta circa ... videbantur:** "the surroundings seemed sufficiently secure." The adjective **tuta** (neuter, plural) is a predicate adjective; **videbantur** needs a subject, which makes it necessary to take the adverb **circa** as almost substantive in nature.

6   **sinistraque manu:** The adjective **sinistra** seems to be excessive, because most would assume that this is Sextus's only free hand, since his right is holding his drawn sword; but the detail brings the action up close.

7–8   **"tace, Lucretia ... ferrum in manu est":** Note how the earlier subordinate clauses, ablative absolutes, and other participial phrases have all given way to short independent clauses and a brief conditional sentence.

7   **inquit:** always used parenthetically, following one or more words (A&G §599.c).

Sex. Tarquinius: No, **Sextus Tarquinius** did not abbreviate his name when he spoke it aloud, and neither should you.

8   **moriere, si emiseris vocem:** a future more vivid condition.

cum pavida ex somno mulier nullam opem, prope mortem
10   imminentem videret, tum Tarquinius fateri amorem, orare,
miscere precibus minas, versare in omnes partes muliebrem
animum. ubi obstinatam videbat et ne mortis quidem metu
inclinari, addit ad metum dedecus: cum mortua iugulatum
servum nudum positurum ait, ut in sordido adulterio necata
15   dicatur. quo terrore cum vicisset obstinatam pudicitiam velut
vi victrix libido, profectusque inde Tarquinius ferox
expugnato decore muliebri esset, Lucretia maesta tanto malo
nuntium Romam eundem ad patrem Ardeamque ad
virum mittit, ut cum singulis fidelibus amicis veniant; ita
20   facto maturatoque opus esse; rem atrocem incidisse.

9   **prope:** adverbial, with **imminentem**, "all but."

10   **tum:** simply "then."

10–11   **fateri ... orare, miscere ... versare:** historical infinitives, used for the imperfect in narrative (A&G §463). Note that, whereas Livy represented directly Sextus's *effective* speech (**tace ... vocem**, lines 7–8), he does not recreate for us Sextus's *ineffective* words.

11   **in omnes partes:** "in all directions."

11–12   **muliebrem animum:** What is the effect of the apparently unnecessary adjective **muliebrem**? We know Lucretia is a woman; do we need to be told that her **animus** is "that of a woman"? One thing the adjective does is identify insistently Tarquin's attempted persuasion as attempted sexual seduction. Moreover, because Romans considered women mentally weaker than men, drawing attention to Lucretia's mind as that of a woman makes her constancy all the more impressive.

13   **mortua:** abl. with **cum**, referring to Lucretia. The participle has a temporal force: "once she was dead."

13-14 **iugulatum servum nudum:** the intended purpose of the lone companion: the slave's dead and naked body will incriminate Lucretia in an act of adultery that is **sordidus** because it is beneath her status socially. Moreover, there will be no witness to contradict Sextus's lies.

14 **necata = necata esse. Lucretia** is the unexpressed subject of the clause.

15-17 **vicisset . . . pudicitiam . . . victrix libido . . . expugnato decore muliebri:** Military metaphors appear regularly in Latin authors' representations of erotic conquest; but in this particular context, with a real war going on at Ardea, they draw attention to the contrast between true martial achievement and this crime; they are also ironic, in that Sextus's act does have political results: It brings down the kingship.

19 **cum singulis fidelibus amicis:** Lucretia wants both reinforcements and discretion; Livy wants four men for narrative purposes: Brutus and Collatinus will be the first pair of consuls at Rome and Lucretius and Valerius their replacements in the first year of the Roman Republic.

20 **facto maturatoque opus esse:** ablatives with **opus est**, "there was need for action and speed" (A&G §497.a). Livy knew his Sallust well, and we can ask if he is thinking of the passage in the *Bellum Catilinae*, where Sallust says there was a debate as to whether military affairs were advanced more by physical force or mental excellence, **nam et prius quam incipias, consulto et, ubi consulueris, mature facto opus est** (1.13–14). If so, the INTERTEXTUAL ALLUSION helps show how Lucretia has already taken counsel with herself and has made her plans.

rem atrocem incidisse: The verb **incidisse** recalls the earlier expression **mentio incidit** (line 15), thus linking the idle talk to the terrible deed.

Lucretia's father and husband arrive, together with P. Valerius and L. Iunius Brutus. Lucretia denounces Sextus Tarquinius and says that her death will bear witness to her innocence. The men try to console her by pointing out that intention is what counts, and she did not intend to commit adultery. But Lucretia remains firm in her dual purpose: to fire up the men to punish Sextus and to herself provide an enduring example of chastity. Moreover, Lucretia's suicide alters the trajectory of the traditional story: She will not be a prize or a marker of political dominance (e.g., Helen; Briseis, the object of contention between Achilles and Agamemnon; Candaules's wife; even the Sabine women early in Livy's history). Lucretia's rape makes her into a symbol of the abused city; her death, which scholars have argued can be seen as a sacrifice, allows the city to be recreated anew in the form of the **res publica**, *which by definition cannot belong to one man.*

Sp. Lucretius cum P. Valerio Volesi filio, Collatinus cum L. Iunio Bruto venit, cum quo forte Romam rediens ab nuntio uxoris erat conventus. Lucretiam sedentem maestam in cubiculo inveniunt. adventu suorum lacrimae obortae,
25 quaerentique viro "satin salve?" "minime," inquit; "quid enim salvi est mulieri amissa pudicitia? vestigia viri alieni, Collatine, in lecto sunt tuo; ceterum corpus est tantum violatum, animus insons; mors testis erit.

21 **Sp. Lucretius:** Lucretia's father is **Spurius Lucretius**. The name **Spurius** means "son of an unknown father." His background, then, unlike that of the Tarquins, is obscure.

P. Valerio Volesi filio: Publius Valerius. This is Valerius's first appearance in the text, as well as the first reference to his father, Volesius. Valerius's participation in these events and his later consulship, both fictions, probably stem from the important role the Valerian clan (the *gens Valeria*) played in the early Republic. One of Livy's sources was an earlier Roman historian, Valerius Antias, who appears to have highlighted and enhanced his Valerian ancestors' achievements.

22   **L. Iunio Bruto:** Lucius Iunius Brutus. Another grandson of Tarquinius Priscus, and cousin of Sextus Tarquinius, Brutus has to this point avoided the danger of being perceived as a threat to the throne by acting as if he were **brutus**, that is, "devoid of intelligence." This pretense is also the explanation (AETIOLOGY) of the Roman cognomen **Brutus**. Two of Julius Caesar's assassins, Marcus Iunius Brutus and Decimus Iunius Brutus, proudly claimed descent from this ancestor who had expelled kings from early Rome.

24   **suorum:** the m. pl. as a noun: "one's relatives" or "kinsmen." While Lucretia is not the grammatical subject, she is the focus of attention in this sentence as well as the previous one.

obortae = obortae sunt.

25   **satin salve = satisne salve,** "is all well?"

25–26   **quid ... salvi est: Salvi** is partitive gen.: "what [of] safety is there?"

26   **amissa pudicitia:** a conditional use of the ablative absolute (A&G §420.4).

26–27   **vestigia viri alieni, Collatine, in lecto sunt tuo:** Lucretia's words are pointed and specific; the initial **vestigia** focuses the listeners'—and the readers'—minds on the physical traces of Sextus's recent crimes; the concrete nouns are **vestigia** and **lecto**; the opposition is between **alieni** and **tuo**, with the delay of the adjective **tuo** drawing attention to it.

27   **ceterum:** "however."

27–28   **corpus ... animus:** Lucretia draws the distinction between mind and body, which both she and the men will develop in the following sentences.

corpus est tantum violatum: Note the position of **tantum**, which gives Lucretia's statement the meaning "*only* my body has been violated."

sed date dexteras fidemque haud inpune adultero fore. Sex.
30 est Tarquinius, qui hostis pro hospite priore nocte vi armatus mihi sibique, si vos viri estis, pestiferum hinc abstulit gaudium." dant ordine omnes fidem; consolantur aegram animi avertendo noxam ab coacta in auctorem delicti: mentem peccare, non corpus, et unde consilium afuerit
35 culpam abesse. "vos," inquit, "videritis, quid illi debeatur: ego me etsi peccato absolvo, supplicio non libero; nec ulla deinde inpudica Lucretiae exemplo vivet." cultrum, quem sub veste abditum habebat, eum in corde defigit prolapsaque in volnus moribunda cecidit. conclamat vir paterque.

29 **date dexteras fidemque:** Lucretia turns from addressing her husband to a plural command—and to a ZEUGMA: the men are to give her their hands and their promise. Note also the ALLITERATION of *d* sounds.

haud inpune adultero fore: Haud inpune is LITOTES.

fore = futurum esse.

29-32 **Sex. est Tarquinius ... gaudium:** both highly emotional as Lucretia chokes out her words, and possibly archaic, in what has been called the *guttatim* ("drop-by-drop") style: **hostis pro hospite, priore nocte, vi armatus.**

30 **hostis pro hospite:** Note the PARANOMASIA, the use of words with similar sounds but very different meanings.

31 **mihi sibique:** datives with **pestiferum**. The protasis, **si vos viri estis**, outlines the condition under which **sibique** is valid.

32 **gaudium:** can refer to a physical or sensual delight as well as to the emotion of joy.

dant ... consolantur: The initial position of the verbs focuses attention on the men's ready response to Lucretia's request (**"date ..."**).

ordine: "one after another."

32-33 **aegram animi:** With adjectives, Latin uses an objective genitive (for an object of reference, A&G §349, sometimes called a genitive of specification). English would use a prepositional phrase, "sick in mind."

33 **avertendo:** a gerund with a direct object, **noxam**.

ab coacta: substantive: "from the victim."

delicti: objective genitive with **auctorem**.

35 **vos . . . videritis:** The **vos** is emphatic. **"It is for you to see to."** The jussive subjunctive rarely occurs in the perfect except in prohibitions; but the Ciceronian exception given by A&G §439 is a good parallel: **Epicurus hoc viderit**, "Let *Epicurus* look to this."

quid illi debeatur: This indirect question is the object of **videritis**.

36 **peccato . . . supplicio:** ablatives of separation with **absolvo** and **libero**. Lucretia continues to think along the lines of the mind/body division; she frees her mind from the **peccatum** but will exact the **supplicium** from her body.

37 **Lucretiae exemplo:** that is, no woman will commit adultery and, citing Lucretia as a precedent, claim to have been raped.

37-38 **cultrum . . . eum:** Although Lucretia is still the subject, the word order makes the knife the focus of attention.

quem sub veste abditum habebat: Lucretia can plot and plan just as well as Sextus.

38 **in corde defigit:** The precise physical detail recalls the equally precise detail of Sextus's initial attack (**sinistraque manu mulieris pectore oppresso**, line 6) and again brings the scene into sharp focus.

39 **moribunda:** "dying." Adjectives ending in –**bundus** –**a** –**um** are verbal and have an active force.

conclamat vir paterque: Note the return to the historical present as Lucretia's male relatives react together (see A&G §317.b for the singular verb with double subject). Their cry may reflect the Roman custom of calling out the name of the dead.

Brutus astounds the other men by boldly taking the initiative from Lucretia as he takes the knife from her body and by recasting the rape as a perversion of kingship and violation of Rome. Lucretia demanded that the men swear an oath of personal vengeance against Sextus; Brutus's oath includes the entire Tarquin family and involves changing Rome's political structure. At first the knife is the focus of attention as Lucretia's connections pledge their faith; then Lucretia's body, carried into the public sphere, becomes the new focus of attention as the revolutionary impulse expands outward.

[59] Brutus illis luctu occupatis cultrum ex volnere Lucretiae extractum manantem cruore prae se tenens, "per hunc," inquit, "castissimum ante regiam iniuriam sanguinem iuro, vosque, di, testes facio, me L. Tarquinium Superbum
5 cum scelerata coniuge et omni liberorum stirpe ferro, igni, quacumque denique vi possim, exsecuturum nec illos nec alium quemquam regnare Romae passurum." cultrum deinde Collatino tradit, inde Lucretio ac Valerio, stupentibus miraculo rei, unde novum in Bruti pectore ingenium. ut
10 praeceptum erat iurant; totique ab luctu versi in iram, Brutum iam inde ad expugnandum regnum vocantem sequuntur ducem.

1–2   **Brutus ... tenens:** a very extended noun modifier, another example of Livy's putting participles (**occupatis, extractum, manantem, tenens**) to hard use.

illis ... occupatis: ablative absolute, referring to Lucretius and Collatinus, and making their emotional reaction a contrasting backdrop for Brutus's decisive words and deeds.

cultrum ... extractum manantem: direct object of **tenens**.

ex volnere Lucretiae extractum manantem cruore: volnere = **vulnere**. Note the chiastic word order and the change in the tense and voice of the participles.

2   **hunc:** demonstrative adjective, modifying **castissimum ... sanguinem** (line 3).

3   **ante regiam iniuriam:** Brutus calls Sextus's crime a "royal" wrong, thus implicating the entire royal family.

4   **vosque, di, testes facio:** an APOSTROPHE to the gods.

4–7   **me ... exsecuturum [esse] nec ... passurum [esse]:** Indirect speech often omits the verb **esse** from the future active infinitive.

4–5   **L. Tarquinium Superbum cum scelerata coniuge et omni liberorum stirpe:** Brutus does not even name Sextus. The oath comprehends the entire nuclear royal family. In Livy Book 2 it expands so as to comprehend the entire Tarquin clan.

5–6   **ferro, igni, quacumque denique vi possim:** Again, note the comprehensive nature of the oath.

6   **denique:** "finally" or "in short."

7–8   **cultrum deinde ... inde:** Brutus gives the knife to Collatinus, then, presumably, takes it back and gives it to Lucretius and Valerius in turn.

8   **tradit:** Note that the main verbs in this passage (**iurant** [line 10], **sequuntur** [line 12], etc.) are in the historical present.

     stupentibus: The shock of Brutus's sudden transformation helps Lucretius and Valerius forget their grief.

9–14   **miraculo rei, unde novum ... ingenium [esset] ... miraculo ... rei novae:** Both instances of **rei** are objective genitive. Note the emphasis on newness and strangeness.

11   **Brutum ... vocantem:** a more compressed expression than a relative clause, such as **Brutum, qui ... vocabat**. Again, the Latin word order focuses attention on Brutus.

     iam inde: "from that point on."

     ad expugnandum regnum: gerundive with **ad** expressing purpose after **vocantem**.

12   **ducem:** a predicate accusative, "they follow, Brutus ..., as leader" (A&G §392 and §393).

elatum domo Lucretiae corpus in forum deferunt
concientque miraculo, ut fit, rei novae atque indignitate
homines. pro se quisque scelus regium ac vim queruntur.
movet cum patris maestitia, tum Brutus castigator
lacrimarum atque inertium querellarum auctorque quod
viros, quod Romanos deceret, arma capiendi adversus hostilia
ausos. ferocissimus quisque iuvenum cum armis voluntarius
adest; sequitur et cetera iuventus.

16 **movet:** The initial position of the word focuses attention on the impact of Brutus's speech.

cum ... tum ...: "both ... and even ..." (A&G §549.b).

17 **lacrimarum ... querellarum:** objective genitives after **castigator**.

17–18 **quod viros, quod Romanos deceret:** implied indirect statement after **auctor**. Note the ANAPHORA of **quod**.

18 **arma capiendi:** objective genitive after **auctor**.

adversus: prep. + acc. Here, with **ausos**.

19 **ausos:** The perfect participle of this semi-deponent verb takes a direct object (**hostilia**).

ferocissimus quisque iuvenum: "all the fiercest of the young men" (i.e., one after another in the order of their fierceness, A&G §313.b).

20 **sequitur et cetera iuventus:** The scene closes with an emphasis on the youth (collective) now mobilized and active.

The Tragedy of Lucretia by Sandro Botticelli (1445–1510) depicts Brutus standing over the body of Lucretia (center) surrounded by the *iuventus*. Botticelli, a native of Florence, Italy, incorporated a statue of the biblical David with the head of Goliath in the center background of the painting to symbolize revolt against tyranny. The painting is now housed in the Isabella Stewart Gardner Museum in Boston, Massachusetts. (Public Domain)

Events move from Collatia to Rome. At Collatia, Lucretia's body, carried into the forum, sparked the revolution; now, at Rome, in the Roman Forum, Brutus's words continue to fan the flames.

  inde patre praeside relicto Collatiae custodibusque datis,
ne quis eum motum regibus nuntiaret, ceteri armati duce
Bruto Romam profecti. ubi eo ventum est, quacumque
incedit armata multitudo pavorem ac tumultum facit; rursus
25 ubi anteire primores civitatis vident, quidquid sit haud temere
esse rentur. nec minorem motum animorum Romae tam
atrox res facit quam Collatiae fecerat. ergo ex omnibus
locis urbis in forum curritur. quo simul ventum est, praeco
ad tribunum celerum, in quo tum magistratu forte Brutus
30 erat, populum advocavit. ibi oratio habita nequaquam eius
pectoris ingeniique quod simulatum ad eam diem fuerat,
de vi ac libidine Sex. Tarquini, de stupro infando Lucretiae
et miserabili caede, de orbitate Tricipitini, cui morte filiae
causa mortis indignior ac miserabilior esset.

21   **inde:** indicates a new stage in the action.

  praeside: "as a garrison."

  Collatiae: locative (A&G §427.3).

22   **ne quis: quis = aliquis.** This negative purpose clause is introduced by **custodibusque datis**.

  motum: from **moveo**; a political movement.

  regibus: the Tarquins.

22–23   **duce Bruto:** abl. abs.

23   **profecti = profecti sunt.**

  ubi . . . ventum est: here and below (**quo simul ventum est**, line 28), impersonal. But it works to translate it personally, "when they arrived."

24–28 **incedit ... facit ... vident ... rentur ... facit ... curritur:** a series of historical presents.

24 **armata multitudo:** "the throng of men, armed as it was."

rursus: "on the other hand."

25 **primores civitatis:** Brutus and Collatinus are of the royal family.

quidquid sit: subjunctive because this is part of the viewers' thoughts.

25–26 **haud temere esse:** LITOTES.

26 **nec minorem motum ...:** The comparison is **nec minorem motum ... Romae ... quam Collatiae.**

28 **curritur:** impersonal, like so many verbs of motion and conflict in military or paramilitary contexts.

29 **ad tribunum celerum:** In early Rome, the **tribunus celerum** was the commander of cavalry organized by tribes (**celeres,** "the swift").

29–30 **in quo tum magistratu forte Brutus erat:** Giving Brutus a magistracy makes his actions legitimate and explains why he was given the opportunity to address the citizens in an assembly.

30–31 **eius pectoris ingeniique:** a genitive of quality (A&G §345.a).

32–33 **de vi ac libidine ... de stupro ... et ... caede, de orbitate:** Note the ANAPHORA, with the repetition of **de** taking the place of coordinating conjunctions. Brutus faces the challenge of rousing the people at Rome by relating events that took place at Collatia. Neither the perpetrators (Sextus, here in the subjective genitive) nor the victims of these crimes (Lucretia, Tricipitinus, here in the objective genitive) are present: Sextus is (presumably) back at Ardea; Lucretia died and was displayed to the people at Collatia; and her father is at Collatia keeping guard.

33 **Tricipitini:** Lucretius's cognomen, it commemorates a three-headed deity, presumably the focus of a family cult.

morte: ablative of comparison. The two items being compared are **causa mortis** (the subject of **esset**) and **morte filiae.**

34 **esset:** The subjunctive conveys this clause as part of Brutus's speech.

Brutus's speech moves from Sextus's crime against Lucretia and her father to the general wrongs done by the king against the Roman people. He reaches further into the past to remind his listeners of the murder of King Servius Tullius that brought the last Tarquin to the throne. The people order that Tarquinius Superbus and his immediate family go into exile.

35 addita superbia ipsius regis miseriaeque et labores plebis in fossas cloacasque exhauriendas demersae; Romanos homines, victores omnium circa populorum, opifices ac lapicidas pro bellatoribus factos. indigna Ser. Tulli regis memorata caedes et invecta corpori patris nefando vehiculo
40 filia, invocatique ultores parentum di. his atrocioribusque, credo, aliis, quae praesens rerum indignitas haudquaquam relatu scriptoribus facilia subicit, memoratis incensam multitudinem perpulit ut imperium regi abrogaret exsulesque esse iuberet L. Tarquinium cum coniuge
45 ac liberis.

35 **addita superbia: addita = addita est;** the verb goes on to acquire two new subjects: **miseriae,** "woes," and **labores.**

35-36 **in fossas cloacasque exhauriendas:** Brutus mentions the work on the sewer but not the more exalted work on the temple of Jupiter.

36 **demersae:** with **plebis**, both literal and metaphorical: "plunged down."

36-37 **Romanos homines:** Add **dixit**. This is indirect speech.

37-38 **opifices ac lapicidas:** not honorable labor, but the tasks of slaves; and, in contrast to **bellatores**, not at all heroic.

38 **factos = factos esse.**

indigna: The position of this adjective makes it the prominent idea (A&G §597).

Ser. Tulli: Servius was murdered in a conspiracy led by his son-in-law Tarquinius Superbus (father of Sextus) and daughter, Tullia, who compounded her crime by driving her carriage over his dead body.

39 **memorata = memorata est.**

39-40 **invecta ... filia:** a second subject for **memorata** [**est**]: "and that his daughter *rode* over his body." The participle contains the main idea (A&G §497). **Corpori** is dative with **invecta**.

nefando vehiculo: a transferred epithet; it was the deed that was unspeakable.

40 **invocati = invocati sunt.**

di: in apposition to **ultores parentum**. The delayed word order, HYPERBATON, places emphasis on the gods as literally the final avengers of the wronged.

40-42 **his atrocioribusque ... aliis ... memoratis:** Livy is fond of extended ablative absolutes that contain within themselves other clauses, as here, **quae ... subicit**.

41 **credo:** Livy inserts himself editorially here.

praesens rerum indignitas: "immediate outrage at events."

haudquaquam: adverb with **facilia**.

42 **relatu:** supine with **facilia**.

scriptoribus: Livy's point is that it is difficult to capture in writing the intense emotions of the moment.

perpulit: Brutus is the subject of the verb.

43-44 **ut ... abrogaret ... iuberet:** result clauses after **perpulit**.

43 **regi:** dative of separation with **abrogaret** (A&G §381).

44 **L. Tarquinium cum coniuge ac liberis:** The expression echoes Brutus's own oath (line 5).

ipse iunioribus, qui ultro nomina dabant, lectis armatisque
ad concitandum inde adversus regem exercitum Ardeam in
castra est profectus: imperium in urbe Lucretio, praefecto urbis
iam ante ab rege instituto, relinquit. inter hunc tumultum
50 Tullia domo profugit exsecrantibus quacumque incedebat,
invocantibusque parentum furias viris mulieribusque.

46 **ipse . . .:** Now that Brutus has finished speaking, the narrative shifts to the actions inspired by the speech.

iunioribus . . . lectis armatisque: another ablative absolute with an embedded relative clause.

47 **ad concitandum . . . exercitum:** a gerundive expressing purpose with **est profectus**.

47-48 **Ardeam in castra:** the spatial goals of **est profectus**.

48-49 **Lucretio, praefecto urbis iam ante ab rege instituto:** Lucretia's father provides important institutional continuity between the regal period and the revolution and, in Book 2, between the revolution and the Republic.

49 **inter:** "amid."

50-51 **exsecrantibus . . . invocantibus . . . viris mulieribusque:** another complex ablative absolute.

51 **parentum furias:** These are the Furies who avenge the murder of parents, the same Furies, or class of Furies, that in Greek mythology hounded Orestes after he killed his mother, Clytemnestra.

The Furies, often depicted with snakes for hair, torment Orestes. Hippolyte Berteax (1843–1926), a French painter of portraits and murals, chose this scene to symbolize tragedy. This painting adorns the ceiling of the Théâtre Graslin in Nantes, France. The story of Orestes is most famously told in Aeschylus's trilogy the *Oresteia*. (© Creative Commons 3.0/Selbymay)

The news of revolution brings Tarquinius Superbus to Rome; but the Romans refuse him entrance. He and two of his sons go into exile together, among the Etruscans. They return in Book 2 to try to retake Rome. Sextus goes to Gabii, where the people hold a grudge against him, and he is killed there.

[60] harum rerum nuntiis in castra perlatis cum re nova trepidus rex pergeret Romam ad comprimendos motus, flexit viam Brutus—senserat enim adventum—ne obvius fieret; eodemque fere tempore diversis itineribus Brutus
5 Ardeam, Tarquinius Romam venerunt. Tarquinio clausae portae exsiliumque indictum: liberatorem urbis laeta castra accepere, exactique inde liberi regis. duo patrem secuti sunt, qui exsulatum Caere in Etruscos ierunt. Sex. Tarquinius Gabios tamquam in suum regnum profectus ab ultoribus
10 veterum simultatium, quas sibi ipse caedibus rapinisque concierat, est interfectus.

1   **harum rerum:** objective genitive with **nuntiis**, and thus part of the ablative absolute. Its position at the beginning of the sentence serves as a link between episodes.

1-2   **cum . . . pergeret:** a temporal **cum**-clause describing the circumstances that accompanied or preceded the main verb, **flexit** (A&G §564).

    re nova: "unforeseen event." The ablative is causal (A&G §404) and explains **trepidus**.

2   **ad comprimendos motus:** the accusative of the gerundive with **ad**, expressing purpose (A&G §506).

3   **senserat enim adventum:** Livy is fond of parentheses. They are a feature of his style. **Brutus** is the subject of the verb.

3-4   **ne obvius fieret:** This avoidance explains why there is not yet a violent clash between the two leaders. Brutus again anticipates his opponent's moves and outwits him.

4   **diversis itineribus:** ablative of manner (A&G §412).

4–5 **Brutus Ardeam, Tarquinius Romam:** The parallel construction reinforces the impression of their simultaneous arrival. **Ardeam** and **Romam**, as well as **Caere** (line 8) and **Gabios** (line 9), are accusatives of place to which (A&G §427).

5 **Tarquinio:** dative with **clausae** and **indictum**. Note the chiastic arrangement of nouns and participles: **clausae portae exsiliumque indictum**.

6 **liberatorem urbis:** Together with the name Brutus, this expression brings to mind the assassins of Julius Caesar, termed **liberatores** by Cicero. Again, note the CHIASTIC construction, which produces a sense of ANTITHESIS, as well as the impression that Brutus entered the camp from one gate and Tarquinius Superbus's children were driven out by the other:

```
         A                            B        B              A
liberatorem urbis laeta castra accepere exactique inde liberi
    regis
```

7 **accepere = acceperunt.**

exactique = exactique sunt.

8 **exsulatum:** supine after a verb of motion (**ierunt**).

Caere: accusative of **Caere, Caeritis**, *n*. Caere was in southern Etruria, about thirty miles northwest of Rome.

9 **Gabios:** a city of Latium, about eleven miles east of Rome.

tamquam in suum regnum profectus: The worst of the Tarquins, Sextus feels no shame, no remorse, and his outward behavior does not even show acknowledgment that he is going into exile.

10 **veterum simultatium:** objective genitive. Sextus had helped his father capture the town of Gabii by treachery and violence. The quarrels are "old" only relative to the recent events.

L. Tarquinius Superbus regnavit annos quinque et viginti. regnatum Romae ab condita urbe ad liberatam annos ducentos quadraginta quattuor. Duo consules inde comitiis
15 centuriatis a praefecto urbis ex commentariis Ser. Tulli creati sunt, L. Iunius Brutus et L. Tarquinius Collatinus.

12-14 **annos quinque et viginti . . . annos ducentos quadraginta quattuor:** accusatives expressing extent of time (A&G §423).

13 **regnatum:** an impersonal use of the passive, "there was kingship" (A&G §207).

ab condita urbe ad liberatam [urbem]: The participle, not the noun, contains the idea: "from the founding to the freeing of the city" (A&G §497).

14-15 **comitiis centuriatis:** an expression of time when, although the main idea in English is that of place: "at the centuriate assembly." The centuriate assembly was the voting assembly of Roman male citizens arranged in military units according to property qualifications. Tradition (including Livy earlier in Book 1) attributed its institution to Servius Tullius.

15 **a praefecto urbis:** Livy draws attention to Lucretius's official role in order to show that the transition from monarchy to republic involved already sanctioned authority.

ex commentariis Ser. Tulli: Even creating a new political system involves consulting the past, selectively, because Servius Tullius was, according to Livy, the last truly good king.

15-16 **creati sunt:** with a predicate nominative (here **consules**) "were elected."

16 **L. Iunius Brutus et L. Tarquinius Collatinus:** The names of the first two consuls conclude the account of the monarchy—and Book 1—an expression that is characteristic of Livy's account of the republic: an annual notice of the officials elected. The sentence thus brings closure to Book 1 as it sets in place the structure that will govern Book 2 and those that follow.

Sallust

Bellum Catilinae 1–9
Standard Level and Higher Level

— Introduction to Sallust —

Gaius Sallustius Crispus (ca. 86–35 BCE) came probably from the local aristocracy of the Sabine town Amiternum, about 85 miles northeast of Rome. Sallust entered politics as a troublemaking plebeian tribune in 52 BCE. He was expelled from the Senate in 50, allegedly for moral turpitude, but more likely because of enmity created in 52 (he had acted against Cicero, among others). Having joined Caesar's side in the civil war against Pompey, Sallust took part in the first African campaign of 46 and was then appointed governor of Africa Nova (formerly the kingdom of Numidia). On his return to Rome, he faced charges of extortion but escaped trial. Sometime shortly afterward, however, recognizing that his public life was over, Sallust took to writing history.

The *Bellum Catilinae* (*BC*), written sometime in the 40s, most likely after Caesar's assassination, is, as far as we know, the earliest (and shortest) of Sallust's works. The *BC* tells the story of a conspiracy that took place in 63 BCE, in which a group of disaffected and indebted nobles, with L. Sergius Catilina at their head, tried to bring down the government by killing the current consuls. One of those consuls was Cicero. Cicero caught wind of the plot and attacked Catiline in the Senate. Catiline left Rome for Etruria and the army he had raised there. Useful evidence, in the form of letters to Catiline from the conspirators, was given up by some Allobrogian Gauls, whom the members of the conspiracy had tried to win over as allies. Cicero had Catiline's co-conspirators arrested and, after a debate in the Senate, executed. Catiline himself died fighting. Cicero's four famous speeches against Catiline are alluded to indirectly and are mentioned directly only in passing. (Aside from personal animosity, Sallust may have wanted to avoid overlap with Cicero's speeches, which were—and still are—in circulation.)

Sallust was a younger contemporary of the major figures in this history: Catiline (108–62 BCE); Caesar (100–44 BCE); Cato (95–46 BCE); and Cicero (106–43 BCE), who played an important role in these events although he does not figure largely in Sallust's account of them.

The International Baccalaureate prescribes *BC* 1–2 and 5–9 for the Villains option. This reader also provides *BC* 3–4 for additional context.

— Introduction to *Bellum Catilinae* —

The writing of history at Rome began in the third century BCE, with a work in Greek by a senator named Fabius Pictor; in the second century, the poet Ennius wrote a Latin hexameter poem called the *Annales*, which gave an account of Rome's history from the city's foundation to his own time; during the same period, the elder Cato wrote the *Origines*—histories of Italian towns, including Rome—also in Latin. The late second and early-mid first century produced a number of writers who chronicled the events of Roman history consular year by consular year, in a method that came to be called the annalistic style. Yet, aside from Caesar's *Commentarii*, Sallust's first two works, the *Bellum Catilinae* and the *Bellum Iugurthinum*, are the earliest historiographical works in Latin that have survived complete. They stand out from their surroundings because they are not annalistic chronicles, but monographs, each dealing with a particular conflict, that of Rome with Catiline, or that of Rome with Jugurtha.

Sallust (like Livy) viewed history as dependent on the actions of individuals, who act according to character. He thus explains historical change as a function of changes in personal and national character rather than shifts in economics, social structure, or politics. Accordingly, the *BC* includes character sketches, both for individuals and for entire peoples; it also includes short, fiery speeches from the mouth of Catiline and two longer, paired, speeches by Cato and Caesar debating what to do with the captured conspirators.

This passage contains the first half of Sallust's preface, which occupies over a sixth of the *BC*. Its main arguments are that one should not pass one's life in **silentium** (*both* not speaking out *and* not being spoken of); the mind is superior to the body in both peace and war; likewise, one can become distinguished both by acting well on behalf of the state and by speaking well, although it is more difficult to win *gloria* by the latter.

Sallust felt that the historian's language needed not simply to record events but also to convey in its style the nature of the political situation. If the political situation was unbalanced and hard to grasp, its written representation should present the same challenges for both writer and readers. Sallust took as stylistic models the abrupt and unbalanced language of the Greek historian Thucydides as well as the old-fashioned and terse Latin of the elder Cato. Sallust's style is marked by Thucydidean abruptness, Catonian brevity, and a paradoxical combination of archaism and novelty.

— *Bellum Catilinae* 1–9 —

Sallust begins by drawing a set of contrasts, first between human beings and other living creatures, then between the mind, **animus,** *and the body,* **corpus.** *The mind rules, the body obeys; humans share the possession of mind with the gods, of body with beasts. The idea was a commonplace (*TOPOS*). Plato says much the same thing at greater length in Republic 586a, where he refers to those who, knowing neither wisdom nor virtue, occupy themselves with gluttony and sensuality and move at random throughout life like sheep or cattle.*

[1] omnis homines, qui sese student praestare ceteris animalibus, summa ope niti decet, ne vitam silentio transeant veluti pecora, quae natura prona atque ventri oboedientia finxit. sed nostra omnis vis in animo et corpore sita est: animi
5   imperio, corporis servitio magis utimur; alterum nobis cum dis, alterum cum beluis commune est.

1   **omnīs homines:** This accusative comes first because it is the topic of the sentence (A&G §597).

   Omnis is first for emphasis: *"every* man." The **-īs** spelling is regular for the accusative plural of two-termination adjectives and for some nouns of the third declension (A&G §73, §74, and §114.a).

   sese = **se**; the reduplication may have been originally emphatic.

   praestare: + dative, literally, "to stand before," metaphorically, "to surpass."

   summa ope: instead of **summo opere.** Another ARCHAISM.

2   **decet:** the main verb of the sentence; **decet** takes an impersonal construction with subject infinitive **niti** and accusative object (**omnis homines**).

   ne ... transeant: a purpose clause; **vitam transire** suggests passivity as opposed to the more vigorous activity conveyed by the usual expressions for living, **vitam/aetatem agere.** The expression fittingly introduces the imagery of pasturing animals that follows: One can move through life as grazing animals move through the landscape.

silentio: ablative of manner, with **silentium** meaning not the active "keeping silent," but the passive, "the state of not being talked about," or "obscurity."

3   **pecora:** farm animals, especially sheep and cattle.

natura: This is Nature as a power determining the physical properties of plants and animals.

prona atque ventri oboedientia: predicate accusatives with **quae ... finxit** (A&G §393). The verb **oboedire** takes the dative. Animals, especially grazing animals, look downward, focusing their attention on their food, so that their physical habits reinforce the METAPHOR of obedience to the belly.

4   **sed:** here introducing a new topic.

nostra: The contrast is with animals.

5   **utimur:** + ablative.

5-6   **alterum ... alterum:** the quality of having an **animus** and the quality of having a **corpus**.

6   **beluis: Beluis** offers a sharper contrast with **dis** than **animalibus**, because the first sentence makes clear that humans are **animalia** too; it is the **cetera animalia** that pass their lives in obscurity.

quo mihi rectius videtur ingeni quam virium opibus gloriam quaerere et, quoniam vita ipsa, qua fruimur, brevis est, memoriam nostri quam maxume longam efficere. nam
10 divitiarum et formae gloria fluxa atque fragilis est, virtus clara aeternaque habetur.

7 **quo:** "for this reason." A relative at the beginning of an independent sentence or clause often connects it to the previous sentence or clause. Translate it with an English demonstrative with or without "and" (A&G §308.f).

rectius: predicate adjective describing **quaerere** and **efficere**; comparative, because it introduces the comparative construction with **quam**. The full construction would be **quo mihi rectius videtur ingeni opibus gloriam quaerere quam virium opibus gloriam quaerere**... The omission of words (ELLIPSIS) keeps the focus on the contrast of mind and body, now rephrased as that of **ingenium** (here "intellect") and **vires** (here "strength or vigor of body").

8–9 **vita... brevis, memoriam... longam:** Note the contrast between the physical (and transient) and the abstract (and more permanent). Note also that Sallust has switched the order in which he presents things having to do with the body and things having to do with the mind.

8 **qua:** abl. with **fruimur**.

9 **nostri:** objective genitive.

quam maxume longam: maxume = archaic spelling for **maxime**; **quam** + superl.: "as ___ as possible"; **longam** is a predicate accusative.

10 **gloria... virtus:** a new opposition; but **gloria** itself is not in opposition to **virtus**; what defines the **gloria** also matters, that is, **divitiae et forma**.

fluxa atque fragilis: Note the ALLITERATION of the paired words as well as the ANTITHESIS that connects the two clauses by the contrast between **gloria** and **virtus** instead of a conjunction. Note also Sallust's tendency to use pairs of nouns and adjectives: **divitiarum et formae; fluxa atque fragilis; clara aeternaque.** Yet to avoid the monotony of parallel construction, he links the members of each pair differently, with **et, atque,** and **-que**.

The goddess Virtus personifies valor and military strength. She is dressed as an Amazon, wearing boots and a helmet, and holding a lance in her right hand. The inscription dedicates the work to Virtus: *Deae Virtuti fatalis neg(otiator) A(uli?) Laeti Grati lib(ertus) v(otum) s(olvit) l(ibens) m(erito)*. This third-century CE limestone relief, found in western Germany, is in the collection of the Römisch-Germanisches Museum in Köln, Germany. (© Creative Commons 3.0/Hannibal21)

Sallust continues to discuss the function and utility of mind and body as he introduces a new topic: the source of military success. For the sake of VARIATIO, *and perhaps also to emphasize how the functions of mind and body are intertwined, he continues to change the order in which they or their uses appear: body vs. mind, then mind vs. body.*

> sed diu magnum inter mortalis certamen fuit, vine corporis an virtute animi res militaris magis procederet. nam et, prius quam incipias, consulto et, ubi consulueris, mature facto opus
> 15   est. ita utrumque per se indigens alterum alterius auxilio eget.

12   **sed:** again introducing a new topic.

   mortalis: The ending **–is** is accusative. Sallust uses **mortales** frequently as an alternative to **homines**.

   certamen: here, "dispute."

12–13   **vine corporis an virtute animi:** The addition of **vis** and **virtus** provides another way of varying the contrast between **corpus** and **animus**. The particles **-ne . . . an** offer a choice of two possible answers: "whether A . . . or B."

13   **res militaris:** military affairs or practices, the new topic, hinted at, perhaps, with the repeated uses of **virtus** ("manliness," "courage") in the previous sentences.

   procederet: subjunctive in indirect question in secondary sequence after **certamen fuit**.

13–14   **et . . . et:** "it is both the case that . . . and that . . ."

   prius quam incipias . . . ubi consulueris: present subjunctive and perfect subjunctive, used in the second person generalizing "you."

14   **consulto . . . facto:** ablatives with **opus est**, "there is need of." The perfect passive participle is here used as a verbal noun (A&G §497.a). Compare Lucretia's message to her husband and father in the selection from Livy Book 1 (58.20) in this volume.

   mature: here, "quickly."

15   **utrumque:** "each [thing] of the two."

per se: "in and of itself."

indigens . . . eget: Sallust continues to balance the claims of mind and body by using related words (**indigeo** < *indu* [an archaic form of *in*] + *egeo*).

alterum alterius: alter . . . alter = "the one . . . the other." Note here the gender of both and the case of **alterius** (dependent on **auxilio**); it is often not necessary to include "the one" in translating. "Each . . . the other."

eget: + ablative **auxilio**, although the verb often takes the genitive.

*Sallust sees two stages in the development of rule (**imperium**): first an uncorrupted age, then one in which the desire for rule led to wars of expansion. Here too intellect predominated. Maintaining supremacy, however, demands constant effort; otherwise vices creep in, and someone better takes over.*

[2] igitur initio reges—nam in terris nomen imperi id primum fuit—divorsi pars ingenium, alii corpus exercebant: etiam tum vita hominum sine cupiditate agitabatur; sua cuique satis placebant.

1   **igitur:** resumes the argument.

        initio: adverbial: "in the beginning."

        in terris: "in the world."

        imperi: The real topic, **imperium**, "empire," is added as an aside.

        id: that is, **reges**, here standing in for the abstract "monarchy."

2   **divorsi:** archaic spelling for **diversi**.

        pars . . . alii: note the INCONCINNITAS, instead of a parallel construction, such as **pars . . . pars** or **alii . . . alii**. In describing this first phase of kingship, Sallust could well have in mind Odysseus, who used his intellect, **ingenium**, and Achilles, who used his physical ability, **corpus**. Both kings were made famous by the Homeric epics about the Trojan War, which according to post-Homeric tradition was the first great conflict between **Graecia** and **Asia**. Although both heroes pillaged and plundered, neither was greedy for expanded rule.

3   **vita . . . agitabatur: vitam agitare = vitam agere**. The frequentative **agitabatur** in place of **agebatur** is an ARCHAISM.

Achilles, whose mother disguised him as a woman and brought him to the household of King Lycomedes to prevent him from dying in the Trojan War, reveals his identity by selecting a weapon from gifts that Odysseus brought. A prophecy stated that the Greeks could not win the war without Achilles, so Odysseus was sent to bring him to Troy. Odysseus's ruse recalls his **ingenium**, while the dagger reflects Achilles's heroism in battle. *Achilles Discovered among the Daughters of Lycomedes*, by Jean Lemaire (1598–1659), is housed in the Los Angeles County Museum of Art. (Courtesy of www.lacma.org) (Public Domain)

5   postea vero quam in Asia Cyrus, in Graecia Lacedaemonii
    et Athenienses coepere urbis atque nationes subigere,
    lubidinem dominandi causam belli habere, maxumam
    gloriam in maxumo imperio putare, tum demum periculo
    atque negotiis compertum est in bello plurumum ingenium
10 posse. quod si regum atque imperatorum animi virtus in
    pace ita ut in bello valeret, aequabilius atque constantius
    sese res humanae haberent neque aliud alio ferri neque
    mutari ac misceri omnia cerneres. nam imperium facile
    iis artibus retinetur, quibus initio partum est. verum ubi pro
15 labore desidia, pro continentia et aequitate lubido atque
    superbia invasere, fortuna simul cum moribus inmutatur.
    ita imperium semper ad optumum quemque a minus bono
    transfertur.

5   **postea vero:** Sallust introduces the next phase.

    Asia: here, Asia Minor, or the Near East.

    Cyrus: the Great King of Persia, conqueror in the mid-sixth century BCE of the peoples of the Near East and Asia, thus ruler of the Persian Empire.

5-6 **Lacedaemonii et Athenienses:** The discussion moves from Cyrus and his empire to the Spartans (**Lacedaemonii**) and Athenians, who defeated the Persian Empire in the fifth century BCE, then turned against one another in the Peloponnesian Wars.

6   **coepere = coeperunt.** Sallust regularly contracts the third person plural perfect active indicative ending –**erunt** into –**ere**. This can generally be distinguished from a present active infinitive because it is built on a perfect stem (e.g., **fuere, habuere,** and **cepere** instead of **esse, habere,** and **capere**).

6-7 **subigere, habere, putare:** complementary infinitives with **coepere**.

7   **dominandi:** objective genitive with **causam**.

    habere: "to consider."

8	**tum demum:** emphatic, "not until then," "only then."
8–9	**periculo atque negotiis:** abstractions for physical fighting and for mental fighting by means of strategy, tactics, and diplomacy.
9	**plurumum:** archaic spelling for **plurimum**; adverbial, with **posse**, "to be the most powerful."
10	**quod si:** "but if."
	regum atque imperatorum: kings and everyone else who has **imperium**.
11–13	**valeret... haberent... cerneres:** present contrary to fact condition with a double apodosis. Note the shift in subject to the general "you" in the second apodosis.
12	**sese... haberent:** used reflexively with an adverb of manner (here **aequabilius atque constantius**), **habere** means "to be (so situated)."
	alio: adv. with **aliud**, "one in one direction, one in another."
13	**mutari ac misceri:** Note the ALLITERATION of the two passive infinitives.
13–17	**nam imperium... ita imperium:** Ancient political theory held that the three forms of state were unstable and liable to degenerate over time into their unworthy opposites: monarchy to tyranny; aristocracy to oligarchy; democracy to ochlocracy (mob rule).
14–16	**pro labore desidia, pro continentia et aequitate lubido atque superbia:** Note how the abstractions multiply.
15	**lubido:** archaic spelling for **libido**.
16	**invasere = invaserunt**. The METAPHOR personifies the subjects **desidia**, **lubido**, and **superbia** as invading enemies. See note on line 6.
	fortuna simul cum moribus: The connection between a change in morals and a change in fortune is not just temporal; it is also causal, as the next sentence makes clear.
17	**ad optumum quemque:** "to each man, according as he is the best."

*Excellence (**virtus**) lies at the heart of all human endeavors. Sallust has no time for those who, slaves to their appetites, achieve nothing and pass through life as strangers to it. The person who strives after the glory won by achievement can be said truly to live.*

quae homines arant, navigant, aedificant, virtuti omnia
20 parent. sed multi mortales, dediti ventri atque somno, indocti incultique vitam sicuti peregrinantes transiere; quibus profecto contra naturam corpus voluptati, anima oneri fuit. eorum ego vitam mortemque iuxta aestumo, quoniam de utraque siletur. verum enim vero is demum mihi vivere atque
25 frui anima videtur, qui aliquo negotio intentus praeclari facinoris aut artis bonae famam quaerit.

19   **quae:** an internal accusative of **arant, navigant,** and **aedificant,** "what men achieve by plowing, sailing, etc." These occupations embrace land and sea. Note the ASYNDETON, which helps Sallust achieve BREVITAS.

omnia: generalizes and sums up **quae homines arant, navigant, aedificant.**

20   **parent:** + dat., "are subject to."

multi mortales: Note the ALLITERATION brought about by Sallust's using **mortales** instead of **homines.**

ventri: recalls the **pecora** who are **ventri oboedientia** (1.3).

somno: a wider meaning than simply sleep, more like lethargy or sloth.

20–21   **indocti incultique:** near synonyms, "untaught and unpolished." PLEONASM for the sake of the alliteration of **in-**.

21   **sicuti peregrinantes:** Animals pass through life in silence; these humans are like foreigners or aliens.

transiere = transierunt.

quibus: a connecting relative; dative with **voluptati** and **oneri** (line 22) in a double dative construction.

23 **iuxta:** adv., "alike."

aestumo: "I value."

24 **siletur:** impersonal, "there is silence," or "no one speaks."

verum enim vero: emphatic.

demum: gives emphasis to **is**.

24-25 **vivere atque frui anima:** PLEONASM.

25 **aliquo negotio:** dat. with **intentus**.

negotio: literally the *absence* of **otium**.

25-26 **praeclari facinoris aut artis bonae:** compare the genitive above: **divitiarum et formae** (page 190, line 10).

Sallust points out that there is more than one way of winning glory. He zeroes in on one field of achievement in particular, that is, service to the **res publica**. *One can serve the republic with words as well as deeds, although writing down the deeds of others is both difficult and wins less glory. It is hard because writing well is hard; but also because readers impute evil motives to authors. In a sentence that recalls Pericles's Funeral Oration in Thucydides, Book 2, Sallust points out that if you criticize bad behavior, readers think you are jealous; if you write about great acts of courage, people are willing to believe you only insofar as they think they are capable of the same feats.*

sed in magna copia rerum aliud alii natura iter ostendit. [3] pulchrum est bene facere rei publicae, etiam bene dicere haud absurdum est; vel pace vel bello clarum fieri licet; et qui fecere et qui facta aliorum scripsere, multi laudantur. ac mihi quidem, tametsi haudquaquam par gloria sequitur
5 scriptorem et actorem rerum, tamen in primis arduum videtur res gestas scribere: primum, quod facta dictis exaequanda sunt; dehinc, quia plerique, quae delicta reprehenderis, malevolentia et invidia dicta putant, ubi de magna virtute atque gloria bonorum memores, quae sibi
10 quisque facilia factu putat, aequo animo accipit, supra ea veluti ficta pro falsis ducit.

27 **in magna copia rerum:** Sallust begins with the wealth of opportunities for winning fame. **Res** here means "affairs" or "activities."

aliud alii: "a different one (**iter**) to each."

natura: personified here.

1 **pulchrum:** predicate adjective modifying **bene facere**. Here it means "noble" or "honorable."

1–2 **pulchrum est bene facere … bene dicere haud absurdum est:** The figure of CHIASMUS joins the two ideas to create a sense of ANTITHESIS. Note the parallel constructions in the rest of the sentence: **vel pace vel bello … et qui fecere et qui facta aliorum scripsere.**

	rei publicae: dative with **bene facere,** "to do a service (to)."
2	**haud absurdum est:** LITOTES.
	fieri: "to become."
2–3	**et qui … et qui:** The relative clauses been placed before the antecedent clause.
	et … et …: "both … and."
3	**fecere … scripsere = fecerunt … scripserunt.** See note on page 196, line 6.
4	**mihi:** dative of the person who "sees" or "thinks" is regular with **videor.**
	haudquaquam: LITOTES: "in no way."
	gloria sequitur: Like **natura,** above (2.27), **gloria** is mildly personified.
5	**rerum:** objective genitive.
	in primis: "chiefly."
6	**res gestas:** "achievements," the usual expression.
6–7	**facta dictis exaequanda sunt: Dictis** is abl. of means; **ex-** has the sense of "throughout."
7	**plerique:** as a noun, "most people."
	quae = [illa] quae.
7–8	**delicta reprehenderis:** perfect subjunctive with the generalizing "you."
8	**malevolentia et invidia:** "ill will and spite." Note the PLEONASM.
	dicta = dicta esse.
10	**supra ea = quae supra ea sunt,** with **ea** referring back to **quae … putant.**
11	**pro falsis:** "as unreal."
	ducit: metaphorical, "considers," "thinks."

Having sketched the history of empires, Sallust now gives a brief autobiography, starting with his early enthusiasm for politics, then telling of his disillusionment and withdrawal.

      sed ego adulescentulus initio, sicuti plerique, studio ad rem publicam latus sum ibique mihi multa advorsa fuere. nam pro pudore, pro abstinentia, pro virtute audacia, largitio,
15 avaritia vigebant. quae tametsi animus aspernabatur insolens malarum artium, tamen inter tanta vitia imbecilla aetas ambitione corrupta tenebatur; ac me, cum ab reliquorum malis moribus dissentirem, nihilo minus honoris cupido eadem, qua ceteros, fama atque invidia vexabat.

12   **sed:** once again, a new topic.

      adulescentulus: temporal use, "as mere youth . . ." Note also the diminutive **adulescentulus** instead of **adulescens**.

12–13 **rem publicam:** here "political life."

13   **ibique** = **et in ea (re publica)**; an illustration of Sallust's fondness for PARATAXIS.

      mihi: dat. with **advorsa**.

      advorsa = **adversa**; archaic spelling.

14   **pro . . . pro . . . pro:** Note the ANAPHORA. One of the features of Latin prose is a fondness for a series of three.

14–15 **audacia, largitio, avaritia:** As in the earlier description of **imperium** (2.1–18), here too a series of abstractions controls the environment. Such a series of nouns without connectives is called a CONGERIES or "heap." Note too that "recklessness," "extravagance," and "greed" do not exactly match **pudor, abstinentia,** and **virtus** point for point. This is another way in which VARIATIO produces a sense of surprise.

15   **quae:** direct object of **aspernabatur**.

15–17	**animus … insolens … imbecilla aetas:** A pair of negatives (**in-**, **im-**) emphasizes Sallust's youthful naiveté and passivity: His was not active evildoing. Note the CHIASTIC word order of nouns and adjectives.
16	**malarum artium:** objective genitive with **insolens**.
17	**corrupta:** predicate nominative with **tenebatur**; agrees with **aetas**.
17–19	**me … cupido … vexabat:** Note that again the abstraction **cupido** is personified.
18	**honoris:** objective genitive with **cupido eadem** (line 19).
19	**qua ceteros = qua ceteros vexabat.**
	fama atque invidia: abl. of means.

Having withdrawn from political life, Sallust turned to writing history. He considered his withdrawal an advantage: Because he was no longer involved in politics, he could present a nonpartisan account of events. The historian finally identifies his topic and explains why he chose it.

[4] igitur ubi animus ex multis miseriis atque periculis requievit et mihi reliquam aetatem a re publica procul habendam decrevi, non fuit consilium socordia atque desidia bonum otium conterere neque vero agrum colundo
5   aut venando servilibus officiis, intentum aetatem agere; sed, a quo incepto studioque me ambitio mala detinuerat, eodem regressus statui res gestas populi Romani carptim, ut quaeque memoria digna videbantur, perscribere, eo magis, quod mihi a spe, metu, partibus rei publicae animus liber
10 erat. igitur de Catilinae coniuratione, quam verissume potero, paucis absolvam; nam id facinus in primis ego memorabile existumo sceleris atque periculi novitate. de cuius hominis moribus pauca prius explananda sunt, quam initium narrandi faciam.

1–3   **ubi ... requievit ... decrevi:** Sallust conflates mind and person. His **animus** had a rest; *he* decided.

1   **multis miseriis atque periculis:** Note the ALLITERATION and PLEONASM.

2   **a re publica procul:** "far from politics."

3–4   **socordia atque desidia:** more PLEONASM of near synonyms.

4   **bonum otium conterere:** precisely what the regal youths were doing in the Livy passage in this volume (1.57.12–13).

4–5   **neque vero agrum colundo aut venando:** gerunds in the dative with **intentum**.

5   **servilibus officiis:** Farming had been an aristocratic occupation. The elder Cato's treatise pointed out that "our ancestors, when they praised a good man, called him a good farmer and a good husbandman" (**bonum agricolam bonumque colonum**). Hunting, also once an aristocratic and heroic, indeed even royal occupation, had become disreputable as well.

intentum aetatem agere: resumes the idea of being **aliquo negotio intentus** in 2.9.

6   **ambitio mala:** Sallust makes the abstraction **ambitio** the agent. He is the object of its action.

7   **res gestas populi Romani:** "the achievements of the Roman people." The Roman historians' way of referring to their material. Compare Livy's use of a similar expression in the opening of his history (Pref. 1: **facturusne operae pretium sim si a primordio urbis res populi Romani perscripserim...**).

carptim: "selectively."

8–9 **eo magis, quod...:** "all the more, because..."

9   **mihi:** dative of possession with **animus liber erat**.

a spe, metu, partibus rei publicae: the prepositional phrase follows **liber**.

10 **de Catilinae coniuratio:** This phrase, which appears again at 23.4.3, gave the work its title.

verissume = verissime.

11 **paucis = paucis verbis.**

11–12 **id facinus ... ego memorabile existumo:** The expression looks back to **ut quaeque memoria digna videbantur** (lines 7–8).

in primis: "especially."

12 **novitate:** "the unusual nature," or "novelty."

12–13 **de cuius hominis moribus:** a connecting relative, with the effect of **sed de eius hominis moribus**.

14 **narrandi:** an objective genitive of the gerund.

*Sallust organizes his famous character sketch of Catiline around the contrast between mind and body that he introduced in the first sentences of the BC. Several of the abstract concepts that shape historical developments and personal character (**vis, ingenium, virtus, audacia, largitio, avaritia**, etc.) reappear, some in altered forms.*

[5] L. Catilina, nobili genere natus, fuit magna vi et animi et corporis, sed ingenio malo pravoque. huic ab adulescentia bella intestina, caedes, rapinae, discordia civilis grata fuere ibique iuventutem suam exercuit.

1 **L. Catilina, nobili genere natus:** Given Catiline's **genus nobile**, it is all the more noteworthy that Sallust never calls him **Lucius Sergius Catilina**, his full name, including that of his *gens*, the Sergii, a very old clan that claimed Trojan ancestry. The *gens Sergia* was patrician and of ancient distinction, having produced, among others, L. Sergius Fidenas, the consul of 437 and 429 BCE who earned his cognomen for a victory over the nearby town of Fidenae. By omitting the name of the *gens*, Sallust may be implying that Catiline is not worthy of the name.

natus: + abl. of origin.

magna vi: descriptive ablative.

1–2 **et animi et corporis:** By reverting to his opening discussion of mind and body and showing that Catiline's **vis** transcends division between the two, Sallust both emphasizes Catiline's human potential and builds him up as a danger to the community.

vi ... ingenio: The first major contrast is not between mind and body—in Catiline's case they seem to work together—but between **vis** and **ingenium**.

2 **malo pravoque:** PLEONASM for the sake of maintaining the pattern of doublets that was established with **et animi et corporis**.

ab adulescentia: Sallust draws a contrast here between Catiline's interests as a youth and Sallust's own.

3   **bella intestina ... discordia civilis:** Note the ASYNDETON in the heaping up, or CONGERIES, of abstract nouns. Note also how the two noun/adjective pairs **bella intestina ... discordia civilis**, which are almost synonyms, open and close the sequence.

4   **ibique = et in illis.**

   iuventutem suam exercuit: Catiline does not passively "pass through life" (**transire vitam/aetatem**); the verb **exerceo** means "to train by practice, to exercise, to occupy (one's time) actively."

This famous painting depicts Cicero accusing Catiline, who sits apart from the other senators, of conspiracy. This meeting of the Senate took place in the temple of Jupiter Stator, but the artist, Cesare Maccari (1840–1919) sets it in the Curia. The Senate often met in buildings other than the Curia. For example, the Senate was meeting in the Theater of Pompey the day of Julius Caesar's assassination. (© 2018 Bridgeman Art Library)

5   corpus patiens inediae, algoris, vigiliae supra quam cuiquam credibile est. animus audax, subdolus, varius, cuius rei lubet simulator ac dissimulator, alieni adpetens, sui profusus, ardens in cupiditatibus; satis eloquentiae, sapientiae parum. vastus animus inmoderata, incredibilia, nimis alta semper
10 cupiebat.

5   **inediae, algoris, vigiliae:** Note again the ASYNDETON. Sallust describes Catiline's body with one adjective, **patiens**, followed by a CONGERIES of nouns that are genitive objects of **patiens**, all to reinforce the point that Catiline is not like those who are **ventri atque somno dediti**.

5–6 **supra quam cuiquam credibile est:** The superhuman capacity of an archvillain is a TOPOS. Livy, for example, writing twenty years later, describes the Carthaginian Hannibal in terms that make an INTERTEXTUAL ALLUSION to Sallust's description and thus compare the two threats to Rome: **Nullo labore aut corpus fatigari aut animus vinci poterat. Caloris ac frigoris patientia par; cibi potionisque desiderio naturali, non voluptate modus finitus; vigiliarum somnique nec die nec nocte discriminata tempora; id quod gerendis rebus superesset quieti datum** (21.4.5).

6   **animus:** Catiline's mind is described at far greater length than his body: first by a CONGERIES of adjectives (**audax, subdolus, varius**); then by a pair of related nouns (**cuius rei lubet simulator ac dissimulator**); then by a series of participial phrases, the first two joined by ANTITHESIS (**alieni adpetens, sui profusus, ardens in cupiditatibus**); then by a statement arranged in CHIASMUS that produces ELLIPSIS of both the verb **erat** and any expression of possession, such as a possessive dative.

cuius rei: objective genitive with **simulator ac dissimulator**.

lubet: archaic spelling for **libet**.

7   **alieni adpetens, sui profusus:** picks up the ideas of **largitio** and **avaritia** in Sallust's autobiography; **sui** is objective genitive after **profusus**.

8 **satis eloquentiae, sapientiae parum:** This part of the description comes to an end with a CHIASTIC formation of words. Once again, ANTITHESIS takes the place of a conjunction.

eloquentiae, sapientiae: partitive genitives dependent on **satis** and **parum**.

9 **vastus ... semper:** The description of Catiline's **animus** continues, with some extravagant language: What does **vastus** mean here?

inmoderata, incredibilia, nimis alta: more ASYNDETON and INCONCINNITAS. What Catiline's **animus** wants is twice expressed negatively by the repeated prefix **in-**; then the sequence is broken by **nimis**, an expression of excess.

10 **cupiebat:** In this and the following passages Sallust portrays desire as a quality that can be good or bad depending on its object.

A transitional passage that moves from the mind of Catiline to the character of the Roman people.

> hunc post dominationem L. Sullae lubido maxuma invaserat rei publicae capiundae; neque id quibus modis adsequeretur, dum sibi regnum pararet, quicquam pensi habebat. agitabatur magis magisque in dies animus ferox inopia rei familiaris et
> 15 conscientia scelerum, quae utraque iis artibus auxerat, quas supra memoravi. incitabant praeterea corrupti civitatis mores, quos pessuma ac divorsa inter se mala, luxuria atque avaritia, vexabant.

11 **post dominationem L. Sullae:** L. Cornelius Sulla dominated Roman politics in the 80s BCE. His reign of terror brought about the deaths of hundreds of aristocrats.

lubido maxuma = libido maxima. Libido is a stock trait of the stereotypical tyrant.

invaserat: We have already seen personified **libido**, as well as **desidia** and **superbia**, as invading enemies.

12 **rei publicae capiundae:** (= **capiendae**), obj. gen. after **lubido**.

id quibus modis adsequeretur: an indirect question introduced by **neque ... quicquam pensi habebat**; the direct object of **adsequeretur** is **id**.

13 **dum ... pararet: dum** + subjunctive in a proviso, a "provided that ..." clause (A&G §528).

pensi: partitive gen. with **quicquam**.

13–16 **agitabatur ... incitabant:** Note both verbs' position at the beginning of their sentences. The focus is on the action.

14 **in dies:** "daily."

animus ferox: After the battle at the end of the *BC*, Catiline is found still breathing and still displaying in his expression his **ferociam animi**.

15 **quae utraque:** that is, **inopia** and **conscientia**.

17 **pessuma ac divorsa:** archaic spellings for **pessima ac diversa**.

luxuria atque avaritia: opposing forces, **divorsa inter se**, because anyone who spends on luxury is not accumulating wealth.

This bust, an Augustan-era copy of a second-century BCE portrait identified as Sulla, is now in the collection of the Munich Glyptothek in Germany. A similar bust identified as Sulla's enemy Marius, also in the the Munich Glyptothek's collection, may have been designed as a companion to the Sulla portrait. (© Creative Commons 2.0/Carole Raddato)

Sallust digresses in order to give a brief history of Rome, starting with the tradition that it was founded by Trojans who came to Italy under Aeneas's leadership together with the native inhabitants of the area.

  res ipsa hortari videtur, quoniam de moribus civitatis tempus
20 admonuit, supra repetere ac paucis instituta maiorum domi
  militiaeque, quo modo rem publicam habuerint quantamque
  reliquerint, ut paulatim inmutata ex pulcherruma atque
  optuma pessuma ac flagitiosissuma facta sit, disserere.

19 **res ipsa:** The *OLD* has nineteen main entries for **res**. Here **res ipsa** means "the subject itself."

  hortari: takes as objects **supra repetere** and **disserere**.

  videtur: The passive of **video** generally means "to seem," "to appear."

  tempus: here, "occasion."

20 **admonuit:** with **de**, "has stirred the memory about," "put in mind of . . ."

  supra: adv. with **repetere**, "to look further back" (in time).

  paucis = paucis verbis.

  instituta: n. pl., object of **disserere**.

21–22 **quo modo . . . quantamque . . . ut:** introducing indirect questions, all of which explain and elaborate upon **instituta maiorum**.

22 **paulatim:** The process was imperceptible until seen from a distance in time.

22–23 **pulcherruma atque optuma:** ablatives with **ex**. These are archaic spellings of **pulcherrima atque optima**. Note the extremes conveyed by these and the following superlatives.

23 **pessuma ac flagitiosissuma:** archaic spelling of **pessima ac flagitiosissima**; here predicate nominatives.

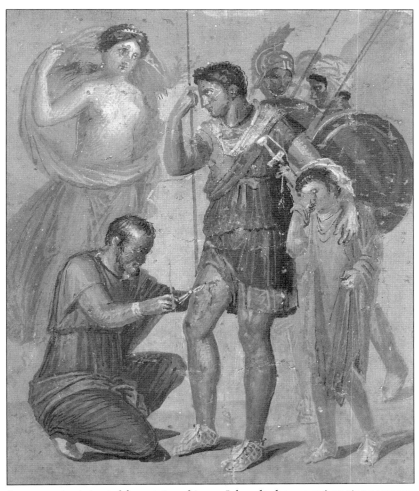

Aeneas, center, is treated for an injury; his son, Iulus, also known as Ascanius, accompanies him. The physician Iapyx uses a medicinal herb provided by Venus, who stands in the background. Vergil relates this episode in *Aeneid* 12.391–429. This first-century CE fresco from the triclinium in the House of Siricus in Pompeii is now in the Naples National Archaeological Museum. (Creative Commons/Marie-Lan Nguyen)

Rome's history began with its founding by Trojan refugees and native Italians.

> [6] urbem Romam, sicuti ego accepi, condidere atque habuere initio Troiani, qui Aenea duce profugi sedibus incertis vagabantur, cumque iis Aborigines, genus hominum agreste, sine legibus, sine imperio, liberum atque solutum.
> 5 hi postquam in una moenia convenere, dispari genere, dissimili lingua, alii alio more viventes, incredibile memoratu est, quam facile coaluerint: ita brevi multitudo dispersa atque vaga concordia civitas facta erat.

1   **urbem Romam:** Note how the topic is brought to the fore, even though it is not the subject of the verb. Tacitus may allude to this passage in the first sentence of his *Annals* (1.1): **Urbem Romam a principio reges habuere.**

       sicut ego accepi: Sallust's nod to the fact that there were multiple versions of Rome's foundation and, although the truth is impossible to find, one has to start somewhere.

1–2   **condidere atque habuere = condiderunt atque habuerunt.** See note on page 196, line 6.

2   **Troiani:** the first subjects of the main verbs. The Trojans take precedence over the Aborigines.

       Aenea duce: ablative absolute.

2–3   **sedibus incertis:** ablative absolute. In contrast to the **Aborigines** who follow, the **Troiani** once had a fixed **sedes**, or "place of residence" (Troy). In coming to Italy, they are seeking another.

3   **cumque iis Aborigines:** Although the Aborigines were in Italy first, the Trojans, city dwellers, receive first billing as founders of the city.

       Aborigines: Ancient sources disagreed as to the origins of the Aborigines; some said they were autochthonous (literally, that they arose from the soil itself, i.e., that they had always inhabited Italy); others that they came from Greece.

3-4 **genus hominum agreste, sine legibus, sine imperio, liberum atque solutum:** in APPOSITION to **Aborigines**. Note how the string of descriptors for **genus** begins with an adjective, continues with two prepositional phrases that elaborate on the idea of **agreste** by showing what the **genus agreste** lacks (laws and **imperium**), and concludes with two more adjectives joined by **atque**. **Liberum** here has the meaning "politically free" (*OLD* s.v. **liber** 2) and **solutum** the meaning "not subject to external restraints" (*OLD* s.v. **solutus** 11).

5 **hi:** the subject under discussion, both the **Troiani** and the **Aborigines** as they are coming together. They are the subject of **convenere** as well as of **quam facile coaluerint**.

in una moenia: moenia is n. pl. acc.: "within one [set of] walls." The emphasis is on unification.

5-6 **dispari genere, dissimili lingua:** descriptive ablatives. Note the ASYNDETON and the effect of ANAPHORA produced by repetition of **dis-**.

6 **alii alio more:** "each group in a different manner."

memoratu: supine with **incredibile**.

7 **quam ... coaluerint:** indirect question.

ita brevi: adverbial, "in such a short time."

7-8 **dispersa atque vaga: Dispersa** perhaps alludes to the Aborigines' lack of organization implied in **agreste** and **solutum** (line 4); and **vaga**, of course, recalls the verb **vagabantur** (line 3) and thus the Trojans' wandering. By making both adjectives the attributes of the one **multitudo**, Sallust further emphasizes the idea of unification.

8 **concordia:** ablative of means or causal ablative.

*Military expansion grows from jealousy (**invidia**). Romans have first to defend themselves; then they form military alliances. A Senate takes shape, made up of a selection of wise elders. After kingship deteriorates into tyranny, the Romans create for themselves a political system that includes checks and balances: a dual magistracy and annually elected officials.*

    sed postquam res eorum civibus, moribus, agris aucta satis
10 prospera satisque pollens videbatur, sicuti pleraque
    mortalium habentur, invidia ex opulentia orta est. igitur
    reges populique finitumi bello temptare, pauci ex amicis
    auxilio esse; nam ceteri metu perculsi a periculis aberant. at
    Romani domi militiaeque intenti festinare, parare, alius
15 alium hortari, hostibus obviam ire, libertatem, patriam
    parentisque armis tegere. post, ubi pericula virtute
    propulerant, sociis atque amicis auxilia portabant magisque
    dandis quam accipiundis beneficiis amicitias parabant.
    imperium legitumum, nomen imperi regium habebant.
20 delecti, quibus corpus annis infirmum, ingenium sapientia
    validum erat, rei publicae consultabant; hi vel aetate vel curae
    similitudine patres appellabantur.

9   **sed:** The conjunction introduces another new stage in the discussion.

    res eorum ... aucta: This developing **res** is not yet a **res publica**.

    civibus, moribus, agris: a CONGERIES of nouns; all ablatives of specification.

9–10 **satis prospera satisque pollens:** predicate nominatives with **videbatur** ("seemed"). Note the ALLITERATION.

10–11 **sicuti pleraque ... habentur:** "as is the case with most human affairs."

11   **invidia ex opulentia orta est:** Sallust represents ill will as arising almost inevitably from another's wealth.

12-13	**temptare ... esse:** historical infinitives, ARCHAISMS.
12	**pauci ex amicis:** With groups of people, such as **amicis**, the regular construction is **ex** + abl. instead of partitive genitive.
13	**auxilio:** Dative expressing purpose is a common construction with **auxilium**.
	a periculis aberant: with perhaps a stronger negative sense than the Latin implies: "failed them in their dangers."
16	**parentis:** accusative plural.
	post: adv., "afterward," modifying the entire sentence. This marks a transition to a new stage for the **res**.
17-18	**portabant ... parabant:** Although few of the Romans' friends were any help to them, they were generous in bringing aid to others.
	magisque dandis quam accipiundis beneficiis: a gerundive. **Beneficiis** is to be taken with both **dandis** and **accipiundis**.
19	**imperium legitumum nomen imperi regium:** The ANTITHESIS is between the legally founded constitution of the **imperium** and its regal name.
20	**quibus:** dative of possession.
20-21	**corpus ... validum:** Note the ANTITHESIS between **corpus** and **ingenium** created by the parallel word order.
21	**rei publicae:** dative.
21-22	**aetate ... similitudine:** causal ablatives: "on account of."
22	**patres:** These are the first set of regal advisors, which devolved into the Roman Senate. As **patres** they gave their name to the patrician order.

> post, ubi regium imperium, quod initio conservandae
> libertatis atque augendae rei publicae fuerat, in superbiam
> 25 dominationemque se convortit, inmutato more annua
> imperia binosque imperatores sibi fecere: eo modo minume
> posse putabant per licentiam insolescere animum humanum.

23 **post:** The adverb introduces the next phase: kingship deteriorates.

23–24 **conservandae libertatis atque augendae rei publicae:** gerundives in the genitive of purpose.

24 **superbiam:** an allusion to Rome's last Tarquin king, who exemplified this quality (cf. Livy 1.57–60).

Here is a case where **superbia** has invaded and, if Sallust knows a version of the Lucretia story, **libido** as well (cf. **ubi ... lubido atque superbia invasere**, Sallust *BC* 2.5). So, as happens, **imperium** will shift to the better man, or in this case, men.

25 **inmutato more:** Sallust has pointed out that when morals (**mores**, pl.) change, then **fortuna simul cum moribus inmutatur** (2.5); now a custom or practice (**mos**, sg.) has changed, with the result implied that **fortuna** will change too.

25–26 **annua imperia binosque imperatores:** The two structural checks on power in the Roman Republic were the limiting of the length of office to one year and the duplication of the head magistrates (note **imperia**, plural). The consuls, each with power of veto, could limit one another's influence.

26 **eo modo:** by electing officials annually.

27 **animum humanum:** The discussion returns, once again, to the **animus**.

A famous legend states that the Cumaean Sibyl offered to sell Tarquinius Superbus nine books of prophecies at a high price. He refused, so she burned three of the books and offered the remaining six books at the same price, which he again refused. The Sibyl burned three more books, after which Tarquinius agreed to buy the last three books at the original price. The books were housed in the temple of Jupiter on the Capitoline and were consulted by order of the Senate during times of crisis. The illustration comes from a fifteenth-century German translation of Boccaccio's *De mulieribus claris*. (© Creative Commons 2.0/kladcat)

*Sallust's version of Rome's history after the expulsion of the Etruscan kings focuses on the vigorous cast of mind of the liberated city, and especially the young men's desire for glory (**cupido gloriae**). Their competition for glory, Sallust asserts, led to an amazingly swift growth in Roman power. In their desire to be conspicuous for excellence and their love of weapons and warhorses, the youth of early Rome fit into the pattern of the Homeric heroes.*

[7] sed ea tempestate coepere se quisque magis extollere magisque ingenium in promptu habere. nam regibus boni quam mali suspectiores sunt semperque eis aliena virtus formidulosa est. sed civitas incredibile memoratu est adepta
5   libertate quantum brevi creverit; tanta cupido gloriae incesserat. iam primum iuventus, simul ac belli patiens erat, in castris per laborem usum militiae discebat magisque in decoris armis et militaribus equis quam in scortis atque conviviis lubidinem habebant.

1   **sed:** here again marking a transition to a new line of argument.

ea tempestate: an ARCHAISM for **eo tempore**.

se quisque ... extollere: The pronoun **quisque**, "each," is in apposition with the plural subject of **coepere**, "they began each to elevate himself more." The reflexive **se** is in its usual position with **quisque**.

2   **ingenium in promptu:** The phrase **in promptu** here means "in full view." A man's fellow citizens could see his virtues and reckon his value accordingly.

regibus: dative with **suspectiores** (A&G §383). Note the change in the tense of the verbs from the perfect, **coepere**, to the present, **sunt** and **est**, as Sallust explains men's new-found desire for prominence by stating some eternal truths (**semper ... est**) about the paranoia of kings.

3   **eis = regibus.**

aliena virtus: "excellence that belongs to another."

4	**civitas:** Sallust has placed **civitas**, the subject of the indirect question **quantum brevi creverit**, at the beginning and outside of the question, so as to focus attention on it as the topic under discussion: "But as to the *city* . . ."
	memoratu: supine with **incredibile est**.
4–5	**adepta libertate:** an ablative absolute; this is an unusual passive use of the participle of the deponent verb **adipiscor**.
5–6	**tanta . . . incesserat:** This independent clause in the pluperfect explains the results outlined in the previous sentence.
	cupido gloriae: Note the abstract subject. **Gloriae** is an objective genitive with **cupido**.
6	**iam primum:** "to begin with," "first of all."
	iuventus: a collective singular, "the youth," that is, the young men of military age.
	simul ac: "as soon as."
	belli: objective genitive with **patiens**.
7	**per laborem:** Translate **per** here as "by reason of" or "by means of."
	usum militiae: practical, as opposed to theoretical, experience of warfare.
7–9	**discebat . . . habebant:** The imperfect tense conveys the sense that this was the regular custom, repeatedly practiced.
8	**decoris armis et militaribus equis:** glorious weaponry, warhorses. Preference for weaponry and warhorses is a stock character trait of a formidable warrior, whether friend or foe. For example, Livy says of the Carthaginian Hannibal that he did not care what he ate or wore but that his weapons and horses were notable: **armi atque equi conspiciebantur** (21.4).
8–9	**scortis atque conviviis:** Compare the pleasure-seeking regal youths in Livy 1.57–60.
9	**lubidinem habebant:** "took pleasure in." Note that the young men are the subject and **lubidinem** the object of **habebant**. Compare the **libido** that *seizes* Sextus Tarquinius in Livy 1.57.

10 igitur talibus viris non labor insolitus, non locus ullus asper aut arduus erat, non armatus hostis formidulosus: virtus omnia domuerat. sed gloriae maxumum certamen inter ipsos erat; se quisque hostem ferire, murum ascendere, conspici dum tale facinus faceret, properabat; eas divitias,
15 eam bonam famam magnamque nobilitatem putabant. laudis avidi, pecuniae liberales erant; gloriam ingentem, divitias honestas volebant. memorare possem quibus in locis maxumas hostium copias populus Romanus parva manu fuderit, quas urbis natura munitas pugnando ceperit, ni ea res
20 longius nos ab incepto traheret.

10 **talibus viris:** dative with the adjectives **insolitus, asper, arduus,** and **formidulosus.**

10–11 **non ... non ... non:** The ANAPHORA conveys heightened emotion.

asper aut arduus: Note the ALLITERATION.

11 **formidulosus:** The repetition of this adjective contrasts the youth of the early Republic, who did not fear even an armed enemy, with kings who are terrified at anyone else's excellence.

11–12 **virtus ... domuerat:** another independent clause in the pluperfect that summarizes and explains the previous statement, "courage had conquered all."

12 **sed gloriae:** "but as to glory, the greatest contest for it ..." **Gloriae** is objective genitive with **maxumum certamen.**

12–13 **inter ipsos:** a contest among themselves as opposed to conflict with the enemy.

13–14 **se quisque ... properabat:** "each hurried to bring it about that he ..."

14–15 **eas divitias, eam ... nobilitatem:** The pronouns that we would expect to be the neuter **ea** and **id** ("*those* [things] were riches; *that* [thing] was a good reputation and great renown") have been attracted into the gender of the nouns.

16	**laudis avidi, pecuniae liberales:** Note the double ANTITHESIS: praise and money; greed and generosity.
17-20	**possem ... traheret:** a present contrary-to-fact condition.
19	**fuderit ... ceperit:** perfect subjunctives in indirect questions.
	urbis = urbes.
	pugnando: the ablative of the gerund, here expressing means (A&G §507).
	ni = nisi.
	ea res: "the subject." Here that means telling the stories of old-time Roman heroism.
20	**longius:** comparative with the sense of excess, "too far."

It was a commonplace of Roman literature that even Achilles would have been forgotten without a Homer to sing his praises; likewise, other heroic figures, both Greek and Roman, depended on writers to preserve their glory and fame. Moreover, it sometimes happened that writers were so talented as to make the deeds they recorded appear greater than they really were. This is what happened with Athens, claimed Sallust; whereas in contrast Rome lacked great writers at first, because men of talent preferred doing great deeds to writing about those of others.

[8] sed profecto fortuna in omni re dominatur; ea res cunctas ex lubidine magis quam ex vero celebrat obscuratque. Atheniensium res gestae, sicuti ego aestumo, satis amplae magnificaeque fuere, verum aliquanto minores tamen
5 quam fama feruntur. sed quia provenere ibi scriptorum magna ingenia, per terrarum orbem Atheniensium facta pro maxumis celebrantur. ita eorum qui ea fecere virtus tanta habetur, quantum ea verbis potuere extollere praeclara ingenia. at populo Romano numquam ea copia fuit, quia
10 prudentissumus quisque maxume negotiosus erat; ingenium nemo sine corpore exercebat; optumus quisque facere quam dicere, sua ab aliis benefacta laudari quam ipse aliorum narrare malebat.

1   **profecto** = "assuredly."

    fortuna ... dominatur: Note the PERSONIFICATION. Sallust returns to the present tense for his truisms.

2   **ex lubidine ... ex vero:** Translate **ex** as "according to."

3   **Atheniensium:** Note how the word order focuses attention immediately on the Athenians.

    res gestae: "accomplishments," "achievements."

    aestumo: The verb means to put a price on something or calculate its value.

4	**verum ... tamen:** "but nevertheless."
	aliquanto: abl. of degree of difference.
5	**quam:** The comparison is compressed by the ELLIPSIS of a second **fuere** to contrast reality and reputation: **Atheniensium res gestae ... minores [fuerunt] quam fama feruntur**. Note the ALLITERATION in **fama feruntur** that is characteristic of Sallust.
	ibi: i.e., in Athens.
5-6	**scriptorium magna ingenia:** "great talents of writers," instead of **scriptores magni ingenii**, "writers of great talent."
7	**pro maxumis:** "as if the greatest."
	ita: "and so." Note that Sallust introduces an independent clause here, instead of a result.
8-9	**praeclara ingenia:** Again, talent is the topic, not specific persons.
9	**populo Romano:** dative of possession.
10	**prudentissumus quisque:** "all the wisest men," that is, one after another in the order of their wisdom (A&G §313.b).
	ingenium: here "intellect."
11	**optumus quisque:** "all the best men."
11-12	**facere quam dicere:** The pairing—and the opposition—is natural, traditional, and heroic: In the *Iliad*, Achilles says that his father taught him to be a speaker of words and a doer of deeds; and yet he is known for his deeds; and in the Embassy scene of Book 9, when he is withdrawn from the fighting and therefore pointedly *not* doing deeds, Achilles appears playing a lyre and singing of the glorious deeds of men.
12-13	**sua ab aliis benefacta laudari quam ipse aliorum narrare malebat:** Consider how Sallust would have had to rephrase either side of the comparison in order to make a completely parallel construction; then note how his switching from the passive **laudari** to the active **narrare** keeps **optumus quisque** the focus of attention.

A paragraph full of abstractions: Aside from the personal subjects of some of the verbs (the Romans of old, and over-bold soldiers), and other nouns identifying categories of people (cives, amicos, hostem), the only concrete entities in this paragraph are signa (standards) and loco (position), and even these appear in references to unspecified situations. Note how Sallust repeatedly presents moral character as a series of choices between two actions or tendencies.

[9] igitur domi militiaeque boni mores colebantur, concordia maxuma, minuma avaritia erat, ius bonumque apud eos non legibus magis quam natura valebat. iurgia, discordias, simultates cum hostibus exercebant, cives cum
5 civibus de virtute certabant. in suppliciis deorum magnifici, domi parci, in amicos fideles erant. duabus his artibus, audacia in bello, ubi pax evenerat aequitate seque remque publicam curabant. quarum rerum ego maxuma documenta haec habeo, quod in bello saepius vindicatum est in eos
10 qui contra imperium in hostem pugnaverant quique tardius revocati proelio excesserant,

1 **domi militiaeque:** both locatives (A&G §427.a). This is a traditional collocation for both spheres of action: "at home and at war."

boni mores: "good character."

2 **concordia maxuma, minuma avaritia:** Note the CHIASMUS and the ANTITHESIS.

ius bonumque: The two nouns (**bonum** is substantive) are tightly bound together as subject of the singular **valebat. Ius** refers to a natural law.

3 **apud eos:** "among them."

non legibus magis quam natura: This highly idealized and morally superior past resembles the "Golden Age" of mythology, in which laws did not exist because they were not necessary. People behaved well naturally.

3-4   **iurgia, discordias, simultates:** a CONGERIES of near-synonyms for strife.

4-5   **cum hostibus ... cives cum civibus:** The ANTITHESIS of **cives**, "as citizens," with **hostibus** replaces a connective. Note the ALLITERATION of **cives cum civibus**.

5-6   **in suppliciis ... domi ... in amicos:** Note the variation and again the ASYNDETON.

6   **in amicos:** "toward their friends."

duabus his artibus: His points forward to **audacia** and **aequitate**; note the ALLITERATION as well as the CHIASTIC arrangements of these two "arts" and the conditions of war (**in bello**) and peace (**ubi pax evenerat**).

7-8   **seque remque publicam:** -que ... -que is a poetic construction, rare in prose.

8   **quarum rerum:** relative used as a connective (A&G §308.f); in the objective genitive, with **documenta**.

8-9   **maxuma documenta haec habeo:** "I consider these to be the greatest proofs."

9-14 **quod in bello ... vindicatum est ... in pace vero, quod ... agitabant, et ... malebant:** the proofs pointed to by **haec**.

9   **vindicatum est:** impersonal passive with **in** + acc.: "punishment was inflicted upon ..."

10   **contra imperium:** Here **imperium** must mean the "order of command," "authority." Notable examples of Romans fighting against orders include the son of the great T. Manlius Torquatus. During a Roman conflict with the Gauls, T. Manlius obtained permission from his commanding officers to challenge an enemy soldier to single combat, fought the enemy, and killed him. A generation later, in a similar situation, his son imitated his father's deed but failed to ask permission first. As consul, Manlius was then obliged to order the execution of his son. (See Livy 7.9 and 8.7 for the stories.)

tardius: modifies **proelio excesserant**.

11   **revocati:** temporal, "when recalled" (A&G §496).

quam qui signa relinquere aut pulsi loco cedere ausi erant;
in pace vero, quod beneficiis quam metu imperium agitabant,
et accepta iniuria ignoscere quam persequi malebant.

12   **loco cedere:** "to give ground" or "fall back"; see *OLD s.v. cedere* 3.b. For the ablative without a preposition in expressions of place from which, see A&G §428.f.

   ausi erant: an ironic use of the verb: "had the nerve" or "dared" to flee.

13   **beneficiis quam metu:** with acts of kindness rather than fear: Sallust again avoids an exact parallel between the items compared: on the one hand, multiple, individual acts of kindness; on the other, abstract, unspecified fear.

14   **accepta iniuria:** ablative absolute; the *idea* of a wrong received continues on as the unspoken object of **persequi**.

   ignoscere quam persequi: "to forgive rather than follow up."

LIVY

***Ab Urbe Condita* 3.44–48**
Higher Level Only

— Introduction to Livy —

Information on the life and works of Livy may be found in the introduction to the Standard Level and Higher Level section (page 153).

— Introduction to *Ab Urbe Condita* 3.44–48 —

At the heart of Books 1–5 Livy places a story of freedom lost and then recovered only through bloody sacrifice. During a period of political strife between patricians and plebeians, the Senate sent three commissioners to Athens to study Solon's law code. When they returned, Rome suspended its annually elected consulships and plebeian tribunate for a year, electing instead a board of ten (*decemviri*) to draft and post a law code (the Ten Tables). When one year's term did not produce a sufficiently comprehensive set of laws, the Roman people voted for a second term of rule by the *decemviri*. This second term added additional provisions to the law code that became known as the Twelve Tables; but these additional laws included one forbidding marriage between patricians and plebeians; moreover, the *decemviri* themselves began to display cruelty, arrogance, and violence, traits of the stereotypical tyrant. Two unspeakable crimes (*duo nefanda facinora*) precipitated the end of their reign. The first, an egregious act of violent cruelty, took place in the army camp in Sabine territory, where the *decemviri* contrived the ambush and murder of an outspoken critic, L. Siccius; a second took place in Rome.

In the second episode, which appears here, the violence of the most prominent *decemvir*, Appius Claudius, finds its outlet in sexual desire, *libido*, and leads to an attempt to rape the maiden Verginia. Appius's *libido* can be seen as analogous to lust for political power and Verginia as a symbol of the Roman plebeians. Because Livy sets her up as a sacrifice, Verginia never speaks; her male connections (fiancé, uncle, and father) speak and act for her. But women support her as well, both individually (her nurse) and collectively (the Roman plebeian matrons). The casting of the episode calls to mind a Greek tragedy, with named characters set apart from a chorus that witnesses and comments on events. Like Lucretia's death, Verginia's leads to a change in the structure of Roman government: a return to annually elected consuls and the restoration of the tribunate. In relating the dispute over Verginia's status, Livy presents legal affairs, including technical language, anachronistically, as he retrojects constitutional developments of the mid-Republic into Rome's more distant past.

Livy introduces the story of Verginia by comparing it overtly to the story of Lucretia, particularly as to outcome. Other points of contact are made implicitly throughout by means of INTRATEXTUAL ALLUSIONS. *The notes will point out some of them.*

[44] sequitur aliud in urbe nefas ab libidine ortum, haud minus foedo eventu quam quod per stuprum caedemque Lucretiae urbe regnoque Tarquinios expulerat, ut non finis solum idem decemviris qui regibus sed causa etiam
5   eadem imperii amittendi esset. Ap. Claudium virginis plebeiae stuprandae libido cepit. pater virginis, L. Verginius, honestum ordinem in Algido ducebat, vir exempli recti domi militiaeque.

1   **sequitur ... ortum:** The initial position of the verb "there follows," together with the "another" of **aliud nefas,** connects this story to the immediately preceding account of the ambush of L. Siccius. **Sequitur** is a historical present. On prose word order, see A&G §597.

   in urbe: The urban location is contrasted to that of the Siccius affair, which took place in the army camp.

   ab libidine: an ablative of source with **ortum** (A&G §403).

2   **foedo eventu:** ablative of quality or descriptive ablative (A&G §415).

2-3 **per stuprum caedemque Lucretiae:** The **nefas** acts "through" the **stuprum caedemque,** which are its means or instrument. Note that as an active force, **nefas** influences events, whereas **libido** manipulates human beings.

   quod ... expulerat = quam illud nefas quod expulerat.

3-5 **ut ... esset:** result clauses (use **esset** twice, with both **non ... solum ...** and **sed ... etiam ...**).

   non finis solum idem ... sed causa etiam eadem: Note the emphasis placed on **finem** and **causa** by **solum** and **etiam.** The "same end" is change in government.

4   **decemviris ... regibus:** datives of possession with [**esset**].

5   **imperii amittendi:** the objective genitive of the gerundive after a noun (here **causa**) or adjective (A&G §504).

5–6   **Ap. Claudium virginis plebeiae stuprandae libido cepit:** Compare the similar phrasing of the Lucretia story (1.57.31–32): **ibi Sex. Tarquinium mala libido Lucretiae per vim stuprandae capit.**

       Ap. Claudium: Appius Claudius, one of the **decemviri**, a member of the ancient and patrician Claudian family, early arrivals to Rome from Sabine territory. The *gens Claudia* held its first consulship in 495 BCE and was famous for its arrogance and high-handed behavior.

       virginis plebeiae stuprandae: a gerundive in the objective genitive after **libido** (A&G §504).

6   **L. Verginius:** probably a made-up name for a fictitious father but appropriate for the father of a girl whose **virginitas** is a central feature of the story.

7   **ordinem ... ducebat:** "was commanding a century" or "was serving as centurion."

       in Algido: a mountain in Latium, south of Tusculum.

       vir exempli recti: genitive of quality (A&G §345).

perinde uxor instituta fuerat liberique instituebantur.
10 desponderat filiam L. Icilio tribunicio, viro acri et pro causa plebis expertae virtutis. hanc virginem adultam forma excellentem Appius amore amens pretio ac spe perlicere adortus, postquam omnia pudore saepta animadverterat, ad crudelem superbamque vim animum convertit.

9 **perinde:** "likewise," "in like manner."

uxor instituta fuerat liberique instituebantur: The repetition of the verb emphasizes the continuity of the family's virtuous way of life, one shared by Verginius and wife, and passed down carefully to the children.

10–11 **desponderat filiam . . . virtutis:** Observe where Livy places the details describing the main actors in this story. We learn very little about Verginia when Livy first presents her as Icilius's betrothed; instead we learn quite a lot about the character of her husband-to-be (he is **acer**, he is a man of **virtus**). Livy introduces him here from the point of view of Verginia's father who is carefully choosing a worthy husband for his daughter.

10 **L. Icilio tribunicio:** As a former tribune of the plebeians, Lucius Icilius is the patricians' natural enemy.

viro acri: dat. in apposition to **L. Icilio**.

11 **expertae virtutis:** genitive of quality (A&G §345).

hanc virginem: the word order shifts focus from father and fiancé to Verginia. We see her now as she appears to the love-crazed eyes of Appius Claudius.

forma: ablative of specification with **excellentem**, "excelling in beauty" (A&G §418).

12 **amore amens:** This alliterative pair linking love and madness appears in Roman poetry as well.

pretio ac spe: ablative of means, "with money and expectation." How Appius was able to get messages to Verginia is unclear. Perhaps he tried to convey them via an attendant.

13 **omnia pudore saepta:** Note the spatial METAPHOR: Verginia is securely defended by her own virtuous character. Literally: "all things were surrounded," with the meaning "she was surrounded on all sides."

13–14 **ad crudelem superbamque vim:** The phrase encompasses three traits of the stock tyrant: **crudelitas**, **superbia**, and **violentia**.

14 **animum convertit:** The compound **animadverterat** "he had noticed" anticipates the related expression **animum convertit**.

*Appius works his evil indirectly, through M. Claudius, his **cliens** (probably either a less powerful relative or an ex-slave). M. Claudius takes advantage of Verginia's presence in the public world of the Forum to claim her as his slave, so that he can hand her over to Appius.*

15　M. Claudio clienti negotium dedit ut virginem in servitutem adsereret neque cederet secundum libertatem postulantibus vindicias, quod pater puellae abesset locum iniuriae esse ratus. virgini venienti in forum—ibi namque in tabernaculis litterarum ludi erant—minister decemviri libidinis manum
20　iniecit, serva sua natam servamque appellans, sequique se iubebat: cunctantem vi abstracturum.

15　**clienti:** The relation between patron, *patronus*, and *cliens* was mutually beneficial, with the *patronus* protecting his *cliens* and the *cliens* rendering his *patronus* various services in return.

15–16　**ut . . . adsereret neque cederet:** substantive clauses of purpose explaining **negotium** (A&G 562.a).

in servitutem adsereret: adserere in servitutem, "to claim as a slave," opposite to **adserere in libertatem,** "to claim as free."

16　**secundum:** prep. + acc., "in favor of."

postulantibus: dat. with **cederet.**

17　**vindicias:** direct object of **postulantibus.** The noun **vindiciae** (rarely singular) indicates the temporary possession of disputed property granted to one side or the other by the *praetor* (judge).

abesset: subjunctive in an explanatory **quod**-clause that is part of Appius's thinking (**ratus**); see A&G §540.

iniuriae: dat. with **locum. Locum** here has the sense of "opportunity."

18　**virgini venienti:** dat. with **iniecit.** The word order focuses our attention first on Verginia, then on her surroundings.

18–19　**ibi namque . . . erant:** Livy is fond of parenthetical explanations. This one adds a specific topographical detail that helps readers picture events even as it delays the account of M. Claudius's action.

19 **litterarum ludi:** grammar, or elementary school; this is probably an anachronistic reference. **Ludi** most likely arose at Rome with the influx of Hellenism and the development of a Latin literature in the third century BCE. Livy needs to explain why a virtuous young woman was in the marketplace. This passage *does* suggest that readers of Livy's time would not find it unusual for an adolescent girl to receive some kind of formal education.

20 **serva sua natam servamque:** The word order preserves the logical argument: being born from Claudius's slave woman would make Verginia his slave.

20–21 **sequique se iubebat:** Part of the legal process of bringing someone to law was to request them to join the plaintiff before the judge's platform, the **tribunal**.

21 **cunctantem vi abstracturum:** the participle with conditional force (A&G §496) + future infinitive for a future more vivid condition in indirect speech. (Assume a verb of speaking, such as **dixit**.)

Verginia is terrified beyond the ability to speak or act. She is, however, not alone: First her nurse and then the onlookers in the Forum come to her aid. A crowd gathers and M. Claudius makes his case before Appius, as prearranged.

    pavida puella stupente ad clamorem nutricis fidem Quiritium implorantis fit concursus. Vergini patris sponsique Icili populare nomen celebrabatur. notos gratia eorum, turbam
25 indignitas rei virgini conciliat. iam a vi tuta erat, cum adsertor nihil opus esse multitudine concitata ait; se iure grassari, non vi. vocat puellam in ius. auctoribus qui aderant ut sequerentur, ad tribunal Appi perventum est.

22 **pavida:** an adjective also used of Lucretia when awakened by Sextus Tarquinius.

ad clamorem: ad + acc., "in response to."

fidem Quiritium: The "allegiance/loyalty of the **Quirites**." An appeal to the multitude, out of which grew the Roman citizen's right of *provocatio*. Livy describes the decemvirate as a magistracy *sine provocatione*, that is, against whose decisions there was no right of appeal. After the abolition of the decemvirate, the tribune Valerius, according to Livy, sponsored a law (which may be fictitious) restoring the right of *provocatio*.

Quiritium: the name of the citizens of Rome as a collective of civilians, used in solemn addresses and appeals.

23 **fit concursus:** Everyone in hearing distance rushes to the spot. The impersonal expression focuses attention on the fact of the gathering where bringing in a new group of human subjects (e.g., **omnes concurrunt**) would distract from it.

24 **populare:** "liked" or "admired by the general public."

celebrabatur: continuous action, "was on everybody's lips."

notos: the friends and acquaintances of Verginius and Icilius.

notos ... turbam: The ANTITHESIS takes the place of a connective.

gratia: here "popularity" or "esteem."

25   **rei:** objective genitive with **indignitas**.

        virgini: dat. with **conciliat**.

        multitudine concitata: abl. with **opus esse** (A&G §497.a). The force is on the participle: "for the mob being stirred up."

27   **grassari:** here "to proceed," but often a word with violent or lawless connotations. It is used of robbers, pirates, and other predatory people.

        vocat … in ius: the technical term for the first move in a legal process (already implied in **sequique se iubebat** [lines 20–21]): the plaintiff requests the defendant to join him in court before the *praetor*.

        auctoribus qui aderant: "with those who were present advising." **Auctoribus** is a one-word ablative absolute, because of the omission of an antecedent (e.g., *illis*) of the relative clause: e.g., *illis auctoribus qui aderant*; **auctoribus** is predicate, because the full expression is **auctor esse** (with **ut/ne** + subjunctive), "to advise." Classical Latin does not use a present participle of **esse**.

28   **ut sequerentur:** the substance of the advice; the verb is plural to include the nurse.

        perventum est: another impersonal construction. Again, the focus is on the gathering as readers imagine Verginia approaching the tribunal, her nurse following, and the bystanders collecting around them.

notam iudici fabulam petitor, quippe apud ipsum auctorem
30   argumenti, peragit: puellam domi suae natam furtoque inde
in domum Vergini translatam suppositam ei esse; id se indicio
compertum adferre probaturumque vel ipso Verginio iudice,
ad quem maior pars iniuriae eius pertineat; interim dominum
sequi ancillam aequum esse.

29   **notam iudici fabulam:** Note the emphatic position of the adjective; **iudici** is dative with **notam**.

29–30   **auctorem argumenti:** "the originator of the plot."

30–31   **puellam … suppositam … esse:** the core of the indirect statement; within are the two participial phrases **domi suae natam** and **furtoque inde in domum Vergini translatam**.

        domi suae: locative.

        furto: ablative of means.

31   **ei = Verginio**; dat. with **suppositam**.

31–32   **id se … compertum adferre probaturumque:** Note the transition from past participle to present infinitive to future.

32   **ipso Verginio iudice:** concessive use of the ablative absolute, "even if …"

33   **pertineat:** subjunctive, because this is a subordinate clause in indirect statement.

33–34   **dominum sequi ancillam:** "that the slave follow her master." M. Claudius's expression recalls the words of those who advised **ut sequerentur**.

In the left panel, Verginius kills Verginia; in the right, Appius presides over the trial of Verginia. Verginius pleads his case as M. Claudius looks on. The illustration comes from a fifteenth-century German translation of Boccaccio's *De mulieribus claris*. (© Creative Commons 2.0/kladcat)

*Verginia's supporters ask Appius to adjourn the case until her father should return. Their words counter M. Claudius's **aequum esse** with **iniquum esse**. Appius agrees to do so.*

35   advocati puellae, cum Verginium rei publicae causa dixissent abesse, biduo adfuturum si nuntiatum ei sit, iniquum esse absentem de liberis dimicare, postulant ut rem integram in patris adventum differat, lege ab ipso lata vindicias det secundum libertatem, neu patiatur virginem adultam famae
40   prius quam libertatis periculum adire.

[45] Appius decreto praefatur quam libertati faverit eam ipsam legem declarare quam Vergini amici postulationi suae praetendant; ceterum ita in ea firmum libertati fore praesidium si nec causis nec personis variet; in aliis enim
5   qui adserantur in libertatem quia quivis lege agere possit, id iuris esse:

35   **advocati:** not advocates here in the legal sense of the term, but simply witnesses and supporters.

cum . . . dixissent: The **advocati** said three things: **Verginium . . . abesse; biduo adfuturum . . .; iniquum esse absentem . . . dimicare.** The **cum**-clause sets up the circumstances for the main clause, **postulant . . .**, which balances the three statements with three requests: **ut . . . differat; vindicias det; neu patiatur.**

rei publicae causa: that is, on military business.

36   **biduo:** abl. of time within which.

37   **integram:** The matter should be taken up anew and from the beginning.

37-38   **in patris adventum:** Here **in** + acc. = "until."

38   **lege ab ipso lata:** The law was carried by Appius in his first year as one of the **decemviri**.

39-40 **famae ... libertatis:** (objective) genitives of the person or thing endangered, with **periculum**.

40 **periculum adire:** "to risk."

1 **decreto:** dat. with **praefatur**.

quam ... faverit: indirect question in the primary sequence with a perfect subjunctive. This indirect question is the object of the verb **declarare**.

libertati: dat. with **faverit**.

1-2 **eam ipsam legem declarare:** the core of Appius's prefatory statement, "the law itself makes clear ..."

3 **ceterum:** neuter singular as an adverb, perhaps here slightly adversative: "however that may be ..."

3-4 **ita ... fore ... si ... variet:** future more vivid condition in indirect statement.

3 **in ea = in lege.**

4 **causis nec personis:** datives of reference, also known as datives of advantage and disadvantage (A&G §376).

variet: here intransitive, with the unspoken **lex** as the subject.

in aliis enim: "for in the case of others."

5 **lege agere:** "legally bring an action," "act in accordance with the law."

6 **id iuris esse:** "this is the law," that is, the request is legal. **Iuris** is partitive genitive.

in ea quae in patris manu sit neminem esse alium cui dominus possessione cedat. placere itaque patrem arcessiri, interea iuris sui iacturam adsertorem non facere quin ducat
10 puellam sistendamque in adventum eius qui pater dicatur promittat.

7   **in ea quae in patris manu sit:** "in the case of a woman who is in her father's **manus**." **Manus** was a technical term for the status of a woman who was under the legal control of her father or her husband.

8   **placere:** impersonal. This is legalistic language.

9   **iuris sui iacturam . . . non facere:** "would not cast away his own rights"; **iuris sui** is an objective gen. with **iacturam**.

   adsertorem: that is, M. Claudius.

9-11   **quin ducat puellam sistendamque . . . promittat:** On **quin** with the subjunctive, see A&G §558. Note the word order, which focuses attention on **ducat puellam** and **sistendam**, but not on **promittat**.

10   **sistendamque:** with **promittat**, "and promise that she be made to appear," a predicate accusative use of the participle.

In this wedding scene from a sarcophagus, Venus Felix crowns the bride and a Genius, a spirit believed to accompany a man throughout his life, attends the groom. A wife could come under the legal control, or *manus*, of her husband through one of three types of marriage, though in other types of marriage the wife remained under the *manus* of her father. This third-century CE sarcophagus is in the collection of the Naples National Archaeological Museum. (© Creative Commons 2.5/Marie-Lan Nguyen)

Verginia's grandfather Numitorius and fiancé Icilius intervene. Livy describes Icilius as an otherwise cool-headed young man, but one who sees the attack on Verginia as a step too far. Pushed out of the way by one of the lictors, he responds with a passionate speech arguing that Appius's destroying the political rights of the plebeians is bad enough; he should stop before attacking the modesty of women and children.

adversus iniuriam decreti cum multi magis fremerent quam quisquam unus recusare auderet, P. Numitorius, puellae avus, et sponsus Icilius interveniunt; dataque inter turbam via, cum
15 multitudo Icili maxime interventu resisti posse Appio crederet, lictor decresse ait vociferantemque Icilium submovet. placidum quoque ingenium tam atrox iniuria accendisset. "ferro hinc tibi submovendus sum, Appi" inquit, "ut tacitum feras quod celari vis. virginem ego hanc sum
20 ducturus nuptamque pudicam habiturus.

12 **adversus:** prep. + acc. **iniuriam**; the phrase modifies **fremerent**.

12–13 **cum multi magis fremerent quam quisquam unus recusare auderet:** The **magis ... quam** construction compares the two actions: "it was more the case that **multi ... fremerent ...** than that ... **unus auderet**."

13 **P. Numitorius:** Publius Numitorius. The name of Verginia's grandfather was derived from that of Numitor, the grandfather of Romulus and Remus. The *gens Numitoria* was an old plebeian clan, with its first attested member being Lucius Numitorius, the plebeian tribune of 470 BCE.

14 **interveniunt:** another historical present.

dataque inter turbam via: Livy's narrative repeatedly conveys the sense of the witnesses as a barrier protecting Verginia. Here the barrier opens to admit her champions.

14–16 **cum multitudo ... crederet:** explanatory; note the imperfect subjunctive indicating secondary sequence.

15 **Icili maxime:** "that of Icilius in particular."

    resisti posse Appio: an impersonal use of the passive infinitive and the dative: "resistance could be made to Appius."

16 **decresse** = **decrevisse.** Assume **Appium** as the subject. The point of the perfect tense is that Appius has already made his decree, so there is no use arguing.

17 **placidum quoque ingenium:** "a mild nature too," "even a mild nature." The effect of **quoque** is to throw emphasis on the preceding word.

18 **"ferro hinc tibi submovendus...":** The position of the word **ferro** focuses attention on the idea of force. Livy's first oration by a plebeian in direct speech, a short and fiery one, opens very dramatically.

    tibi: dative of agent with the passive periphrastic.

19 **tacitum:** adverbial: "silently."

19–20 **virginem ego hanc sum ducturus nuptamque pudicam habiturus:** The future active participles here express not simple futurity but intent (A&G §499.2). **Ducere** here means "to take in marriage."

proinde omnes collegarum quoque lictores convoca; expediri virgas et secures iube; non manebit extra domum patris sponsa Icili. non, si tribunicium auxilium et provocationem plebi Romanae, duas arces libertatis tuendae, ademistis, ideo
25 in liberos quoque nostros coniugesque regnum vestrae libidini datum est.

21 **proinde omnes collegarum quoque lictores convoca:** At the beginning of their second term, the *decemviri* had shocked the people by going about with twelve lictors each instead of circulating those lictors among themselves as they had the previous year. Livy says that the throng of lictors filled the forum (*forum impleverunt*).

21–22 **expediri virgas et secures iube:** To make matters worse, all hundred and twenty lictors had added the axes to their bundles of rods, and they had started using them.

convoca ... iube: Icilius speaks forcefully, first with a pair of commands, which he counters with a negative statement (**non ... manebit**).

22–23 **domum patris sponsa Icili:** Icilius does not name Verginia. Her identity continues to be defined by relationships to her father and her husband-to-be.

23 **tribunicium auxilium et provocationem:** the plebeian tribunate and the right of *provocatio ad populum*: Tradition assigned the origins of the plebeian tribunate to 494 BCE and the first secession of the *plebs*. The power of the tribunes stemmed from the oath taken by the *plebs* to guarantee their inviolability (*sacrosanctitas*). The plebeian tribunes (originally two, then four, but after 449 BCE ten) could summon the *plebs* to assembly, guide it in forming resolutions (*plebiscita*), which later became binding legislation, and veto any act of a magistrate. The right of *provocatio*, appeal to the Roman people against any act of a magistrate, was traditionally credited to a *lex Valeria*, a law of 509 BCE, the first year of the Republic. (It was named after P. Valerius, who helped expel the Tarquins and became consul after Collatinus left Rome.) That law is probably a fictitious retrojection of a later *lex Valeria* from 300 BCE.

24 **plebi Romanae:** dative of disadvantage with **ademistis** (A&G §376), not dative with **provocationem**. Livy uses **provocatio** either alone or with **ad populum**.

duas arces libertatis tuendae: The METAPHOR suggests that Roman **libertas** is under siege; and it adds to the impression that Verginia is surrounded, first by her modesty, then by the protective bystanders, and now by the metaphorical protection of the tribunate and right of *provocatio*.

libertatis tuendae: the gerundive in the objective genitive.

24-26 **ademistis . . . vestrae libidini:** Icilius is now addressing all the **decemviri**.

25 **in liberos quoque nostros coniugesque: in** + accusative, here expressing hostile intent.

25-26 **regnum vestrae libidini datum est:** personified **libido**, itself portrayed as a tyrant. Note the ANTITHESIS of **nostros** and **vestrae**.

saevite in tergum et in cervices nostras: pudicitia saltem
in tuto sit. huic si vis adferetur, ego praesentium Quiritium
pro sponsa, Verginius militum pro unica filia, omnes
30 deorum hominumque implorabimus fidem, neque tu istud
unquam decretum sine caede nostra referes. postulo, Appi,
etiam atque etiam consideres quo progrediare. Verginius
viderit de filia ubi venerit quid agat; hoc tantum sciat, sibi
si huius vindiciis cesserit condicionem filiae quaerendam
35 esse. me vindicantem sponsam in libertatem vita citius
deseret quam fides."

27-27 **saevite in tergum et in cervices nostras: pudicitia saltem in tuto sit:** Note the abruptness produced by ASYNDETON and the shift from the imperative to the jussive subjunctive; the CHIASTIC arrangement of the nouns; and the ANTITHESIS setting the physical (**tergum, cervices**) against the abstract (**pudicitia**).

28 **in tuto sit: in tuto esse** = "to exist safely."

vis: nominative subject of **adferetur.**

28-30 **ego . . . fidem:** If we fill in the ELLIPSES, the sentence runs: **ego praesentium Quiritium fidem pro sponsa implorabo fidem, Verginius militum pro unica filia implorabit fidem, omnes deorum hominumque implorabimus fidem.**

30-31 **istud . . . decretum:** The demonstrative shows Icilius's contempt.

32 **etiam atque etiam:** "more and more," "ever more urgently," especially with verbs of entreaty.

consideres: subjunctive without **ut** after **postulo.**

quo progrediare: indirect question after **consideres. Progrediare** is the alterative to **progrediaris** for second person singular present deponent subjunctive.

32-33 **Verginius viderit:** "let Verginius see."

33 **ubi venerit:** future perfect indicative, "when he arrives."

quid agat: indirect question after **viderit.**

hoc tantum sciat: "only let him know this." **Hoc** looks forward to **sibi . . . esse** (lines 33–35).

33-35 **sibi . . . condicionem . . . quaerendam esse:** another passive periphrastic with a dative of agent, here in indirect speech.

34 **si . . . vindiciis cesserit:** Here **vindiciis cedere** means to "yield to the claim of ownership."

condicionem: here "a marriage contract." Icilius will have nothing to do with Verginia if her reputation is besmirched by time spent away from her father's house and under the control of M. Claudius and Appius Claudius.

35 **vindicantem . . . in libertatem:** The expression **vindicare in libertatem** means "to claim as free (one who asserts he is wrongly held in slavery)." It can also mean "to free a country or people from oppressive rule." Cicero and Caesar used it this way in discussing party politics, as did Augustus in his *Res Gestae*: **rem publicam dominatione factionis oppressam in libertatem vindicavi.**

Icilius's speech and the presence of the lictors has stirred up the crowd. The situation almost turns violent; but Appius avoids a physical confrontation by deferring for one day his decision as to Verginia's status. This will, he claims, give Verginia's father time to return to Rome so that the matter of her parentage can be looked into properly.

[46] concitata multitudo erat certamenque instare videbatur. lictores Icilium circumsteterant; nec ultra minas tamen processum est, cum Appius non Verginiam defendi ab Icilio, sed inquietum hominem et tribunatum etiam nunc
5   spirantem locum seditionis quaerere diceret. non praebiturum se illi eo die materiam; sed ut iam sciret non id petulantiae suae sed Verginio absenti et patrio nomini et libertati datum, ius eo die se non dicturum neque decretum interpositurum: a M. Claudio petiturum, ut
10 decederet iure suo vindicarique puellam in posterum diem pateretur; quod nisi pater postero die adfuisset, denuntiare se Icilio similibusque Icili, neque legi suae latorem neque decemviro constantiam defore. nec se utique collegarum lictores convocaturum ad coercendos seditionis auctores:
15 contentum se suis lictoribus fore.

1–2   **concitata multitudo erat ... circumsteterant:** A series of short, independent clauses sets the scene.

3   **processum est:** impersonal; with **nec ultra minas** a good way of saying "matters did not go beyond threats," without focusing attention on a subject.

3–5   **cum Appius ... diceret:** "while Appius was saying." Note how Icilius's outburst was in direct speech, whereas Appius's is in indirect.

      non Verginiam defendi ... sed ... hominem ... locum seditionis quaerere: the core of Appius's statement. Vile as Appius is, he has a point: Icilius *is* eager to stir up rebellion as well as defend his fiancée.

4–5	**tribunatum etiam nunc spirantem:** a striking METAPHOR.
5	**locum:** here, "opportunity."
5–9	**non praebiturum ... non dicturum neque ... interpositurum ... petiturum:** future infinitives (**esse** is regularly dropped from the future infinitive in indirect speech).
6	**materiam:** here, "occasion."
7	**id:** the temporary release of Verginia to her family's custody.
	petulantiae suae: The reflexive refers to Icilius as subject of **sciret**.
7–8	**Verginio absenti et patrio nomini et libertati:** Note how the recipients of Appius's concession become progressively more abstract.
10	**vindicarique puellam:** Here **vindicare** means "to set free."
	in posterum diem: Translate **in** as "until."
12–13	**legi suae ... decemviro:** datives with **defore**.
	latorem ... decemviro: Appius himself is both **lator** and **decemvir**.
13	**utique:** adv., "on any account," "at all events."
	collegarum: that is, an additional hundred and eight lictors.
14	**ad coercendos seditionis auctores:** ad + the gerundive expressing the purpose or goal of an action.
15	**fore = futurum esse.**

Having bought a little time, Verginia's supporters withdraw in order to plot their strategy. They send messengers immediately to summon Verginius back to Rome, before Appius can send orders that he be kept in camp under guard. In the meantime, M. Claudius insists on bail being deposited in order to ensure Verginia's appearance in court the next day. The bystanders volunteer to provide this. Touched by their goodwill, Icilius thanks them and promises that he will call upon their help the next day.

  cum dilatum tempus iniuriae esset secessissentque advocati
puellae, placuit omnium primum fratrem Icili filiumque
Numitori, impigros iuvenes, pergere inde recta ad portam, et
quantum adcelerari posset Verginium acciri e castris:
20 in eo verti puellae salutem, si postero die vindex iniuriae ad
tempus praesto esset. iussi pergunt citatisque equis nuntium
ad patrem perferunt. cum instaret adsertor puellae ut
vindicaret sponsoresque daret, atque id ipsum agi diceret
Icilius, sedulo tempus terens dum praeciperent iter
25 nuntii missi in castra, manus tollere undique multitudo
et se quisque paratum ad spondendum Icilio ostendere.

16 **cum dilatum tempus iniuriae esset:** "when the moment of injustice had been postponed."

16–17 **secessissentque advocati puellae:** Verginia's supporters withdraw in order to strategize.

17–19 **placuit . . . e castris:** Note the several ways in which Livy conveys a sense of urgency: **omnium primum . . . impigros iuvenes . . . pergere inde recta ad portam . . . quantum adcelerari posset.**

17–18 **fratrem Icili filiumque Numitori:** Note how the message is borne by members of the two families, Verginia's and that of her fiancé.

20 **in eo:** points ahead to **si . . . esset.**

   verti: "turned" or "hinged."

21 **praesto:** adv., "on the spot," "at one's service."

iussi pergunt: The short sentence emphasizes the young men's swift action in response to their orders.

pergunt... perferunt: The historical present verbs help establish a sense of urgency.

citatisque equis: Compare the young princes in the Lucretia story who expend their energy (and that of their horses) on a frivolous contest (1.57.22).

22 **instaret... ut: instare + ut,** "to be insistent that."

23 **vindicaret... daret:** The subject is Icilius.

sponsores: A **sponsor** is a person who formally guarantees the good faith of another.

23-24 **atque id ipsum agi diceret Icilius:** Icilius was stalling for time.

24 **sedulo tempus terens:** "Carefully" or "diligently" using up time seems almost an oxymoron, because the verb **tero** tends to be used of spending time in frivolous activities. Icilius's stalling is in sharp contrast to the youths in the Lucretia story, who were using time irresponsibly (**otium... terebant**, 1.57.12–13).

dum praeciperent iter: with the subjunctive **dum** here denotes intention. The expression **praecipere iter** means "to get the start on others."

25-26 **manus tollere... ostendere:** historical infinitives, suggesting repeated action.

26 **se... paratum = se paratum esse.**

quisque: Each man promises individually.

ad spondendum: with **paratum**, "ready to stand surety," "ready to act as guarantor."

atque ille lacrimabundus "gratum est" inquit; "crastina die vestra opera utar; sponsorum nunc satis est." ita vindicatur Verginia spondentibus propinquis. Appius paulisper moratus
30 ne eius rei causa sedisse videretur, postquam omissis rebus aliis prae cura unius nemo adibat, domum se recepit collegisque in castra scribit, ne Verginio commeatum dent atque etiam in custodia habeant. improbum consilium serum, ut debuit, fuit, et iam commeatu sumpto profectus Verginius
35 prima vigilia erat, cum postero die mane de retinendo eo nequiquam litterae redduntur.

27 **lacrimabundus:** a rare adj., "in tears."

gratum est: "Thank you."

crastina die: in ANTITHESIS with **nunc**. The adjective **crastina** is formed from the adverb **cras**, meaning "tomorrow." **Dies** is feminine when indicating an appointed day.

29 **spondentibus propinquis:** abl. absolute. So far Icilius has kept the matter within the family circle.

29–33 **Appius . . . habeant:** Note the order of clauses in this sentence: It begins with the participial phrase **paulisper moratus** modifying the subject; the participle **moratus** introduces the purpose clause **ne . . . videretur**; there follows a temporal clause, **postquam . . . nemo adibat**. Then, finally, come the main, independent clauses, **domum se recepit collegisque in castra scribit**, followed by the clauses containing the substance of Appius's message.

This is not an extraordinary sentence; in fact, its structure is regular for Livy: one or more subordinate clauses and/or participial phrases, followed by the main clause, followed by a subordinate clause or clauses and/or ablative absolute. What it does is cast in higher relief the speed expressed in the description of Verginia's supporters, who make their decision immediately (**placuit**) and the young men who take the message: **iussi pergunt citatisque equis nuntium ad patrem perferunt** (lines 21–22).

30 **sedisse:** here in its technical meaning "to sit in an official capacity," as magistrate or judge (*OLD* s.v. **sedeo** 3).

34 **ut debuit:** "as was right." Livy editorializes with this parenthetical statement as well as the adjective **improbum** placed at the beginning of the sentence for emphasis.

34-35 **commeatu sumpto profectus Verginius ... erat:** It is a good habit at first to translate the ablative absolute literally: "leave having been procured," but as often in the case of ablative absolutes, when the subject of the main verb is also obviously the person who carried out the action of the participle in the ablative absolute, it is then possible to retranslate actively, "having procured leave, Verginius ..."

35 **prima vigilia:** The night was divided into four watches, starting at sunset.

35-36 **cum ... redduntur:** The principal action in this sentence is in the temporal clause introduced by **cum** and with its verb in the indicative. The construction inverts the logical relations of the two clauses, so that this use is called *cum inversum* (A&G §546 note 4.a).

postero die mane de retinendo eo nequiquam litterae redduntur: Note the buildup of adverbial elements before the subject and the verb; note also their order: the specific day, the specific time of day, the subject of the letter, its efficacy.

[47] at in urbe prima luce cum civitas in foro exspectatione erecta staret, Verginius sordidatus filiam secum obsoleta veste comitantibus aliquot matronis cum ingenti advocatione in forum deducit. circumire ibi et prensare homines coepit
5 et non orare solum precariam opem, sed pro debita petere: se pro liberis eorum ac coniugibus cottidie in acie stare, nec alium virum esse cuius strenue ac fortiter facta in bello plura memorari possent; quid prodesse si, incolumi urbe, quae capta ultima timeantur liberis suis sint patienda? haec
10 prope contionabundus circumibat homines. similia his ab Icilio iactabantur. comitatus muliebris plus tacito fletu quam ulla vox movebat.

1–2   **at in urbe ... staret:** After an **at** expressing a contrast with the preceding statement, this sentence too sets out the adverbial material first: place, time, and the backdrop against which the main clause takes place.

1   **civitas:** The onlookers are described not simply as a crowd, **multitudo**, as before, but as a citizenry.

2   **erecta:** a METAPHOR meaning not that the citizenry has good posture, but that it is attentive and alert.

    sordidatus: Suppliants and accused persons wore mourning clothes to muster sympathy.

    obsoleta: Like her father's, Verginia's shabby appearance is meant to heighten the pathos of the situation.

3   **comitantibus aliquot matronis:** not just any women, but married, therefore in Roman eyes, respectable, women, representatives of an ordered society.

    advocatione: here a body of legal advisors.

4   **in forum deducit:** The verb **deducere** has a number of specific meanings, including that of bringing someone before the court; the verb can also be used of bringing home a bride; and **deducere in forum** is used of introducing a young man to the forum at the start

of his career. The expression's polyvalence captures Verginia's situation: used of a young woman claimed by someone whose interest is *not* honorable marriage, the verb is ironic; and here, in the forum, is where Verginia will go from being the daughter of a family to being a public figure, a symbol of the plebeians' plight under the *decemviri*.

circumire ibi et prensare homines coepit: almost as if Verginius were canvassing for votes.

5 **et non orare solum precariam opem, sed pro debita petere:** Note the position of the verbs with the expression **non ... solum ... sed ...** The opposition is between *supplicating* for help (**opem**) that depends on the mercy of another (**precariam**) and *requesting* return for services rendered (**pro debita**).

pro debita: "as things owed."

5-6 **se ... stare:** Verginius enters into indirect speech.

7 **strenue ac fortiter:** The qualities of being **fortis** and **strenuus** were often combined as the essence of the ideal male Roman.

8 **quid prodesse:** "what good is it?"

incolumi urbe: a concessive use of the ablative absolute.

9 **quae ... ultima timeantur ... sint patienda:** Livy has switched his subordinate verbs from the imperfect (**possent**) to the present subjunctive in order to render Vergilius's rhetorical question more vivid.

capta = **capta urbe**, a conditional use of the ablative absolute.

9-10 **haec prope contionabundus circumibat homines:** A little RING COMPOSITION brings full circle a passage that began with **circumire**. **Haec** is the direct object of the verbal adjective **contionabundus**. Like **his**, and **similia**, it denotes things people say.

10 **his:** dative with **similia**.

11-12 **comitatus muliebris plus tacito fletu quam ulla vox movebat:** Although grammatically the comparison is between **comitatus muliebris** and **ulla vox**, the logical comparison is between their silent tears and any talk.

Appius ascends the tribunal, interrupts the proceedings, and, after offering a specious pretext for his decision, decrees Verginia to be a slave.

    adversus quae omnia obstinato animo Appius—tanta vis amentiae verius quam amoris mentem turbaverat—in
15 tribunal escendit, et ultro querente pauca petitore quod ius sibi pridie per ambitionem dictum non esset, priusquam aut ille postulatum perageret aut Verginio respondendi daretur locus, Appius interfatur. quem decreto sermonem praetenderit, forsan aliquem verum auctores antiqui
20 tradiderint: quia nusquam ullum in tanta foeditate decreti veri similem invenio, id quod constat nudum videtur proponendum, decresse vindicias secundum servitutem.

13   **adversus:** prep. + acc. **quae omnia** (a connective relative); the entire phrase modifies the ablative absolute **obstinato animo**.

13-18   **Appius ... escendit ... Appius interfatur:** Note that Appius is the subject of the main verbs that convey what his position allows him—the right to climb the tribunal; the right to interrupt other speakers.

13-14   **tanta vis ... turbaverat:** Livy is fonder of parenthetical statements than are most Latin historians.

   vis amentiae verius quam amoris: a variation on the **amans/amens** theme.

   Note that **verius** is the comparative adverb, not **magis**, as one might expect. The contrast between truth and falsehood runs through this passage.

15   **ultro:** adv., here, "unprovoked."

   querente pauca: "saying a few words of complaint."

15-16   **quod ius ... dictum non esset:** the substance of the complaint.

16   **per ambitionem:** the seeking for support by Verginius and Icilius.

17-18   **respondendi ... locus:** objective gen., "opportunity/chance of responding."

18-19 **quem decreto sermonem praetenderit:** indirect question after **tradiderint.**

decreto: dat. with **praetenderit.**

19-20 **forsan ... tradiderint:** concessive. This is clearly Livy's own opinion.

19 **aliquem verum = aliquem sermonem verum.**

auctores antiqui: By referring to the "authorities of old," Livy nods to the tradition of historical writing.

20 **quia nusquam ullum in tanta foeditate:** Livy's language is strong and vehement.

21 **decreti:** subjective (possessive) genitive with **tanta foeditate.**

veri: gen. with **similem**, again assuming **sermonem.**

21-22 **id ... nudum videtur proponendum:** a gerundive expressing obligation. Although the construction **id ... videtur proponendum** is probably personal, it works best to translate **videtur** as impersonal, "it seems ... "

21 **quod constat:** "which is agreed."

22 **decresse vindicias secundum servitutem:** Livy has maintained suspense by deferring **servitutem** to the end.

The reaction to Appius's decree is astounded silence at first; then the women collectively give voice to their grief; their lament provides a chorus to Verginius's emotional outburst.

    primo stupor omnes admiratione rei tam atrocis defixit; silentium inde aliquamdiu tenuit. dein cum M. Claudius
25 circumstantibus matronis iret ad prehendendam virginem, lamentabilisque eum mulierum comploratio excepisset, Verginius intentans in Appium manus, "Icilio" inquit, "Appi, non tibi filiam despondi et ad nuptias, non ad stuprum educavi. placet pecudum ferarumque ritu promisce in
30 concubitus ruere? passurine haec isti sint, nescio: non spero esse passuros illos, qui arma habent."

23   **primo:** with **inde**, and **dein**, marks the stages in events.

23-24 **stupor ... silentium:** Note how the abstractions come to the fore as the subjects of the transitive verbs.

      rei ... atrocis: objective gen. with **admiratione**.

24-26 **cum M. Claudius ... iret ... eum ... comploratio excepisset:** Note how Claudius goes from being the subject of the first **cum**-clause to the object of the second.

25   **circumstantibus matronis:** The married women form both an audience of onlookers and a barrier—one morally although not physically forceful—around Verginia.

      ad prehendendam virginem: ad + gerundive expressing purpose. The use of **virginem** singles out Verginia from the surrounding **matronae**. The verb for arresting a person, **prehendere**, means to seize physically, and thus emphasizes the predatory nature of Claudius's action.

27   **Verginius intentans in Appium manus:** As M. Claudius reaches out to seize Verginia (**ad prehendendam virginem**), her father extends his hands toward Appius.

27-28 **Icilio ... tibi:** datives with **despondi**.

28 **ad nuptias, non ad stuprum:** Here **ad** refers to the end or purpose in mind.

29 **placet:** impersonal.

pecudum ferarumque ritu: a contrast between the society of humans, which is supposed to be orderly, and the random mating of animals, both wild and domestic.

promisce: adv.

30 **passurine ... sint:** the subjunctive of the first periphrastic conjugation in an indirect question about the future.

isti: a contemptuous reference to mere onlookers, in contrast to **illos**.

31 **esse passuros:** future infinitive after **spero**. For verbs of hoping, expecting, and the like taking the construction of indirect speech, see A&G §579.c.

qui arma habent: a descriptive relative clause, with the verb therefore in the indicative.

An official calls for silence, and an enraged Appius declares that he has discovered signs of sedition in the city. Accordingly, he has brought an armed following for the purpose of preventing civil unrest. He orders one of his lictors to clear away the crowd so that he can seize Verginia.

cum repelleretur adsertor virginis a globo mulierum circumstantiumque advocatorum, silentium factum per praeconem.

[48] decemvir alienatus ad libidinem animo negat ex hesterno tantum convicio Icili violentiaque Vergini, cuius testem populum Romanum habeat, sed certis quoque indiciis compertum se habere nocte tota coetus in urbe factos esse ad
5 movendam seditionem. itaque se haud inscium eius dimicationis cum armatis descendisse, non ut quemquam quietum violaret, sed ut turbantes civitatis otium pro maiestate imperii coerceret. "proinde quiesse erit melius. i," inquit, "lictor, submove turbam et da viam domino ad
10 prehendendum mancipium." cum haec intonuisset plenus irae, multitudo ipsa se sua sponte dimovit desertaque praeda iniuriae puella stabat.

47.32–48.10   **cum repelleretur ... cum haec intonuisset:** A pair of circumstantial **cum**-clauses describe the background to important steps in the narrative: the quieting of the crowd so that Appius can speak, and the crowd's desertion of Verginia.

32   **virginis:** objective gen. with **adsertor**.

32–33   **mulierum circumstantiumque advocatorum:** genitive of material with **globo**.

33   **factum = factum est.**

per: "through the agency of."

1	**animo:** abl. of specification with **alienatus**.
1–3	**negat... tantum... sed... quoque:** "says that not only... but also." **Tantum** places emphasis on **hesterno**, and **quoque** on **certis**.
4	**compertum se habere:** The perfect passive participle with **habere** (A&G §497.b) means almost the same as the perfect of the verb (here it would be **compertum esse**), but **habere** indicates that the *effect* of the verb is continuous.
	nocte tota: abl. of time when.
4–5	**ad movendam seditionem:** ad + gerundive expressing purpose.
5	**se haud inscium = se haud inscium esse.** Note the LITOTES.
5–6	**eius dimicationis:** objective gen. with **inscium**.
7	**turbantes = illos turbantes.**
	otium: direct object of **turbantes**.
7–8	**pro maiestate imperii:** "in the interest of the dignity of his office."
8	**proinde:** This adverb links Appius's direct speech to the indirect speech that preceded it.
	quiesse = quievisse. The infinitive is the subject of **erit**.
	melius: predicate adjective in agreement with the infinitive **quiesse**.
9	**i:** imperative of **ire**. The first of Appius's three arrogant commands.
9–10	**ad prehendendum mancipium:** This gerundive with **ad** shows how a spatial expression (the lictor is to clear a path to Verginia) can overlap with an expression of purpose.
10	**intonuisset:** a striking verb that suggests Appius imposes his authority in a Jove-like manner.
11	**multitudo ipsa se sua sponte dimovit:** The crowd parts before the lictor needs to part it. Note the word order, which keeps the intensifying adjective, reflexive pronoun, and reflexive adjective together.
	praeda: in APPOSITION to **puella**.
12	**iniuriae:** genitive with **praeda**.

Verginius asks permission to take his daughter and nurse aside and question the nurse. He does not say why Verginia needs to be present, but Appius does not object. Perhaps the idea is that if Verginia hears the nurse admit to her father that Verginia is not his daughter, she will accept the fact of her enslavement to Appius. Verginius's motive is of course to isolate his daughter near a place where he can lay hands on a weapon.

tum Verginius ubi nihil usquam auxilii vidit, "quaeso" inquit, "Appi, primum ignosce patrio dolori, si quo inclementius in te
15 sum invectus; deinde sinas hic coram virgine nutricem percontari quid hoc rei sit, ut si falso pater dictus sum aequiore hinc animo discedam." data venia seducit filiam ac nutricem prope Cloacinae ad tabernas quibus nunc novis est nomen atque ibi ab lanio cultro arrepto, "hoc te uno quo
20 possum" ait "modo, filia, in libertatem vindico." pectus deinde puellae transfigit respectansque ad tribunal "te" inquit, "Appi, tuumque caput sanguine hoc consecro."

13   **auxilii:** partitive genitive with **nihil**.

13–14   **quaeso ... ignosce:** The two verbs are in a paratactic construction; that is, neither is subordinate to the other.

14   **patrio dolori:** dat. with **ignosce**.

quo = aliquo, "in any way."

14–15   **in te sum invectus:** The passive of **inveho** means "to ride, drive, sail in to attack," and (metaphorically), "to attack verbally." The English expression "to inveigh against" preserves the Latin, but not the METAPHOR, of attack.

15   **sinas = sinas me**; subjunctive without **ut**, after **quaeso**.

coram virgine: coram + abl., "in the presence of."

16   **quid hoc rei sit:** indirect question. **Rei** is another partitive genitive: "what of a matter is this?" "what is this matter?"

16–17   **si falso pater dictus sum ... discedam:** "if I have (in fact) been called father falsely ... I might withdraw."

17 **data venia:** ablative absolute.

17-21 **seducit . . . transfigit:** The present indicative verbs convey events vividly.

18 **prope Cloacinae = prope templum Cloacinae.** This is the shrine of Venus Cloacina, that is, the goddess of the Cloaca Maxima, Rome's main sewer, originally a stream that drained the Forum, but which had been made into a sewer under the Tarquins. The reference to Cloacina, then, is an INTRATEXTUAL ALLUSION calling to mind the tyranny of the Tarquins, under whom the people were "plunged down" into constructing the sewer (**in fossas cloacasque exhauriendas demersae**, page 178, line 36); but it also invokes the goddess in her role as purifier. A shrine to Venus Cloacina appears on a silver denarius of 42 BCE.

18-19 **quibus nunc novis est nomen:** the "New Shops." Livy identifies not only an old and famous landmark (the Cloaca Maxima) but also a change in the landscape of his own time (**nunc**). Any Roman could see the place and reimagine the revolutionary events that took place there. **Novis** is dative by attraction into the possessive dative of **quibus**.

19 **ab lanio:** The butcher's shop provides a convenient weapon. Moreover, Verginius's use of a butcher's knife puts Verginia in the position of a lamb or pig, that is, a domestic, and therefore potentially sacrificial, animal.

19-20 **hoc te uno quo possum . . . modo:** Note the word order, which keeps the pronouns (**hoc, te**) together, and the short relative clause, **quo possum**, that defines **uno . . . modo**. Translate "in the only way I can."

20-22 **vindico . . . consecro:** Livy's narrative brings together words and actions in a manner that calls to mind sacrificial ritual. With the verb **vindico** Verginius defines his act of killing his daughter as an assertion of her freedom; he kills her; then, turning to the tribunal, with the verb **consecro** he redefines the murder into a blood sacrifice that is at the same time a curse on Appius. Compare Lucretia's words before her suicide, as well as Brutus's in response to it (1.58.35–37; 1.59).

An outcry follows as Verginius makes his escape and Icilius and Numitorius take on roles as public speakers similar to those played by Brutus and Collatinus in the story of Lucretia. One striking difference is the presence of the chorus of women. Lucretia's story allowed her to speak but set her (and her voiceless serving women) apart from the regal wives. Verginia's story does not give its central victim a voice; but it allows Roman plebeian matrons to express themselves collectively on private concerns in a manner that complements the men's complaints about public affairs.

*In the aftermath of these events, Appius goes into exile; the army and the plebeians go on strike, withdrawing first to the Aventine Hill, then to the Sacred Mount (**Mons Sacer**), until the **decemviri** are removed from office and replaced, first with military tribunes, then with consuls once again. Appius returns to Rome and is arrested but kills himself before his trial.*

    clamore ad tam atrox facinus orto excitus Appius
    comprehendi Verginium iubet. ille ferro quacumque ibat
25 viam facere, donec multitudine etiam prosequentium tuente
    ad portam perrexit. Icilius Numitoriusque exsangue corpus
    sublatum ostentant populo; scelus Appi, puellae infelicem
    formam, necessitatem patris deplorant. sequentes clamitant
    matronae: eamne liberorum procreandorum condicionem,
30 ea pudicitiae praemia esse?—cetera quae in tali re muliebris
    dolor, quo est maestior imbecillo animo, eo miserabilia magis
    querentibus subicit. virorum et maxime Icili vox tota
    tribuniciae potestatis ac provocationis ad populum ereptae
    publicarumque indignationum erat.

23   **clamore ... orto:** causal ablative explaining **excitus**; Livy introduces a series of short clauses and sentences that reflect the speed of events.

        ad: "in response to."

24   **iubet:** the first in a series of historical presents (**ostentant, deplorant, clamitant**), all verbs denoting some form of communication. Together they quicken the pace of the narrative.

        ille: The ANTITHESIS with **Appius** takes the place of a conjunction.

25   **facere:** historical infinitive, "he kept making."

25–26   **exsangue corpus sublatum:** A direct translation of the perfect passive participle is clumsy and is better replaced with an active construction, such as "the bloodless body, which they had taken up..."

27   **ostentant:** a frequentative, which denotes a forcible or repeated action; because the men lament multiple topics, the sense of repeated action is probably the strongest here.

27–28   **scelus Appi, puellae infelicem formam, necessitatem patris:** Two instances of CHIASMUS and the resulting ANTITHESIS take the place of connectives in this list.

28   **clamitant:** another frequentative, again with multiple objects: **eamne... esse?** and **cetera** (lines 29–30).

29–30   **eamne... ea...:** Note the ANAPHORA, here conveying heightened emotion: "was *this* the condition... were *these* the prizes?" The women's role is to present grief; the men's, in contrast, anger. With the nouns **condicionem... praemia**, the women cast their complaints in legal/military terms that point to their interest in the city's future.

31   **quo... eo:** correlative: "the more... the more."

imbecillo: lacking in intellectual strength; presumably not trained by philosophy to cope with **dolor**.

magis: with **subicit**.

32   **subicit:** not a historical but a gnomic or aoristic present, i.e., a statement of a general truth (A&G §465).

virorum et maxime Icili: Once again, ANTITHESIS, here with **matronae**, serves in place of a conjunction.

vox tota: "all the talk." Icilius now leaves the mourning of Verginia to the women.

33–34   **tribuniciae potestatis... provocationis... ereptae... publicarum... indignationum:** objective genitives with **vox tota**.

33   **provocationis ad populum ereptae:** The participle, not the noun, contains the main idea: "the snatching away of the right of **provocatio**" (A&G §497).

34   **publicarumque indignationum:** public resentments, as opposed to the private, here the violation of a father's authority over his daughter.

Heinrich Friedrich Füger (1751–1818) was a German painter of court portraits and historical scenes. His *Death of Virginia* depicts Verginia, now dead, in the arms of her nurse as Verginius (center) accuses Appius (right, in toga). The painting is now in the Staatsgalerie Stuttgart in Stuttgart, Germany. (© José Luiz Bernardes Ribeiro / CC BY-SA 4.0)

Appendix 1: Historical Timeline

Date	Historical and Political Events	Significant texts/ literary events
BCE		
ca. 1180	Traditional date of the fall of Troy	
753	Traditional date of the founding of Rome	
510	Traditional date of the expulsion of the Etruscan king Tarquinius Superbus	
509	The beginning of the Republic	
451–450	Development and publication of Rome's first law code, the Twelve Tables, under the Decemvirs	
264–241	First Punic War	
218–201	Second Punic War	
149–146	Third Punic War	
106	Birth of Pompey the Great	Birth of Cicero
108	Birth of L. Sergius Catilina	
100		Birth of Julius Caesar
86		Birth of Sallust

70		Birth of Vergil
65		Birth of Horace
64		Possible date for birth of Livy
63	Cicero's consulship; Catilinarian conspiracy; birth of Octavian (Augustus)	
60	Caesar, Crassus, and Pompey make agreement known as the First Triumvirate	
59		Possible date for birth of Livy
50–45	Civil War between Caesar and Pompey the Great	
48	Battle of Pharsalus; death of Pompey the Great	
44	Assassination of Julius Caesar	
44–40		Sallust's *Conspiracy of Catiline* appears
43–31	Civil War	
43	Mark Antony, Octavian, and Lepidus make agreement known as the Second Triumvirate; proscription and murder of Cicero	
ca. 41–ca. 34		Horace works on first book of *Satires*
36	Defeat of Sextus Pompey at Naulochus	
35	Death of Sextus Pompey	

Appendix 1: Historical Timeline

ca. 35		Death of Sallust
31	Octavian defeats forces of Antony and Cleopatra at Battle of Actium	
30	Suicides of Antony and Cleopatra	
29	Octavian celebrates a triple triumph over Egypt, Dalmatia, and Illyria	
ca. 29–19		Vergil works on the *Aeneid*
27	Octavian "restores" government to Senate and people; receives name Augustus	
ca. 26		Livy 1–5 published
ca. 23		Publication of first three books of Horace's *Odes*
19		Death of Vergil
8		Death of Horace; death of Maecenas

CE

12		Possible date for death of Livy
14	Death of Augustus	
14–37	Reign of Tiberius	
17		Possible date for death of Livy
37–41	Reign of Gaius (Caligula)	
38–41		Birth of Martial
41–54	Reign of Claudius	
54–68	Reign of Nero	

69	"Year of Four Emperors": Galba, Otho, Vitellius, and Vespasian	
69–79	Reign of Vespasian	
79–81	Reign of Titus	
80	Opening of Colosseum	
81–96	Reign of Domitian	
102–104		Death of Martial

Appendix 2: Meter

Dactylic Hexameter
(Horace, *Satire* 1.6; Martial 6.64; Vergil, *Aeneid*)

The meter of the *Iliad*, the *Odyssey*, the *Aeneid*, and Ovid's *Metamorphoses*, the *dactylic hexameter* is the meter of ancient epic. It is also the meter of such didactic (teaching) poems as Hesiod's *Theogony* and Lucretius's *De Rerum Natura* as well as that of satirical and pastoral verse and some of Martial's poems. The *dactylic hexameter* consists of six (*hex* = six) metrical feet, called *dactyls* (*dactylos* = finger), each formed by one long syllable followed by two shorts: (– ᴗ ᴗ). The two short syllables (ᴗ ᴗ) can be replaced by one long (–) anywhere in the first five feet, although Latin poets rarely do so in the fifth foot. (When they do, the effect is noticeable.) The last foot is always treated as two long syllables (whether long or short by nature, that last syllable is treated as a long). A hexameter line, then, has from twelve to seventeen syllables:

$$- \smile\smile \mid - \smile\smile \mid - \smile\smile \mid - \smile\smile \mid - \smile\smile \mid - \, -$$

A *caesura* (from *caedere*, to cut) occurs whenever a word break falls within a metrical foot. Each line generally has one principal *caesura*, falling usually after the long syllable of the third or fourth foot. It is generally accompanied by a break in sense. When the main *caesura* falls in the fourth foot, there is usually an additional *caesura* in the second.

— Other Dactylic Meters —

Elegiac Couplet
(Martial 10.10, 11.32, 11.56)

The *elegiac couplet* consists of a dactylic hexameter followed by a "pentameter" (a line that is not really five feet, but 2½ + 2½ feet). This is the traditional meter of epigram, mournful laments, and love elegy.

$$- \smile\smile \mid - \smile\smile \mid - \smile\smile \mid - \smile\smile \mid - \smile\smile \mid - \, \smile$$
$$- \smile\smile \mid - \smile\smile \mid - \parallel - \smile \smile \mid - \smile \smile \mid -$$

Note the *caesura* after the first half of the second line. The words that end each half line are often grammatically connected. Note also that in the "pentameter" one long syllable can replace two shorts only in the first half of the line.

Elegiac couplets are generally self-contained. That is, there is usually a break in thought at the end of each pair of lines.

Hendecasyllables
(Martial 1.35, 1.41, 10.20, 11.6, 12.61)

Hendecasyllables take their name from the Greek word for "eleven," *hendeca*. Catullus frequently uses this meter, as does Martial.

x x − ᴗ ᴗ − ᴗ − ᴗ − x

(Each of the first two syllables may be either long or short, but they cannot *both* be short at the same time.) There is usually a *caesura* after the fifth or sixth syllable.

Sapphic Strophes
(Horace, *Ode* 1.2)

This meter, which takes its name from the poet Sappho of Lesbos, is one of Horace's favorites. It consists of three Sapphic *hendecasyllables* and one Adonic (− ᴗ ᴗ − −).

— Iambic Meters —

Iambic Strophes
(Horace, *Epode* 7)

Iambic strophes consist of an *iambic trimeter* followed by an *iambic dimeter*. An iamb consists of a short syllable followed by a long (ᴗ −). The principal *caesura* in the trimeter is after the fifth or seventh syllable (so as not to divide the line equally).

x − ᴗ − x − ᴗ − x − ᴗ −
x − ᴗ − x − ᴗ −

Limping Iambics
(Martial 11.98)

The so-called *limping iambics* take their name from the spondee $(-\ -)$ that replaces the final iamb $(\smile\ -)$ and brings the end of the line to a jolting halt.

$$\times - \smile - \times \parallel - \smile - \smile - - -$$

The *caesura* usually falls after the fifth syllable.

Second Pythiambic
(Horace, *Epode* 16)

Second Pythiambics consist of a dactylic hexameter alternating with iambic trimeter.

$$- \overset{\smile}{\smile} \mid - \overset{\smile}{\smile} \mid - \overset{\smile}{\smile} \mid - \overset{\smile}{\smile} \mid - \overset{\smile}{\smile} \mid - -$$
$$\times - \smile - \times - \smile - \times - \smile -$$

Appendix 3: Glossary of Rhetorical Terms, Figures of Speech, and Metrical Devices

adynaton: an impossibility.

aetiology: a story that explains the origins of, for example, a custom or a place-name.

alliteration: repetition of the same consonant sound at the beginnings of words in a sequence or otherwise closely connected.

anadiplosis: "doubling back," the repetition of a word or several words; specifically, the beginning of a clause with the word that ended the previous clause.

anairesis: "taking away," a series of negatives.

anaphora: repetition of the same word or phrase at the beginning of a series of clauses or phrases.

antithesis: words or ideas set against or opposed to one another in a parallel construction.

apostrophe: a figure of speech in which the writer (or narrator) turns to and addresses an imaginary character, sometimes the reader.

apposition: the placing together of two or more words or phrases that are grammatically parallel.

archaism: the use of an old, or obsolete, and therefore archaic word or form of word.

assonance: repetition of the same vowel sound in words close to one another.

asyndeton: the lack of conjunctives between words or clauses.

brevitas: brevity of diction, expression using as few words as possible.

chiasmus: the reversing of the order of words in pairs of corresponding phrases (ABBA). Chiastic word order displays such reversal.

congeries: a collection, heap, or pile of words or phrases.

ellipsis: omission of a word or words necessary to complete the sense.

exemplum: a paradigm or model, a moralizing story or anecdote.

hypallage: see **transferred epithet**.

hyperbaton: the separation of words that usually belong together.

inconcinnitas: a violation of expectations for parallel construction.

intertextual allusion: a quotation, citation, or other reminiscence of one literary work by another.

intratextual allusion: a quotation, citation, or other reminiscence of one part of a literary work within the text of the same work.

juxtaposition: placing two words side by side to compare or contrast.

litotes: understatement that affirms something by negating its opposite (e.g., "not bad" for "good").

metaphor: an implied comparison, in which a word ordinarily used of one thing is applied to another.

metonymy: the change of a name; the substitution of one word for another with which it stands in close relation.

onomatopoeia: the use of words to imitate other sounds.

oxymoron: the juxtaposition of words that seem to contradict one another.

paronomasia: word play with similar sounding words; etymological word play.

parataxis: the placing of clauses one after another without conjunctions indicating coordination or subordination.

personification: the assigning of personal qualities to a thing.

pleonasm: redundancy, the use of superfluous words.

polyptoton: repetition of the same word, but in different cases.

prolepsis/proleptic: the anticipation of a result of the action of a verb.

rhetorical question: a question that does not expect an answer, but is asked for effect.

ring composition: a narrative structure in which a sequence of ideas moves toward a central point, then moves on from that point in reverse order.

simile: a comparison between two things, using, in English, "like" or "as," in Latin, *ceu, ut,* or *velut.*

synchesis: generally, the "confusion" of word order in a sentence for rhetorical effect; more specifically, interlocking word order.

synechdoche: a form of **metonymy**; the use of the part for the whole or the whole for a part.

tmesis: the separation of two parts of a compound word by an intervening word or words.

topos: a commonplace, a traditional theme in literature.

transferred epithet (hypallage): a figure in which an adjective grammatically modifies a noun other than the one it actually describes.

variatio: deliberate variation of expression, construction, or vocabulary in order to avoid tedious repetition.

zeugma: the linking of two different words to a verb or an adjective that properly goes with only one of them.

Appendix 4: Family Tree of the Tarquins

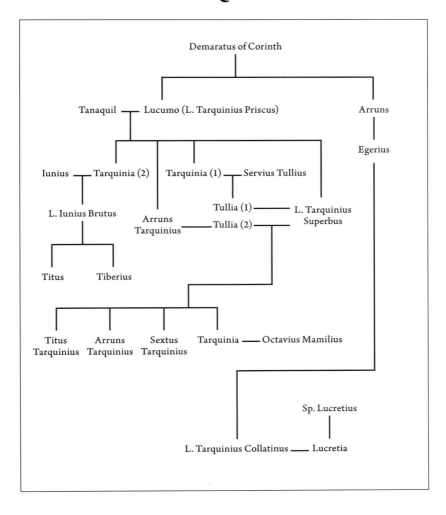

Commentaries for Further Reading

— Horace —

Gowers, Emily. *Horace Satires I*. Cambridge; New York: Cambridge University Press, 2012.

Mankin, David. *Horace Epodes*. Cambridge; New York: Cambridge University Press, 1995.

Meyer, Roland. *Horace Odes Book I*. Cambridge; New York: Cambridge University Press, 2012.

Nisbet, R. G. M., and Margaret Hubbard. *A Commentary on Horace, Odes, Book I*. Oxford: Clarendon Press, 1970.

Nisbet, R. G. M., and Margaret Hubbard. *A Commentary on Horace, Odes, Book II*. Oxford: Clarendon Press, 1978.

Shorey, Paul, and Gordon Jennings Laing. *Horace: The Odes and Epodes*. Boston: B. H. Sanborn, 1923.

Watson, Lindsay. *A Commentary on Horace's Epodes*. Oxford; New York: Oxford University Press, 2003.

— Livy —

Greenough, J. *Livy, Books I and II*. Boston, London: Ginn, 1891.

Ogilvie, R. M. *A Commentary on Livy Books I–V*. Oxford: Clarendon Press, 1965.

— Martial —

Shackleton Bailey, D. R. *Martial, Epigrams*. 3 vols. Loeb Classical Library. Cambridge, Mass.: Harvard University Press, 1993.

Watson, Lindsay, and Patricia Watson. *Martial, Select Epigrams*. Cambridge; New York: Cambridge University Press, 2003.

— Sallust —

McGushin, Patrick. *C. Sallustius Crispus, Bellum Catilinae: A Commentary*. Brill, 1977.

Ramsey, J. *Sallust's Bellum Catilinae*. 2nd ed. American Philological Association Texts and Commentaries. Oxford and New York: Oxford University Press, 2007.

— Vergil —

Harrison, S. J. *Vergil Aeneid 10*. Oxford: Clarendon Press, 1991.

Latin-to-English Glossary

This word list generally follows the definitions given in the *Oxford Latin Dictionary* and to a lesser degree Lewis and Short's *A Latin Dictionary*; it aims at a middle course between simply glossing the words in the text and giving some impression of their range of meaning.

A

a *or* **ab,** *prep. + abl.,* from; away from; by (*agent*)

abditus, -a, -um, *adj.,* hidden, secret

abdo, -ere, -idi, -itum, to conceal, hide

abeo, -ire, -ii/-ivi, -itum, to go away, depart

abicio, -cere, -eci, -ectum, to throw away, throw down, abandon

abigo, -igere, -egi, -actum, to drive away, drive off, reject

abominor, -ari, -atus, *originally of bad omens:* to wish to nullify; *also,* to abhor, detest, execrate

Aborigines, -um, *m. pl.,* a race of pre-Roman inhabitants of Italy

abrogo (1), to repeal (a law); to disregard, repudiate

abscindo, -ere, -scidi, -scissum, to tear off, break away

absolvo, -vere, -ui, -utum, to free from, release; to acquit, declare innocent; to pay off

abstinentia, -ae, *f.,* restraint, self-control, (financial) integrity

abstraho, -here, -xi, -ctum, to drag away, remove forcibly; to remove, take away

absum, abesse, afui, to be absent physically, be elsewhere, not be available; to be distant

absurdus, -a, -um, *adj.,* discordant, awkward, out of place, inappropriate

ac. *See* **atque**

accedo, -ere, -cessi, -cessum, to come to, approach, be added

accendo, -dere, -di, -sum, to set on fire, kindle; to stir up

accio, -ire, -ivi/-ii, -itum, to summon, send for, invite

accipio, -ipere, -epi, -eptum, to receive; to accept as valid

accresco, -ere, -crevi, -cretum, to increase, become greater

acer, acris, acre, *adj.,* sharp, fierce, bitter

acerbus, -a, -um, *adj.,* harsh, bitter, violent, grievous, severe

acetum, -i, *n.,* sour wine, vinegar

acies, -ei, *f.,* sharp edge; line of sight; army about to engage; line of battle

Acron, -onis, *m.,* Acron, a Greek killed by Mezentius in *Aeneid* 10
actor, -oris, *m.,* performer, doer
acuo, -uere, -ui, -utum, to sharpen, make keener, intensify
ad, *prep. + acc.,* to, toward
adcelero (1), to quicken one's pace, cause to travel faster; to act quickly
addo, -ere, -idi, -itum, to add in, insert; to attach
adeo, -ire, -ivi/-ii, -itum, to go to, approach
adfecto (1), to aspire to, strive after, grasp
adfero, -rre, attuli, adlatum, to bring along, deliver, fetch; to add (to something), confer
adficio, -icere, -eci, -ectum, to make an impression upon; to affect, stir; to afflict
adimo, -imere, -emi, -emptum, to remove by force; to take away, deprive of
adipiscor, -ipisci, -eptus, to overtake, reach; to gain, acquire
admiratio, -onis, *f.,* wonder, astonishment, surprise
admoneo, -ere, -ui, -itum, to remind, give advice to, urge, warn
admoveo, -movere, -movi, -motum, to move (something) near (to), bring into contact (with), lead toward, bring up, apply
adorior, -iri, -ortus, to attack, assault; to accost; to attempt

adsequor, -qui, -cutus, to follow, overtake, come upon; to acquire, achieve
adsero, -ere, -ui, -tum, to claim; to liberate; to defend; to assert
adsertor, -oris, *m.,* one who formally asserts the status of another, a claimant (of a person as slave or free)
adsisto, -stere, astiti, to stand nearby, take up a position near
adsum, adesse, adfui, to be present; to have come; to be at hand; to give support (to)
adsto, -are, -iti, to stand by, stand waiting
adsurgo, -ere, -rexi, -rectum, to rise to one's feet (as a mark of respect); to stand up, rise, extend upward
adulescentia, -ae, *f.,* youth, young manhood; the young
adulescentulus, -a, -um, *adj.,* very young; *subst. m.,* young man, a mere youth
adulter, -eri, *m.,* illicit lover, adulterer
adulterium, -(i)i, *n.,* adultery
adultero (1), to commit adultery; to mingle, falsify, corrupt
adultus, -a, -um, *adj.,* full-grown, adult, mature
aduncus, -a, -um, *adj.,* hooked, curved
advenio, -venire, -veni, -ventum, to come (to), arrive (at), reach
adventus, -us, *m.,* arrival
adversus, -a, -um, *adj.,* turned toward, facing

adversus, *prep. + acc.,* against, facing
adverto, -tere, -ti, -sum, to turn or direct toward; to direct (the senses) toward
advocatio, -onis, *f.,* body of legal advisors; the functions of an advocate
advocatus, -i, *m.,* legal assistant, professional advocate; helper, supporter
advoco (1), to call upon, summon; to call together
advorsus. *See* **adversus**
aedes, -is, *f.,* dwelling place, house; temple, sanctuary, shrine
aedifico (1), to erect a building, build, construct
aeger, -gra, -grum, *adj.,* ill, sick
aegroto, -are, -avi, -atum, to be sick; to languish, pine, suffer
aemulus, -a, -um, *adj.,* rivaling, jealous, grudging
Aeneas, -ae, *m.,* Aeneas, son of Venus and Anchises, Trojan refugee and ancestor of the Romans
aequabiliter, *adv., compar.* **aequabilius,** equally, equitably; smoothly, justly
aequalis, -is, *m.,* companion of one's own age; contemporary
aequitas, -atis, *f.,* evenness; fairness, equity
aequor, -oris, *n.,* an even surface; the sea
aequus, -a, -um, *adj.,* level, equal, fair, tranquil, calm

aer, aeris, *m.,* air, the atmosphere, the heavens
aes, aeris, *n.,* copper, bronze, brass
aestumo (1), *archaic for* **aestimo,** to value; to assess, judge; to reckon, consider
aestuo (1), to burn fiercely, be hot, blaze; to seethe, boil up; to be agitated, restless
aestuosus, -a, -um, *adj.,* hot, sultry, seething, raging
aetas, -atis, *f.,* one's age, generation; period or time of life; era
aeternus, -a, -um, *adj.,* eternal, everlasting
aevum, -i, *n.,* time, the past, an age
Africus, -a, -um, *adj.,* of Africa, African; *as subst.,* the southwest wind
agedum. *See* **ago**
agellus, -i, *m.,* small plot of land
ager, -gri, *m.,* field, farmland, arable land, territory, district
Agis, -idis, *m.,* Agis, a Lycian in *Aeneid* 10
agito (1), to set in motion, move, stir, busy oneself, consider
agmen, -inis, *n.,* throng, company, column
ago, -ere, egi, actum, to drive; to set in motion; to proceed, deal with; to transact; to debate
agedum, *a colloquial impv.,* Come!
agrestis, -e, *adj.,* rustic, uncultivated, uncivilized, unsophisticated
aio, *defective verb,* to say

alacer, -cris, -cre, *adj.,* lively, active, eager, keen
albus, -a, -um, *adj.,* white, ghastly (of pallor)
Alcathous, -i, *m.,* Alcathous, a Trojan in *Aeneid* 10
ales, alitis, *m., f.,* bird; a bird whose flight is an omen, *hence,* augury, omen
algeo, -ere, -si, to feel cold, be cold, become cold
Algidus, -i, *m.,* Algidus, a mountain in Latium, south of Tusculum
algor, -oris, *m.,* cold
alieno (1), to transfer to someone else; to give up
alienus, -a, -um, *adj.,* of or affecting others; not one's own
alioqui, *adv.,* in other respects, otherwise
aliquamdiu, *adv.,* awhile, for some time
aliquanto, *adv.,* by some amount, to some extent
aliquis, aliqua, aliquid, *pron.,* someone, something, anyone, anything
aliquo, *adv.,* to some place, somewhere
aliquot, *indecl. adj.,* a number, several, some
aliter, *adv.,* otherwise, differently
alius, -a, -ud, *adj.,* other
alii ... alii, some ... others
Allobrox, -ogis, *m.,* the Allobroges, a Gallic tribe, or member of this tribe
almus, -a, -um, *adj.,* nurturing, kindly

alter, -tera, -terum, *adj.,* a second; another; the other (of two)
altus, -a, -um, *adj.,* high, lofty, deep
ambitio, -onis, *f.,* canvassing for votes, striving after popularity, desire for advancement, ambition
ambo, ambae, ambo, *pl. adj. and pron.,* both
ambulator, -oris, *m.,* itinerant trader, peddler
amens, -ntis, *adj.,* out of one's mind, demented; greatly excited, frantic
amentia, -ae, *f.,* the state of being out of one's mind; excitement, frenzy, infatuation
amicio, -cire, -cui/-xi, -ctum, to cover, clothe; (*passive or reflexive*) to dress
amicitia, -ae, *f.,* friendship
amicus, -a, -um, *adj.,* friendly, supporting politically, loyal, favorable
amicus, -i, *m.,* personal friend; lover; political supporter
amitto, -ittere, -isi, -issum, to dismiss, release, give up; to let slip, forfeit, lose
amnis, -is, *m. and f.,* river
amo (1), to love
amor, -oris, *m.,* love
amplus, -a, -um, *adj.,* large, impressive, extensive
Amycus, -i, *m.,* Amycus, a Trojan in *Aeneid* 10
an, *part.,* whether; or
anceps, -ipitis, *adj.,* doubtful, dangerous, wavering

ancilla, -ae, *f.,* maidservant, handmaid
angustus, -a, -um, *adj.,* narrow, confined, tight, straitened
anima, -ae, *f.,* breath, life, vital principle, spirit, soul
animadverto, -tere, -ti, -sum, to pay attention to; to criticize, judge of; to estimate
animal, -alis, *n.,* living creature, animal; animal other than human, beast
animus, -i, *m.,* mind, soul, heart, courage
   in animo mihi est, I intend
annosus, -a, -um, *adj.,* aged, long lived
annus, -i, *m.,* year
annuus, -a, -um, *adj.,* yearly; year-long
ansa, -ae, *f.,* the handle of a cup or jar
ante, *prep. + acc.,* before, in front of
anteeo, -ire, -ivi/-ii, -itum, to walk in front of; to go before, precede
antiquus, -a, -um, *adj.,* ancient, early; of olden time
Ap. = Appius, -i, *m.,* a Roman *praenomen*
aper, apri, *m.,* wild boar
Apollo, -inis, *m.,* Apollo, son of Zeus and Leto, god of poetry, music, archery
appello (1), to name; to speak to
Appenninus, -a, -um, *also* **Apenn-,** *adj.,* of or originating in the Apennines, a mountain range in Italy
appeto, -ere, -ivi/ii, -itum, to try to reach, make for, desire, seek, seek out, attack, "go for"
Appius, -i, *m.,* Appius, a praenomen, especially of the *gens Claudia*
apto (1), to adapt, fit, apply, adjust
apud, *prep. + acc.,* at, near; at the house of; in the presence of
aquila, -ae, *f.,* eagle; image of an eagle
aquosus, -a, -um, *adj.,* abounding in water, wet, rainy
arbor, -oris, *f.,* tree
arcesso, -ere, -ivi/-ii, -itum, to send for, fetch, summon; to arraign
Ardea, -ae, *f.,* the town of Ardea, south of Rome
ardens, -entis, *adj.,* burning, glowing
ardor, -oris, *m.,* a burning, fire, heat; agitation, passion, intensity
arduus, -a, -um, *adj.,* tall, lofty, on high, steep; difficult, troublesome, arduous
Argous, -a, -um, *adj.,* of the Argo
argumentum, -i, *n.,* a process of reasoning; the plot of a play; a narrative (esp. a fictitious narrative)
arma, -orum, *n. pl.,* arms, weapons
armatus, -a, -um, *adj.,* armed
armentum, -i, *n.,* cattle for plowing; drove, herd
armo (1), to arm, equip
armus, -i, *m.,* the forequarter or shoulder of an animal

aro (1), to plow
Arpinus, -a, -um, *adj.,* of Arpinum, the birthplace of Cicero, southeast of Rome
arrigo, -ere, -exi, -ectum, to make stand upright, stand on end
arripio, -ere, -ui, arreptum, to grasp, take hold of; to arrest; to seize, grab
ars, artis, *f.,* technical skill, craft
arvum, -i, *n.,* an arable field, cultivated land; (*pl.*) fields, country, regions
arx, -cis, *f.,* citadel, a strong point in a city
as, assis, *m.,* copper coin, coin of small value, penny, copper
ascendo, -ere, -di, -sum, to go up, climb, mount, ascend
Asia, -ae, *f.,* the continent of Asia, as known to the ancients; the East; (*spec.*) Asia Minor
asper, -era, -erum, *adj.,* rough, harsh, coarse, bristling
aspernor, -ari, -atus, to push away, scorn, spurn, refuse
assumo, -ere, -psi, -ptum, to add, take on, put on; to assume, take up, acquire
ast, *conj.,* but if, however, whereas, while
astrum, -i, *n.,* star, constellation
at, *conj.,* but
ater, -tra, -trum, *adj.,* black, dark-colored, devoid of light, discolored
Athenae, -arum, *f. pl.,* Athens
Atheniensis, -e, *adj.,* of Athens, Athenian; *subst.,* an Athenian
atque, *conj.,* and
atqui, *conj.,* but, and yet, nevertheless
atrox, -ocis, *adj.,* terrible in appearance; frightful, dreadful
auctor, -oris, *m.,* originator, source, person or thing responsible; author
audacia, -ae, *f.,* daring, bravery; recklessness, impudence
audax, -acis, *adj.,* daring, bold; reckless, audacious
audeo, -ere, ausus sum, to dare, be bold
audio, -ire, -ivi/-ii, -itum, to hear
aufero, auferre, abstuli, ablatum, to carry or fetch away, remove
augeo, -gere, -xi, -ctum, to increase, intensify; to extend, amplify, glorify
augur, -uris, *m.,* an observer and interpreter of bird signs; prophet, seer
aura, -ae, *f.,* breeze
aureus, -a, -um, *adj.,* made of gold, golden
auris, auris, *f.,* ear
aut, *conj.,* or; **aut . . . aut,** either . . . or
autem, *part.,* but, moreover, however
auxilium, -(i)i, *n.,* assistance, help, aid; resource
avaritia, -ae, *f.,* greed
Aventinus, -i, *m.,* or **Aventinum, -i,** *n.,* the Aventine Hill, a hill located outside the original sacred boundary of Rome and associated with the plebeians

averto, -tere, -ti, -sum, to turn aside, divert; to change direction, turn away
avide, *adv.,* greedily, hungrily
avidus, -a, -um, *adj.,* greedy, covetous, avaricious
avis, -is, *f.,* bird
avitus, -a, -um, *adj.,* inherited from one's grandfather, ancestral, family
avolo (1), to fly away, fly off
avus, -i, *m.,* grandfather, ancestor

B
barbarus, -a, -um, *adj.,* foreign, barbarous, uncivilized
Barrus, -i, *m.,* the name Barrus, a character in Horace's *Satires*; the name means "elephant"
basiator, -oris, *m.,* one who kisses
basio (1), to kiss
basium, -i, *n.,* kiss
beatus, -a, -um, *adj.,* happy, prosperous, fortunate, blessed
bellator, -oris, *m.,* warrior, fighter
bellum, -i, *n.,* war; a particular war
belua, -ae, *f.,* beast, brute, monster
bene, *adv., comp.* **melius,** well, fittingly, favorably
benefacio, -facere, -feci, -factum, to do a service (to), confer a benefit (on)
benefactum, -i, *n.,* benefit, service, good deed
beneficium, -i, *n.,* service; kindness
benigne, *adv.,* kindly, benevolently
bibo, -ere, -i, to drink

bibulus, -a, -um, *adj.,* given to drink, absorbent, thirsty
biduum, -i, *n.,* a period of two days
bilis, bilis, *f.,* the fluid secreted by the liver, bile; anger, ill temper, spleen
bini, -ae, -a, *adj.,* two to each, two at a time, a set of two
bis, *adv.,* twice; doubly
blande, *adv., compar.* **blandius,** in a coaxing, flattering, or charming manner
blandior, -iri, -itus (*also* **-io**), to behave or speak ingratiatingly (to); to coax, flatter, charm
blandus, -a, -um, *adj.,* charming, ingratiating, winning, persuasive
bonum, -i, *n.,* the good
bonus, -a, -um, *adj.,* good
brevis, -e, *adj.,* short, brief, small
Britannus, -a, -um, *adj.,* of Britain; *subst.,* a Briton
Brutus, -i, *m.,* Brutus, a Roman cognomen; L. Junius Brutus, the first consul
bucca, -ae, *f.,* cheek

C
C. = Gaius, -i, *m.,* a Roman *praenomen*
caballus, -i, *m.,* undistinguished horse, nag, hack
caco (1), to defecate
cacumen, -inis, *n.,* peak, top (*of an object that tapers*), tip, point, extremity
Cadmus, -i, *m.,* the Greek name Cadmus

cado, -ere, cecidi, casum, to fall, drop, perish; to be killed, fall (*esp. in battle*)
Caecilius, -i, *m.,* Caecilius, an addressee of Martial's poems
Caecubus, -a, -um, *adj.,* of Caecubum, a district in the south of Latium noted for its wine
caecus, -a, -um, *adj.,* not seeing, blind, hidden, obscure
caedes, -is, *f.,* killing, slaughter
Caedicus, -i, *m.,* Caedicus, an Etruscan in *Aeneid* 10
caedo, -dere, cecidi, caesum, to strike, kill, murder; to chop
caeles, -itis, *adj.,* dwelling in heaven; *subst. pl.,* divinities, gods
caelo (1), to adorn; to emboss, engrave
caelum, -i, *n.,* the sky, the heavens
Caere, -itis, *n.,* Caere, a city in Etruria
caeruleus, -a, -um, *adj.,* like the sky, blue; blue-eyed
Caesar, -aris, *m.,* Caesar, the cognomen of the *gens Iulia*, especially that of G. Julius Caesar; the cognomen inherited by Octavian/Augustus and the succeeding emperors
calix, -cis, *m.,* cup, goblet
calo, -onis, *m.,* a servant, especially a soldier's servant or attendant
calx, -cis, *f., (m.),* the back of the foot, heel

Campanus, -a, -um, *adj.,* Campanian, of Campania, a region in southern Italy
campus, -i, *m.,* plain, field; *spec.,* the Campus Martius at Rome
candens, -ntis, *adj.,* shining, white, radiant
canis, -is, *m. and f.,* dog
capella, -ae, *f.,* she-goat
capillus, -i, *m.,* the hair of the head, hair
capio, -ere, cepi, captum, to take, seize, capture, acquire, appropriate, choose
caprea, -ae, *f.,* roe deer
Capua, -ae, *f.,* Capua, a large and prosperous town on the Campanian plain
caput, -itis, *n.,* head
carbo, -onis, *m.,* piece of charcoal
careo, -ere, -ui, -itum (+ *abl.*), to be without, be free from, lack
carmen, -inis, *n.,* solemn or ritual utterance; song, poem
caro, carnis, *f.,* flesh, meat
carpo, -ere, -psi, -ptum, to pluck, pull away, tear to pieces, criticize, carp at
carptim, *adv.,* selectively
carus, -a, -um, *adj.,* expensive, dear; beloved, valued
castigator, -oris, *m.,* one who reproves or corrects
castitas, -atis, *f.,* moral or sexual purity, uprightness, chastity
castra, -orum, *n. pl.,* (army) camp
castro (1), to emasculate, castrate
castus, -a, -um, *adj.,* upright, moral, sexually pure, chaste

casus, -us, *m.,* fall, end, chance, occurrence
catenatus, -a, -um, *adj.,* chained, fettered
Catilina, -ae, *m.,* the name Catiline, *esp.* L. Sergius Catilina
catinus, -i, *m.,* large bowl, dish
Cato, -onis, *m.,* the name Cato, referring either to M. Porcius Cato, the severe politician, farmer, and scholar of the second century BCE, or to his great-grandson M. Porcius Cato Uticensis, a foe of Caesar and a man of moral integrity
Catullianus, -a, -um, *adj.,* of, or characteristic of, Catullus
Catullus, -i, *m.,* Catullus the poet
cavus, -a, -um, *adj.,* hollow, hollowed out; containing caves; porous
caveo, -ere, cavi, cautum, to take precautions, beware, be on one's guard
causa, -ae, *f.,* cause, reason; + *preceding gen.,* for the sake of
cautus, -a, -um, *adj.,* wary, cautious, circumspect, prudent
-ce, *deictic particle added to demonstratives*
cedo, -ere, cessi, cessum, to withdraw, give ground, fall back; to yield
celebratus, -a, -um, *adj.,* famous, widely known, distinguished
celebro (1), to throng, fill, crowd; to praise, extol; to make known; to cause to be honored
celer, -ris, -re, *adj.,* fast, speedy, quick, agile
celo (1), to conceal, hide
celsus, -a, -um, *adj.,* raised, elevated, high, lofty
cena, -ae, *f.,* dinner, supper
ceno (1), to dine, eat dinner
censeo, -ere, -ui, -um, to think, suppose; to recommend
censor, -oris, *m.,* censor, one of two magistrates appointed at Rome every five years for a term of eighteen months. Their duties included to register and classify citizens according to their property; upon finding moral or other delinquencies, to degrade citizens to a lower rank, expel members from the Senate, and deprive members of the equestrian order of their horses and rings; and to administer public finances and see to the building of roads, bridges, and aqueducts.
centum, *indecl. adj.,* one hundred
centuriatus, -a, -um, *adj.,* voting in the *comitia centuriata,* the assembly of the Roman people that chose the higher magistrates and decided on capital offences
centurio, -onis, *m.,* the officer in command of a century, centurion
ceratum, -i, *n.,* ointment made using a base of wax and oil
Ceres, -eris, *f.,* goddess of agriculture; (*meton.*) bread, fruit, grain, food

cerno, -ere, crevi, cretum, to distinguish, discern
certamen, -inis, *n.,* competition, contest, dispute, strife
certo (1), to contend for superiority; to fight, dispute
certus, -a, -um, *adj.,* fixed, settled, sure
cervix, -icis, *f.,* neck
cervus, -i, *m.,* stag, deer
ceterus, -a, -um, *adj.,* the other, the rest; (*n. sg. as adv.*) for the rest, moreover, however that may be
ceu, *part.,* like, as if
Chaeremon, -onis, *m.,* Chaeremon, the addressee of one of Martial's poems
charta, -ae, *f.,* "paper" (made from papyrus); *pl.,* pages containing written works; pages
cicer, -ris, *n.,* chickpea
cimex, -icis, *m.,* bedbug
cinaedus, -i, *m.,* catamite (also used of a man of luxurious or effeminate habits)
cinis, -eris, *m.,* ashes
Cinnamus, -i, *m.,* Cinnamus, the name of a barber mentioned by Martial
circa, *adv.,* round about; *prep.* + *acc.,* around, near, about
circum, *adv.,* around; *prep.* + *acc.,* round about, nearby
circumeo, -ire, -ivi/-ii, -itum, to go around, surround, go the round of
circumfero, -ferre, -tuli, -latum, to carry around, pass around, bring around
circumgemo, -ere, to roar around about
circumsto, -are, -eti/-iti, to stand around, gather round, surround
circumvagus, -a, -um, *adj.,* wandering around, flowing around
Circus, -i, *m.,* a racetrack; *spec.,* the Circus Maximus, the great racetrack and stadium between the Palatine and Aventine in Rome
Cisseis, -idis, *f.,* daughter of Cisseus (Hecuba, queen of Troy)
citatus, -a, -um, *adj.,* made to move quickly; hurried
citus, -a, -um, *adj.,* moving quickly, rapid
civilis, -e, *adj.,* of citizens, civil, civic
civis, civis, *m. and f.,* citizen
civitas, -atis, *f.,* an organized community of citizens; a state
clamito (1), to shout repeatedly; to proclaim
clamor, -oris, *m.,* shout, cry
clamosus, -a, -um, *adj.,* given to shouting; loud, noisy
clarus, -a, -um, *adj.,* bright, distinct; celebrated, famous
Claudius, -a, -um, *adj.,* the name of the *gens Claudia*; the name of members of the *gens Claudia*
claudo, -dere, -si, -sum, to close, shut up, confine
claudus, -a, -um, *adj.,* lame, crippled
clavis, -is, *f.,* key

clavus, -i, *m.,* nail; purple stripe (on a tunic)
cliens, -ntis, *m.,* a person attached to someone more politically powerful or more influential; a client
cloaca, -ae, *f.,* underground drain, sewer
Cloacina, -ae, *f.,* a cult title of Venus ("the purifier")
Clonius, -ii, *m.,* Clonius, a companion of Aeneas in *Aeneid* 10
Cn. = Gnaeus, -i, *m.,* a Roman *praenomen*
clusus *also* **clausus, -a, -um,** *adj.,* shut in, enclosed
coactor, -oris, *m.,* collector (of money, taxes)
coalesco, -escere, -ui, -itum, to grow or be joined together; to unite, become unified
cocus *also* **coquus, -i,** *m.,* cook
coena. *See* **cena**
coepi, -isse, -tum, to begin, commence
coerceo, -ere, -ui, -itum, to restrain, confine, restrict, suppress
coetus, -us, *m.,* meeting, encounter; gathering, assembly
cogitatio, -onis, *f.,* the act of thinking, reflection; intention, design
cogo, -ere, coegi, coactum, to drive together, collect; to compel
cohors, -tis, *f.,* contingent, company, armed force

Colchis, -idis, *f.,* a Colchian woman, *esp.* Medea
Collatia, -ae, *f.,* Collatia, a Sabine town near Rome
Collatinus, -i, *m.,* Collatinus, the name of Lucretia's husband
collaudo (1), to commend, praise, eulogize
collega, -ae, *m.,* colleague, associate
colo, -ere, -ui, cultum, to live in; to cultivate, tend, worship
columba, -ae, *f.,* dove, pigeon
coma, -ae, *f.,* the hair of the head
comes, -itis, *m. and f.,* companion, attendant
comisatio, -onis, *f.,* carousing, revelry
comiter, *adv.,* in a friendly manner, pleasantly
comitium, -i, *n., comitium,* the place of public assembly in the Roman Forum; *pl.,* **comitia centuriata,** an assembly of the Roman people voting by *centuriae* for the purpose of electing magistrates and deciding capital issues
comito (1), to go along with, accompany
commeatus, -us, *m.,* the act of coming and going, passage; leave of absence
commentarius, -i, *m.,* notebook, journal, historical record
commode, *adv., compar.* **commodius,** properly, conveniently, agreeably, pleasantly
communis, -e, *adj.,* shared, joint, common

communiter, *adv.,* together, jointly

comperio, -ire, -i, -tum, to learn, ascertain, establish, verify

compertus, -a, -um, *adj.,* ascertained, proved; *subst. n.,* a fact

compitum, -i, *n.,* a place where three or more roads meet; crossroads, road junction

comploratio, -onis, *f.,* lamentation, mourning

comprehendo, -ere, -di, -sum, to unite, seize

comprimo, -imere, -essi, -essum, to compress, crush, squeeze, suppress, stifle, check

concilio (1), to bring or collect together, unite, join; to endear; to acquire

concilium, -(i)i, *n.,* popular assembly, public meeting

concio *also* **concieo, -ire, -ivi, -itum,** to stir up, set in motion, provoke

concito (1), to set in rapid motion, stir up, rouse, incite

conclamo (1), to shout aloud; to mourn, bewail

concordia, -ae, *f.,* harmony, peace, concord

concubitus, -us, *m.,* the act of lying together (for sleeping or dining); sexual intercourse

concurro, -ere, -curri *or* **-cucurri, -cursum,** to run together, meet, clash

concursus, -us, *m.,* a gathering of a crowd; a running together

condicio, -onis, *f.,* situation, circumstance

condo, -ere, -didi, -ditum, to put or insert into, sheathe (a sword), found (a city), establish, put together

confero, -ere, -tuli, -latum, to bring, carry, convey

congelo (1), to cause to freeze; to make harden; to chill

coniunx, -ugis, *m. or f.,* husband, wife

coniuratio, -onis, *f.,* the taking of an oath together, conspiracy, plot

conparo (1), to match, set against, compare

conscendo, -dere, -di, -sum, to go on board, embark, take ship, mount (a horse)

conscientia, -ae, *f.,* the holding of knowledge in common, complicity

consecro (1), to dedicate, devote

conservo (1), to save, keep unharmed, preserve; to maintain, keep to

considero (1), to examine, take notice of, take into consideration

consilium, -(i)i, *n.,* debate, discussion, deliberation; advice, counsel; a deliberative body

consolor, -ari, -atus, to offer consolation, comfort, solace

conspicio, -icere, -exi, -ectum, to catch sight of, witness; *pass.,* to be visible, be noticed, be the object of attention

constantia, -ae, *f.,* firmness, steadfastness, persistence
constanter, *adv., compar.* **constantius,** equably, steadily, resolutely
consto, -are, -iti, to take up position, stand; to be fixed on, established
constringo, -ere, -strinxi, -strictum, to bind, shackle, fetter, restrain
consul, -ulis, *m.,* consul
consulatus, -us, *m.,* the office of consul, consulship
consulo, -ere, -ui, -tum, to consult, take counsel, decide upon, resolve
consulto (1), to deliberate, debate, consult, discuss
consultum, -i, *n.,* decision, resolution, plan, decree
contagium, -i, *n.,* infection
contemno, -nere, -psi, -ptum, to look down upon, despise, scorn; to disregard; to avoid
contendo, -ere, -di, -tum, to stretch, strain, strive for, seek
contentus, -a, -um *from* **contendo,** *adj.,* strained, exerted
contentus, -a, -um *from* **contineo,** *adj.,* content, satisfied
contero, -terere, -trivi, -tritum, to pound to pieces, wear out; (*of time*) to spend, use up
continentia, -ae, *f.,* restraint, self-control
continuo, *adv.,* immediately, straightway, directly

contionabundus, -a, -um, *adj.,* delivering a public speech
contra, *adv. and prep. + acc.,* in opposition, on the other side; against, facing, toward
convenio, -venire, -veni, -ventum, to meet, come together, converge, agree
conventus, -us, *m.,* meeting, assembly
converto, -tere, -ti, -sum, to cause to turn; to direct one's attention, divert
convicium, -i, *n.,* angry noise, clamor; insulting talk, abuse
convictor, -oris, *m.,* friend, companion
conviva, -ae, *m.,* table companion, guest
convivium, -(i)i, *n.,* party, banquet, feast
convoco (1), to summon together, convoke, assemble
convorto. *See* **converto**
copia, -ae, *f.,* supply, abundance; *pl.,* supplies
cor, cordis, *n.,* heart; as center of thought, memory; as seat of intelligence
coram, *adv.,* face-to-face; in person; publicly; openly; *prep. + abl.,* in the presence of
Cornelius, -i, *m.,* Cornelius; a member of the *gens Cornelia;* *spec.,* one of Martial's addressees
cornu, -us, *n.,* horn; projection; extremity; bugle
corona, -ae, *f.,* garland or crown; circle of bystanders

corpus, -oris, *n.,* body
corrumpo, -umpere, -upi, -uptum, to spoil, harm, ruin, taint, corrupt
Corythus, -i, *m.,* Corythus, an ancient town in Etruria
cottidie, *adv.,* every day, day by day
cras, *adv.,* tomorrow
crastinus, -a, -um, *adj.,* of tomorrow, of the next day; **crastina,** *subst., perhaps m.,* tomorrow, the morrow
credibilis, -e, *adj.,* believable, conceivable, plausible
credo, -ere, -idi, -itum, to entrust, believe, suppose; to rely on
credulus, -a, -um, *adj.,* that easily believes, unsuspecting, trustful
creo (1), to create, produce; to elect, appoint
crepo, -are, -ui, to clatter, crack, rattle, tinkle
cresco, -ere, crevi, cretum, to be born, arise, grow, increase
creta, -ae, *f.,* fine, white clay; chalk
crista, -ae, *f.,* plume, crest
crudelis, -e, *adj.,* cruel, merciless, savage
cruento (1), to stain with blood; to wound
cruentus, -a, -um, *adj.,* bloody
cruor, -oris, *m.,* blood (from a wound, or spilled in battle)
crus, -uris, *n.,* leg, lower leg, shin, shank
cubiculum, -i, *n.,* bedroom
cubile, -is, *n.,* couch, bed
cucullus, -i, *m.,* covering for the head, hood
culcita, -ae, *f.,* stuffed mattress, cushion
culpa, -ae, *f.,* fault, error, blame, guilt
culter, -tri, *m.,* knife (esp. used to slaughter sacrificial victims)
cum, *rel. adv.,* when, since; *prep.* + *abl.,* with; **cum ... tum:** *rel. adv.,* **cum** introduces one of two coexisting circumstances or actions; **tum** indicates the more particular or noteworthy of the two
cunctor, -ari, -atus, to hesitate, delay
cunctus, -a, -um, *adj.,* all
cupiditas, -atis, *f.,* passionate desire, longing; lust, greed, avarice
cupido, -inis, *f.,* passionate desire, longing; **Cupido, -inis,** *m.,* the god Cupid, son of Venus
cupio, -ere, -ivi/-ii, -itum, to desire, wish for
cur, *interr. adv.,* why? for what reason?
cura, -ae, *f.,* trouble, care; anxiety, concern; + **esse,** to be an object of care
Curius, -i, *m.,* a member of the *gens Curia,* an early Roman clan
Curius, -a, -um, *adj.,* having to do with the *Curii*
curo (1), to watch over, care for, look after

curro, -rere, cucurri, -sum, to run, gallop; to hurry

currus, -us, *m.,* chariot, wagon; triumphal chariot

curtus, -a, -um, *adj.,* having a part missing, mutilated; (*of animals*) castrated

curulis, -e, *adj.,* of curule rank (i.e., of consuls, praetors, curule aediles); *subst. f.* = **sella curulis,** the chair of state used by consuls, praetors, and curule aediles

cuspis, -idis, *f.,* sharp point, tip; spear, lance

custodia, -ae, *f.,* protection, safekeeping, defense, guard

custos, -odis, *m. and f.,* guardian, sentry, guard, watch

cyathus, -i, *m.,* ladle

Cyrus, -i, *m.,* Cyrus, ruler of the Persian Empire in the mid-sixth century BCE

D

Dama, -ae, *m.,* Dama, a typical slave name

dam(m)a, -ae, *f.,* a member of the deer family

de, *prep. + abl.,* from, down from, about

debeo, -ere, -ui, -itum, to owe, be indebted, be under obligation

decedo, -dere, -ssi, -ssum, to go away, depart, withdraw; to get out of the way, retreat

decemvir, -ri, *m.,* a member of a board of ten

decerno, -ernere, -revi, -retum, to decide, determine

decet, -ere, -uit, to be proper, be fitting, be right

Decius, -i, *m.,* the Roman plebeian *gens Decia, esp.* P. Decius Mus, both father and son who devoted themselves during the wars of the fourth century BCE

declaro (1), to make known, indicate, reveal, show, declare

decorus, -a, -um, *adj.,* suitable, fitting, seemly

decresco, -escere, -evi, -etum, to grow smaller, dwindle, shrink; to decline, weaken, fade

decretum, -i, *n.,* resolve, order, decree

decus, -oris, *n.,* honor, glory; dignity, decorum; beauty, grace

decutio, -tere, -ssi, -ssum, to cause to fall by shaking, knock down; to shake off

dedecus, -oris, *n.,* discredit, disgrace, dishonor, shame

dedignor, -ari, -atus, to reject, spurn, feel contempt for

deditus, -a, -um, *adj.,* devoted (to); attached (to)

dedo, -ere, -idi, -itum, to give up, surrender

deduco, -ere, -duxi, -ductum, to lead away, escort, accompany

defendo, -dere, -di, -sum, to ward off, defend, protect

defero, -rre, detuli, delatum, to carry, convey, bring; to carry downward; to transfer, pay over; to denounce

defigo, -gere, -xi, -xum, to fix; to attach; to petrify, dumbfound
dehinc, *adv.,* after this, from now on, afterward, next
deicio, -icere, -ieci, -iectum, to throw down; to hurl down, drop, cast (as a lot)
dein *or* **deinde,** *adv.,* then, next; henceforth
delenio, -ire, -ii, -itum, to soothe, mollify, soften
deleo, -ere, -evi, -etum, to remove, expunge; to wipe out, annihilate, abolish
delibutus, -a, -um, *adj.,* thickly smeared
delictum, -i, *n.,* misdeed, offense, fault
delubrum, -i, *n.,* temple, shrine, sanctuary
demens, -ntis, *adj.,* out of one's mind, frenzied
demergo, -gere, -si, -sum, to submerge, bury, engulf
demitto, -ittere, -isi, -issum, to send down, drop, lower, let fall; to cast down, throw, plunge
demum, *adv.,* at last, only then; only this
denique, *adv.,* finally, at last
dens, -ntis, *m.,* tooth
densus, -a, -um, *adj.,* thick, close-knit, closely packed
denuntio (1), to make known in advance; to declare; to serve a summons
deploro (1), to lament, complain of; to despair of, give up
depono, -ere, -posui, -positum, to put aside, set down, lay, place, set
depr(eh)endo, -dere, -di, -sum, to seize; to catch; to detect; to come upon
descendo, -dere, -di, -sum, to go or come down; to get down (from); to make a hostile descent on
desero, -ere, -ui, -tum, to abandon, quit; to leave in the lurch
desidia, -ae, *f.,* idleness, inactivity
desilio, -ire, -ui, to leap or jump down
desino, -inere, -(i)i/-ivi, -itum, to leave off, desist, finish, stop
despondeo, -dere, -di, -sum, to promise (a woman in marriage), betroth; to pledge, promise
desum, -esse, -fui, to be wanting, fail (in respect of)
detineo, -inere, -inui, -entum, to hold, detain; to keep from; to cause to remain
deus, -i, *m.,* god; *pl.,* **dei/di/dii, -orum** *or* **deum** (*poetic also* **divum/ divom**)
devotus, -a, -um, *adj.,* devoted, accursed
dext(e)ra, -ae, *f.,* right hand
Diana, -ae, *f.,* Diana, a Roman goddess identified with the Greek Artemis
dicax, -acis, *adj.,* having a ready tongue

dico, -ere, -xi, -ctum, to talk, speak; to say, disclose
dies, diei, *m. (f.),* day
differo, -rre, distuli, dilatum, to carry off in different directions; to spread abroad; to postpone
digitus, -i, *m.,* finger
digno (1), to consider worthy (*usually pass. + abl.*); *with inf.,* to deign, think fit (to)
dignus, -a, -um, *adj.,* suitable, worthy, deserving
dimicatio, -onis, *f.,* battle, fight; struggle, conflict
dimico (1), to contend in battle; to fight
dimidius, -a, -um, *adj.,* half
dimoveo, -overe, -ovi, -otum, to make a parting in, cleave, cause a group of people to part
Dindymus, -i, *m.,* Dindymus, a slave boy addressed in Martial's poems
Dionysius, -(i)i, *m.,* Dionysius, a Greek personal name
dirus, -a, -um, *adj.,* awful, dreadful, dire
dis, ditis, *adj.,* wealthy, rich
discedo, -dere, -ssi, -ssum, to go off in different directions; to split apart; to go away, withdraw
disco, -ere, didici, to aquire knowledge, learn, be informed of
discordia, -ae, *f.,* disagreement, discord, dissension
discrepo, -are, -avi, to be out of harmony or inconsistent with; to differ in opinion, disagree

disertus, -a, -um, *adj.,* skilled in speaking or writing
dispar, -aris, *adj.,* unlike, dissimilar
dispergo, -gere, -si, -sum, to scatter, disperse; to spread
dissentio, -tire, -si, -sum, to disagree, dissent, differ
dissero, -ere, -ui, -tum, to set in order; to treat of, discuss
dissimilis, -e, *adj.,* unlike, different
dissimulator, -oris, *m.,* a person who conceals (his true purpose or character; his knowledge)
dissipo (1), to spread abroad, scatter, disperse
dito (1), to enrich with money
diu, *adv., compar.* **-utius,** for a long time
diurnus, -a, -um, *adj.,* of or belonging to the day
diversus, -a, -um, *also* **-vor-,** turned or facing in different directions, separated, different
divinus, -a, -um, *adj.,* of or belonging to the gods or a god, divine; able to know future things; *subst.,* fortune-teller
dives, -itis, *adj.,* rich, wealthy
divitiae, -arum, *f. pl.,* wealth, riches
divorsus. *See* **diversus**
do, -are, dedi, datum, to give
doceo, -ere, -ui, -tum, to inform, instruct, demonstrate, teach
doctor, -oris, *m.,* teacher, instructor, trainer
doctus, -a, -um, *adj.,* learned, wise, expert

documentum, -i, *n.,* example (serving as a precedent, warning)
Dolichaon, -onis, *m.,* Dolichaon, a man mentioned in *Aeneid* 10 as father of Hebrus
dolor, -oris, *m.,* physical pain; mental distress, anguish
dolus, -i, *m.,* deliberate performance of an unlawful act, guilty intention; trickery, treachery
domesticus, -a, -um, *adj.,* belonging to the home; household
dominatio, -onis, *f.,* dominion, despotism
dominor, -ari, -atus, to rule, be in control; to dominate
dominus, -i, *m.,* master, lord
domo, -are, -ui, -itum, to subdue, subjugate, defeat, overcome
domus, -us *or* **-i,** *f.,* house, home; **domi militiaeque,** at home and at war
donec, *conj.,* until, as long as
dono (1), to reward (with); to present, give
dormio, -ire, -ivi/-ii, -itum, to be or fall asleep, sleep; to be idle
ducenti, -ae, -a, *adj. num.,* two hundred
duco, -ere, -uxi, -uctum, to lead, guide, bring; to consider
ductus, -us, *m.,* military leadership, command
dulcis, -e, *adj.,* sweet, agreeable, pleasant, charming
dum, *adv.,* yet, now; *conj.,* while (+ *indicative*), provided that (+ *subjunctive*) =
duo, -ae, -o, *adj.,* two
duro (1), to make hard, harden, hold out, endure
durus, -a, -um, *adj.,* hard, harsh, hardy
dux, ducis, *m. or f.,* leader, guide, commander, general

E

e. *See* **ex**
ebrius, -a, -um, *adj.,* drunk, intoxicated
echinus, -i, *m.,* sea urchin; an article of tableware, perhaps a saltcellar
educo (1), to bring up, nurture, rear
educo, -cere, -xi, -ctum, to lead or bring out
effero, -rre, extuli, elatum, to bring out, carry out (*spec. in regard to burial*); to lift, raise, make prominent
efficio, -icere, -eci, -ectum, to manufacture, make, construct; to cause to occur, bring about
effugio, -ugere, -ugi, to flee, run away, escape
egeo, -ere, -ui, to need, want, lack
Egerius, -i, *m.,* Egerius, cousin of Tarquinius Superbus
ego, mei, mihi, me, *pron.,* I
egregius, -a, -um, *adj.,* outstanding, excellent, preeminent

eloquentia, -ae, *f.,* the ability to express oneself in words; the quality of fluid and apt speech, eloquence
emendo (1), to free from faults or errors, correct
emitto, -ttere, -si, -ssum, to send out, dispatch; to release, let loose; to give off, emit
enim, *part.,* for
enimvero, *part.,* well, of course; and, in fact; on the other hand (*strengthens an adversative such as* **verum**)
ensis, -is, *m.,* sword
eo, *adv.,* there, to that place
eo, ire, ivi *or* **ii, itum,** to go, come
eques, -itis, *m.,* cavalryman; *pl.,* cavalry
equito (1), to travel on horseback, ride
equus, -i, *m.,* horse
erectus, -a, -um, *adj.,* upright, perpendicular; bold, assured; alert, attentive
ergo, *adv.,* therefore, then
eripio, -ere, -ipui, -eptum, to seize, snatch away, take by force, carry off
Ericaetes, -is, *m.,* Ericaetes, a Trojan in *Aeneid* 10
Erycinus, -a, -um, *adj.,* Erycinian, having to do with Mt. Eryx; a cult title of Venus; *f. subst.,* Venus
escendo, -dere, -di, -sum, to get up (on a platform, etc.), mount
et, *conj.,* and; *adv.,* even, also; **et . . . et . . .,** both . . . and

etenim, *conj.,* and indeed; the fact is
etiam, *adv.,* still, yet, even now, also
Etruscus, -a, -um, *adj.,* Etruscan; *m. as subst.,* an Etruscan
etsi, *conj.,* even if, although
Euanthes, -is, *m.,* Euanthes, a Phrygian in *Aeneid* 10
Eurus, -i, *m.,* Eurus, the east or southeast wind
evenio, -enire, -eni, -entum, to come out, emerge; to happen, come about; to turn out
eventus, -us, *m.,* outcome, result, success
ex, *prep. + abl.,* from, out of
exaequo (1), to make level or equal; to equal, match
excedo, -dere, -ssi, -ssum, to go away, withdraw, depart; to go or extend beyond
excello, -ere, to be superior in height; to be conspicuous, surpass, excel
excio, -ire, -ivi/-ii, -itum, to call out, summon; to stir into action, rouse
excipio, -ere, -cepi, -ceptum, to accept, receive
excito (1), to rouse, stir; to provoke
exemplum, -i, *n.,* example, specimen, precedent, model
exeo, -ire, -ivi/-ii, -itum, to come or go out, move out from
exerceo, -ere, -ui, -itum, to train by practice, exercise; to occupy, employ

exercitus, -us, *m.,* army
exhaurio, -rire, -si, -stum, to swallow up, remove, drain off, deplete
exigo, -igere, -egi, actum, to drive or force out; to remove, eject; to spend time; to exact (payment, service); to demand
existumo *archaic for* **existimo** (1), to value, esteem, judge
expedio, -ire, -ivi/-ii, -itum, to extricate, disengage, let loose, liberate
expello, -ellere, -uli, -ulsum, to drive or force out; to send into exile; to eject, banish
expers, -rtis, *adj.,* having no share of
expertus, -a, -um, *adj.,* well-proved, tested
expio (1), to make atonement, atone; to purify
explano (1), to expound, explain
expono, -ere, -posui, -positum/-postum, to put out; to abandon, expose
exposta. *See* **expono**
expugno (1), to capture, subdue
exsanguis, -e, *adj.,* bloodless
exsecror, -ari, -atus, to curse, take an oath with a curse to fall on whoever fails to keep it
exsequor, -qui, -cutus, to seek after, pursue; to carry out
exsilium *also* **exilium -(i)i,** *n.,* exile
exspectatio, -onis, *f.,* hopeful waiting, expectancy
exspes, *adj. (only nom. sg.),* without hope
exspiro (1), to breathe out, breathe one's last, die
exsul *also* **exul, -lis,** *m. (f.),* a banished person, an exile
exsulatus *also* **exulatus, -us,** *m.,* banishment, exile
extollo, -ere, to lift up, raise; to praise
extra, *adv. and prep. + acc.,* outside of, beyond
extraho, -ere, -xi, -ctum, to pull out, extract, draw out, bring to light

F
Fabius, -i, *m.,* a member of the *gens Fabia,* an ancient and prestigious Roman clan
Fabius, -a, -um, *adj.,* having to do with the *Fabii*
faber, -bri, *m.,* craftsman, workman, artisan
fabula, -ae, *f.,* talk, tale, legend
facies, -iei, *f.,* external form, appearance, face, countenance
facile, *adv.,* easily
facilis, -e, *adj.,* easy
facinus, -oris, *n.,* deed, act; misdeed, crime
facio, -ere, feci, factum, to do, make, bring about
factum, -i, *n.,* deed, act
facundus, -a, -um, *adj.,* eloquent
faex, -cis, *f.,* wine lees, dregs, sediment
falcifer, -era, -erum, *adj.,* bearing a sickle
fallax, -acis, *adj.,* deceitful, treacherous, deceptive

fallo, -ere, fefelli, falsum, to deceive, trick, cheat, elude, fail, disappoint
falsus, -a, -um, *adj.,* erroneous, untrue; in error, wrong; spurious, imitation
fama, -ae, *f.,* report, rumor, public opinion, reputation, renown
fames, -is, *f.,* hunger, starvation
familiaris, -e, *adj.,* of or belonging to one's household or family; personal, familiar
fanum, -i, *n.,* shrine, sanctuary, temple
far, farris, *n.,* emmer wheat
fasces, -ium, *m. pl.,* a bundle of rods usually with an ax carried by lictors before a magistrate, used for punishment, and signifying his power
fastus, -us, *m.,* pride, haughtiness, conceit
fateor, -eri, -fassus, to concede, acknowledge, admit
fatigo (1), to tire out, weary, exhaust
fatum, -i, *n.,* destiny, fate, calamity, mishap, ruin
faveo, -ere, favi, fautum, to approve, show favor to, take the side of
fax, -cis, *f.,* torch
febricito, -are, -avi, to have a fever
felix, -icis, *adj.,* productive, lucky, auspicious, fortunate, prosperous
fera, -ae, *f.,* wild beast, wild animal
fere, *also* **ferme,** *adv.,* approximately, about

ferio, -ire, to strike, hit; to strike dead, kill
fero, ferre, tuli, latum, to carry; to proceed; to endure; to assign, allege
ferox, -ocis, *adj.,* having a violent or savage nature, fierce
ferreus, -a, -um, *adj.,* of iron or steel
ferrum, -i, *n.,* iron, steel, iron implement, sword; (*meton.*) armed might
fessus, -a, -um, *adj.,* tired, weary, exhausted
festino (1), to make haste, bustle, hurry
fictus, -a, -um, *adj.,* untrue, made up
ficus, -us, *f.,* fig tree, fig
fidelis, -e, *adj.,* faithful, loyal, trustworthy
fides, -ei, *f.,* trust, good faith, credibility
figo, -gere, -xi, -xum, to fix in, insert, fasten, secure
figura, -ae, *f.,* shape, form
filia, -ae, *f.,* daughter
filius, -i, *m.,* son
fingo, -ngere, -nxi, -ctum, to make, compose, contrive, fabricate, make up
finis, -is, *m. and f.,* boundary, end, goal; (*pl.*) the land lying within boundaries, territory
finitimus, -a, -um, *adj.,* bordering upon, adjoining, neighboring
fio, fieri, to be, become, happen
firmus, -a, -um, *adj.,* strong, stout; robust, steady, secure; substantial

Flaccus, -i, *m.,* Flaccus, the addressee of a number of Martial's poems
flagitiosus, -a, -um, *adj.,* disgraceful, shocking, infamous
Flavius, -a, -um, *adj.,* the Roman *gens Flavia; m. or f.,* a member of the *gens Flavia;* Flavius, a teacher of Horace
flavus, -a, -um, *adj.,* yellow, golden; fair-haired
flecto, -ctere, -xi, -xum, to bend, curve; to turn, deflect, avert; to guide; to change, modify
fleo, -ere, -evi, -etum, to weep, bewail, lament
fletus, -us, *m.,* weeping, lamentation
Floralia, -ium, *n. pl.,* a festival held on April 28 in honor of Flora
floreo, -ere, -ui, to bloom, flower
fluo, -ere, fluxi, fluxum, to flow, stream, overflow, spread
fluxus, -a, -um, *adj.,* flowing, loose, unstable, transitory
focus, -i, *m.,* hearth
foeditas, -atis, *f.,* foulness, repulsiveness; disgrace, shame, infamy
foedus, -a, -um, *adj.,* foul, repulsive, horrible
for, fari, fatus, to speak, talk
fore = **futurum esse**
forma, -ae, *f.,* appearance, shape, mode, image, form
formidulosus *also* **formidolosus, -a, -um,** *adj.,* terrifying

formosus, -a, -um, *adj.,* beautiful, handsome
fornix, -icis, *m.,* vault, arch; cellar or other such space used for prostitution; brothel
fors, -tis, *f.,* chance, luck
forsan, *adv.,* perhaps, it may be
forsit, *adv.,* perhaps
fortasse, *adv.,* perhaps, possibly
forte, *adv.,* by chance
fortis, -e, *adj.,* powerful, forceful, bold
fortiter, *adv.,* powerfully, vigorously, boldly
fortuna, -ae, *f.,* Fortune (*personified*); luck, chance, outcome
forum, -i, *n.,* public square, Forum
fossa, -ae, *f.,* ditch, trench
fractus, -a, -um, *adj.,* broken
fragilis, -e, *adj.,* liable to break or crumble, brittle, easily destroyed
fragmen, -inis, *n.,* a piece broken off, fragment
frango, -ngere, fregi, -ctum, to break, shatter, smash
frater, -tris, *m.,* brother
fraternus, -a, -um, *adj.,* of a brother
fraudo (1), to deprive a person of what is rightfully his or hers; to cheat
fremo, -ere, -ui, -itum, to roar, growl; to grumble, clamor for
frequens, -ntis, *adj.,* occurring at close intervals; of constant occurence, regular
fritillus, -i, *m.,* a dicebox

frons, -ntis, *f.,* forehead, brow
fruor, -i, -ctus, to enjoy the proceeds from, profit from, enjoy
frustra, *adv.,* in vain
fuga, -ae, *f.,* the action of taking flight, fleeing, flight
fugax, -acis, *adj.,* prone to run away, elusive, swift, transient
fugio, -ere, fugi, to flee, run away from
fulgeo, -ere, fulsi, to flash, glitter, gleam, glare
fumo, -are, -avi, to emit smoke, give off steam
fundo, fundere, fudi, fusum, to pour, pour out, shed
funus, -eris, *n.,* funeral procession, funeral
furia, -ae, *f.,* rage, fury, frenzy; a Fury; (*pl.*) the Furies, goddesses who take vengeance for guilt
furo, -ere, to behave wildly, rave, rage, be frantic
furor, -oris, *m.,* violent madness, hostile rage, fury
furtum, -i, *n.,* robbery, theft

G
Gabba, -ae, *m.,* Gabba, the name of a professional buffoon
Gabii, -orum, *m. pl.,* the ancient city of Gabii in Latium
Gades, -ium, *f. pl.,* Cadiz, a city in Spain
galea, -ae, *f.,* soldier's helmet
Gallicus, -a, -um, *adj.,* of Gaul, Gallic
Gallus, -i, *m.,* a Gaul
Gallus, -i, *m.,* a castrated priest of the goddess Cybele
gaudeo, -dere, gavisus, to be glad, be pleased, rejoice
gaudium, -ii, *n.,* joy, delight, gladness
geminus, -a, -um, *adj.,* twin
gener, -ri, *m.,* son-in-law
generosus, -a, -um, *adj.,* of noble birth; noble-spirited
genitor, -oris, *m.,* one's father; (*of Jupiter, Neptune*) the creator
gens, gentis, *f.,* race, nation, people; a Roman clan
genus, -eris, *n.,* descent, birth, origin; kind, variety, class; family line; way, method
Germania, -ae, *f.,* Germany
germino (1), to sprout, bud
gero, -ere, gessi, gestum, to bear, carry, carry on; to perform, do; **bellum gerere,** to wage war
gladius, -i, *m.,* also **gladium, -(i)i,** *n.,* sword
gleba, -ae, *f.,* lump of earth, clod
globus, -i, *m.,* compact mass of spherical shape; sphere of a heavenly body; close-packed throng of persons or animals
gloria, -ae, *f.,* praise, honor, distinction; thirst for glory, ambition, pride
grabatus, -i, *m.,* camp bed or pallet
gradus, -us, *m.,* step; firm position of the feet, degree, grade, rank
Graecia, -ae, *f.,* Greece
Graius, -a, -um, *adj.,* Greek

grandis, -e, *adj.*, mature, large, great, weighty, grand
grando, -inis, *f.* (*m.*), hail
grassor, -ari, -atus, to proceed
gratia, -ae, *f.*, favor, gratitude
gratus, -a, -um, *adj.*, grateful, thankful; acceptable, welcome
gravis, -e, *adj.*, heavy, weighty; respectable, venerable
grex, -egis, *m.*, flock, herd, drove, swarm
gurges, -itis, *m.*, whirlpool, eddy
gutta, -ae, *f.*, drop (of liquid); speck
guttus *also* **gutus, -i,** *m.*, narrow-necked vessel, flask

H

habeo, -ere, -ui, -itum, to have, occupy, hold; to have in mind, think, regard
habito (1), to dwell, reside, live
haereo, -rere, -si, -sum, to stick, cling
Hannibal, -alis, *m.*, Hannibal, the Carthaginian leader in the Second Punic War
harundineus, -a, -um, *adj.*, of reeds
hasta, -ae, *f.*, spear, javelin
haud, *part.*, not
haudquaquam, *adv.*, by no means, in no way
Hebrus, -i, *m.*, Hebrus, a character killed in *Aeneid* 10
hesternus, -a, -um, *adj.*, of yesterday; *n. sg. as subst.*, yesterday
heu, *interj. of grief or pain,* alas! oh!

hic, haec, hoc, *pron. adj.*, this
hic, *adv.*, here, in this place; in the present circumstance
hinc, *adv.*, from here, hence
hio, -are, -avi, to be wide open, gape; to have the mouth wide open
hircus, -i, *m.*, he-goat
hirsutus, -a, -um, *adj.*, hairy, rough; thick with foliage
hoc, *adv.*, to this place, for this reason
homo, -inis, *m. or f.*, man; human being
honestus, -a, -um, *adj.*, of good repute, honorable; well-born; decorous, becoming
honor (-os), -oris, *m.*, high esteem; mark of esteem; honor; (high) political office
hora, -ae, *f.*, hour
hortor, -ari, -atus, to urge on, encourage
hospes, -itis, *m.* (*f.*), guest, visitor
hospitalis, -e, *adj.*, hospitable
hostilis, -e, *adj.*, characteristic of an enemy, hostile
hostis, -is, *m. or f.*, enemy
huc, *adv.*, to this place
humanus, -a, -um, *adj.*, of or belonging to human beings, human
humerus, -i, *m.*, shoulder
humus, -i, *f.*, earth, ground, soil
Hydaspes, -is, *m.*, Hydaspes, a character killed in *Aeneid* 10
hymenaeus *or* **-os, -i,** *m.*, the Greek wedding refrain; *usually pl.*, wedding, match

I

iaceo, -ere, -ui, -itum, to lie, lie prostrate; to lie dead
iacio, -ere, ieci, iactum, to throw, toss
iacto (1), to throw, hurl, toss; to jostle, shake; to hurl (remarks), brag; to show off
iactura, -ae, *f.,* the act of throwing overboard; deprivation, loss; expense, cost
iaculor, -ari, -atus, to throw a javelin; to shoot at, strike
iaculum, -i, *n.,* javelin
iam, *adv.,* at this point, now, already
ianua, -ae, *f.,* door
ibi, *adv.,* in that place, there; thereupon
Icilius, -i, *m.,* the name of L. Icilius, Verginia's fiancé
idem, eadem, idem, *pron.,* the same
ideo, *adv.,* for the reason that, therefore
Idus, -uum, *f. pl.,* the Ides; in the Roman calendar the fifteenth day of March, May, July, and October, and the thirteenth of the other months; the day for settling payment
igitur, *conj.,* in that case, then, therefore, consequently
ignarus, -a, -um, *adj.,* ignorant, unaware (of)
ignis, -is, *m.,* fire
ignobilis, -e, *adj.,* unknown, obscure, of low birth, inglorious
ignosco, -noscere, -novi, -notum, to forgive; to make allowances for
ignotus, -a, -um, *adj.,* unknown, unfamiliar, strange
ilex, -icis, *f.,* oak, holm oak
Ilia, -ae, *f.,* Ilia, the mother of Romulus and Remus
ille, illa, illud, *pron. adj.,* he, she, it; that
illic, *adv.,* at that place, over there
illinc, *adv.,* from that place, thence
imago, -inis, *f.,* image, likeness, representation, model; ancestral image, mask
imbecillus, -a, -um, *adj.,* feeble, weak; lacking intellectual or moral strength
imber, -bris, *m.,* rain
imitor, -ari, -atus, to copy, imitate
immanis, -e, *adj.,* savage, brutal; of enormous size, tremendous
immerens, -entis, *adj.,* undeserving, innocent, blameless
immineo, -ere, to overhang; to press upon
immoderatus, -a, -um, *adj.,* boundless, unrestrained, intemperate
immotus, -a, -um, *adj.,* unmoved
immundus, -a, -um, *adj.,* unclean, untidy, slovenly
immuto (1), to alter, modify, change
impastus, -a, -um, *adj.,* hungry, unfed
impavidus, -a, -um, *adj.,* fearless, dauntless

impedio, -ire, -ivi, -itum, to entangle, ensnare, block, hamper, hinder; bind, encircle, embrace
imperator, -oris, *m.,* ruler; commanding officer, general
imperito (1), to be in command, exercise authority or control (over)
imperium, -(i)i, *n.,* supreme power, dominion, rule
impero (1), to demand payment, levy, give orders (to), command
impetus, -us, *m.,* thrust; attack, assault
impiger, -gra, -grum, *adj.,* active, energetic, brisk
impius, -a, -um, *adj.,* showing no regard for moral duties, impious
imploro (1), to ask for help, appeal to for aid
impotentia, -ae, *f.,* weakness, helplessness, lack of self-restraint, immoderate behavior
impudicus, -a, -um, *adj.,* shameless, without modesty
imputatus, -a, -um, *adj.,* unpruned, untrimmed
imus, -a, -um, *adj. superl.,* lowest, deepest
in, *prep.* + *acc.,* into, onto, against; + *abl.,* in, on, in the case of, in relation to
inanis, -e, *adj.,* empty, hollow, unoccupied
inaratus, -a, -um, *adj.,* unplowed
incalesco, -escere, -ui, to grow warm or hot; (*of persons*) to become excited; heated

incedo, -ere, -ssi, to proceed, walk (in a stately manner); march forward, advance
incensus, -a, -um, *adj.,* inflamed
inceptum, -i, *n.,* undertaking, attempt; the theme or subject of a book
incertus, -a, -um, *adj.,* doubtful, uncertain
incido, -ere, -i, incasum, to fall into, come upon, chance upon, happen upon, come across
incipio, -ere, -epi, -eptum, to begin
incito (1), to speed up, urge on, impel, drive; to intensify, increase; to arouse, evoke
inclementer, *adv.,* rudely, harshly
inclino (1), to make tilt, incline; to bend downward; to influence, dispose, affect, alter
incolo, -ere, -ui, to inhabit, dwell in, reside in, live
incolumis, -e, *adj.,* unharmed, safe
incorruptus, -a, -um, *adj.,* intact, unspoiled
incredibilis, -e, *adj.,* incredible, unbelievable
incultus, -a, -um, *adj.,* uncultivated, unkempt, lacking in culture or refinement
incumbo, -umbere, -ubui, to lean forward, lean over, lie down (on)
inde, *adv.,* from that place, from that point, from there, thence, next, then
indicium, -i, *n.,* information, sign, evidence

indico, -ere, -xi, -ctum, to proclaim, declare
indigens, -ntis, *adj.,* needy, not self-sufficient
indigeo, -ere, -ui, to stand in want of, need, require; to lack
indignatio, -onis, *f.,* indignation, resentment, fury; angry outburst
indignitas, -atis, *f.,* shamefulness, humiliation
indignor, -ari, -atus, to take offense at, resent, disdain
indignus, -a, -um, *adj.,* unworthy, not deserving
indocilis, -e, *adj.,* not teachable, not to be taught
indoctus, -a, -um, *adj.,* unlearned, ignorant; untrained
inedia, -ae, *f.,* starvation
ineo, -ire, -ivi/-ii, -itum, to go into, enter
ineptus, -a, -um, *adj.,* lacking in judgment, foolish, silly
iners, -rtis, *adj.,* lacking skill, clumsy; inactive, lazy, having no purpose; without spirit
infandus, -a, -um, *adj.,* unspeakable
infans, -ntis, *adj.,* that cannot speak; *subst., m. and f.,* little child, infant
infelix, -icis, *adj.,* unlucky, ill-fated
infero, inferre, intuli, inlatum, to bring in, carry into; to bring forward; to inflict; **inferre pedem,** to advance, attack

infestus, -a, -um, *adj.,* hostile, aggressive, threatening
inficio, -ere, -eci, -ectum, to stain, tinge, infect, spoil
infidelis, -e, *adj.,* not to be trusted, faithless
infirmus, -a, -um, *adj.,* weak, feeble, ineffectual
infractus, -a, -um, *adj.,* broken
infremo, -ere, -ui, to roar, bellow
infrendo, -ere, to gnash the teeth (in anger)
infrenis, -e, *adj.,* unbridled, unrestrained
ingenium, -(i)i, *n.,* natural disposition, temperament
ingens, -tis, *adj.,* of very great size, huge, great
ingenuus, -a, -um, *adj.,* native to a place, natural; freeborn; (*m. or f., as subst.*) a freeborn man or woman
ingredior, -di, -ssus, to go into, enter upon, embark, advance to the attack
inhonestus, -a, -um, *adj.,* dishonorable, disgraceful, shameful
inhorresco, -escere, -ui, to stand on end, bristle
inicio, -icere, -ieci, -iectum, to throw in or on; to inspire, suggest
iniquus, -a, -um, *adj.,* uneven, unequal, inequitable, unfair
initium, -i, *n.,* beginning
iniuria, -ae, *f.,* wrong, injustice
iniussus, -a, -um, *adj.,* unbidden, unordered

inmuto (1), to change, alter
inominatus, -a, -um, *adj.,* ill-omened
inopia, -ae, *f.,* want, scarcity
inp-. *See also* **imp-**
inprobus, -a, -um, *adj.,* of poor quality, morally unsound, rascally
inpudicus, -a, -um, *adj.,* unchaste, immoral, shameless
inpune, *adv.,* without punishment, with impunity; safely, without harm
inquam, (*with direct speech*) to say
inquietus, -a, -um, *adj.,* restless, impatient
inquino (1), to make dirty, befoul, stain, taint, pollute, debase, contaminate
insanus, -a, -um, *adj.,* of unsound mind, mad, insane
inscius, -a, -um, *adj.,* not knowing, unaware, ignorant
insignis, -e, *adj.,* conspicuous, noteworthy
insisto, -ere, institi, to stand or tread on; to set about, proceed with; to stand
insolens, -ntis, *adj.,* unaccustomed, excessive, immoderate, haughty, arrogant
insolesco, -ere, to become overbearing, grow proud
insolitus, -a, -um, *adj.,* unfamiliar, unaccustomed
insons, -ntis, *adj.,* innocent, guiltless
inspergo, -gere, -si, -sum, to sprinkle, scatter, distribute over

instituo, -uere, -ui, -utum, to put up, establish, appoint
institutum, -i, *n.,* habit, custom, mode of life
insto, -are, -iti, to set foot upon, press on with; to assail, be urgent with or press (*a person*); to attack, loom, threaten
insula, -ae, *f.,* island
insum, inesse, infui, to be in or on
intactus, -a, -um, *adj.,* untouched, uninjured
integer, -gra, -grum, *adj.,* not previously touched, whole, undiminished
intendo, -ere, -di, -tum, to stretch, strain, extend, exert
intento (1), to hold out, point at; to threaten
intentus, -a, -um, *adj.,* intent, attentive, serious, earnest
inter, *prep.* + *acc.,* among, amid, between
interdum, *adv.,* from time to time
interea, *adv.,* in the meantime, meanwhile
interficio, -ere, -feci, -fectum, to put to death, kill
interfor, -ari, -atus, to interrupt, interpose
intericio, -icere, -ieci, -iectum, to throw or place between, insert, introduce
interim, *adv.,* meanwhile, for the time being
interpello (1), to interrupt, impede, get in the way of

interpono, -ponere, -posui, -positum, to place between, insert; to introduce; to interpose (delay)

intersum, -esse, -fui, to intervene; to be present (at); to attend as a participant

intervenio, -ire, -veni, -ventum, to come on the scene; to intervene, occur, crop up

interventus, -us, *m.,* arrival; active interference; intervention, mediation; the occurrence of an event

intestinus, -a, -um, *adj.,* civil, domestic, internal

intono, -are, -ui, to thunder; to utter in thunderous tones

intro (1), to go into, enter

intumesco, -escere, -ui, to become swollen, swell up

inultus, -a, -um, *adj.,* unpunished; unavenged

inuro, -rere, -ssi, -stum, to burn; to brand on, stamp

invado, -ere, -si, -sum, to enter in a hostile fashion, attack, invade; to enter into

inveho, -here, -xi, -ctum, to carry in, import, introduce; to attack (with words), inveigh against; (*pass.*) to ride, drive, sail

invenio, -venire, -veni, -ventum, to encounter, find, come across, discover

invideo, -idere, -idi, -isum, to regard with ill will or envy; to begrudge

invidia, -ae, *f.,* envy, ill will, jealousy, prejudice

invidus, -a, -um, *adj.,* envious, envying

inviso, -ere, -i, to go to see, visit

invito (1), to entertain, offer hospitality to, invite; to request; to incite, provoke

invoco (1), to call to one's side, summon; to call upon, invoke; to ask or pray for

iocosus, -a, -um, *adj.,* full of fun, funny

iocus, -i, *m.,* joke, jest

Iovis. *See* **Iuppiter**

ipse, -a, -um, *demon. pron. and adj.,* himself, herself, itself, the very

ira, -ae, *f.,* anger, rage

irascor, -i, iratus, to become angry

is, ea, id, *adj.,* this, that; *pron. m./f./n.,* he, she, it, they

iste, ista, istud, *pron. and pron. adj.,* that; that of yours

ita, *adv.,* to that extent, so, thus

Italia, -ae, *f.,* Italy

itaque, *adv.,* since, in consequence, so; well then

iter, itineris, *n.,* journey, march, route, road

iubeo, -ere, iussi, iussum, to order, command, bid

iudex, -icis, *m.,* judge, juror, decider

iudicium, -i, *n.,* trial, judgment, decision; judgment, opinion

iugulo (1), to kill by cutting the throat

iungo, -gere, -xi, -ctum, to join physically; to bring close together

iuniores, -um, *m. pl.,* younger men, esp. those of military age (seventeen to forty-six years)

Iunius, -ia, -ium, *adj.,* the name of the Roman *gens Iunia,* to which Brutus belonged

Iuno, -onis, *f.,* Juno, the Roman goddess identified with the Greek Hera

Iuppiter, Iovis, *m.,* Jupiter, the Italian sky god identified with the Greek Zeus, the weather god, the sky

iurgium, -i, *n.,* quarrel, dispute

iuro (1), to swear, take an oath

ius, iuris, *n.,* law, authority, right

iustus, -a, -um, *adj.,* legitimate, rightful, fair

iuvenalis, -e, *adj.,* youthful, young

iuvenis, -is, *adj.,* young; *subst. m.,* young man

iuventa, -ae, *f.,* the period of youth, the state of being young, youth

iuventus, -utis, *f.,* young men collectively, the youth

iuvo, -are, iuvi, iutum, to help, assist, please

iuxta, *adv.,* alike, equally; *prep.* + *acc.,* next to, beside; in conformity with

K

Karthago, -inis, *f.,* Carthage

L

L. = Lucius, -i, *m.,* a Roman *praenomen*

labor, -i, lapsus, to slide, slip, collapse

labor, -oris, *m.,* work, labor, toil

laboriosus, -a, -um, *adj.,* full of labor, wearisome, difficult; industrious; troubled, harassed

laboro (1), to toil, exert oneself, take pains; to be distressed; to work at

labrum, -i, *n.,* lip

Lacedaemonius, -a, -um, *adj.,* of Lacedaemon, Spartan

lacertus, -i, *m.,* arm

lacesso, -ere, -ivi/-ii, -itum, to challenge, provoke, harass, assail

lacrima, -ae, *f.,* tear

lacrimabundus, -a, -um, *adj.,* weeping, in tears

laetor, -ari, -atus, to rejoice, be glad

laetus, -a, -um, *adj.,* happy, exulting, flourishing

Laevinus, -i, *m.,* Valerius Laevinus, a possibly degenerate member of the *gens Valeria*

laevus, -a, -um, *adj.,* left

laganum, -i, *n.,* thin flat cake, pancake

lambo, -ere, -i, to lick

lamentabilis, -e, *adj.,* doleful, mournful, deplorable

lana, -ae, *f.,* fleece, wool

lanio (1), to wound, mutilate, tear

lanius, -i, *m.,* butcher

lapicida, -ae, *m.,* quarrier, stonecutter

lapis, -idis, *m.,* stone, pebble
lapsus, -us, *m.,* falling, collapse, gliding, flowing
Lar, Laris, *m. pl.,* the protecting deities of the city and of households
largitio, -onis, *f.,* a giving of doles; corrupt giving, bribery; bribe
largus, -a, -um, *adj.,* generous, bountiful, plentiful
lasanum, -i, *n.,* chamber pot
Latagus, -i, *m.,* Latagus, a Trojan in *Aeneid* 10
Latini, -orum, *m. pl.,* the Latians, the inhabitants of Latium
Latinus, -a, -um, *adj.,* Latin, of or belonging to Latium
lator, -oris, *m.,* the proposer of a law
latus, -a, -um, *adj.,* broad, wide
laudo (1), to praise, extol
Lavinium, -i, *n.,* Lavinium, a town in Latium said to have been founded by Aeneas
Laurens, -ntis, *adj.,* of or belonging to Laurentum, a coastal town in Latium
lauriger, -era, -erum, *adj.,* bearing laurels; decked with laurels
laus, laudis, *f.,* praise
Lausus, -i, *m.,* Lausus, son of Mezentius in *Aeneid* 10
lavo, -ere/-are, lavi, lautum/ lotum, to wash, bathe
laxus, -a, -um, *adj.,* spacious, loose, slack, hanging loosely, gaping
lectica, -ae, *f.,* litter, sedan
lectus, -i, *m.,* bed, couch

legio, -onis, *f.,* the largest unit of the Roman army, legion, army, host
legitimus, -a, -um, *adj.,* legal, legitimate, lawful
lego, -ere, legi, lectum, to gather, choose, select; to read
leo, leonis, *m.,* lion
Leuconicus, -a, -um, *adj.,* of or belonging to the Gallic tribe of Leucones; *subst. n.,* Leuconian wool
levis, -e, *adj.,* smooth, not rough, slick, slippery
levo (1), to lift or raise up; to relieve; to free from
lex, legis, *f.,* a law, the law, a rule
libellus, -i, *m.,* small book, volume; document, dispatch; public notice
liber, -bri, *m.,* book; any lengthy document
liber, -era, -erum, *adj.,* free, unrestricted, clear, unoccupied
liberalis, -e, *adj.,* of or worthy of a free man; magnanimous, generous, lavish
liberator, -oris, *m.,* one who sets free, deliverer
liberi, -um *or* **-orum,** *m. pl.,* children
libero (1), to free
libertas, -atis, *f.,* freedom
libertinus, -a, -um, *adj.,* of the status of a freedman
libet, -ere, -uit/-itum est *also archaic* **lib-,** *impers.,* it is pleasing
libido, -inis, *f., also archaic* **lub-,** desire, lust, wantonness

Libycus, -a, -um, *adj.,* of or belonging to North Africa
licentia, -ae, *f.,* lack of restraint, disorderliness
liceo, -ere, -ui, to fetch (*with abl. or gen. of price*)
licet, -ere, -uit/-itum est, *impers.,* it is permitted
lichen, -enos, *m.,* a kind of lichen; skin disease, ringworm
lictor, -oris, *m.,* lictor, one of the attendants allotted to Roman magistrates
Ligurra, -ae, *m.,* Ligurra, the addressee of Martial 12.61
limen, -inis, *n.,* threshold
limo (1), to rub smooth, remove the blemishes of, polish, perfect
lingua, -ae, *f.,* tongue; language, dialect
linquo, -ere, liqui, to leave, depart from
linteum, -i, *n.,* linen cloth, sail
lit(t)us, -oris, *n.,* seashore, beach
littera, -ae, *f.,* letter of the alphabet; (*pl.*) written document; letter
loco (1), to place
loculus, -i, *m.,* compartment, box, writing case
locum, -i, *n. or* **locus, -i,** *m.,* place, spot, position; position in society
longe, *adv.,* a long way, far, at a distance
longus, -a, -um, *adj.,* long, extended
loquor, -i, -cutus, to talk, speak
lubet. *See* **libet**
lubido. *See* **libido**

lubricus, -a, -um, *adj.,* slippery, hazardous
luceo, -ere, luxi, to emit light, shine; to glitter, be conspicuous, excel
lucerna, -ae, *f.,* oil lamp
Lucretia, -ae, *f.,* Lucretia, wife of Collatinus
Lucretius, -i, *m.,* Lucretius, father of Lucretia
luctus, -us, *m.,* sorrow, mourning, grief
lucubro (1), to work by lamplight
ludo, -ere, -si, -sus, to play, sport, play a game; to joke, trifle, make fun of
ludus, -i, *m.,* sport, play, game, frivolity
lumbus, -i, *m.,* hips, loins
lumen, -inis, *n.,* light, the light of day, the light enjoyed by the living
lupus, -i, *m.,* wolf
lustra, -orum, *n. pl.,* den of vice
lusus, -us, *m.,* the act of playing, game, joke, prank
lutum, -i, *n.,* mud
lux, lucis, *f.,* light, daylight; **prima luce,** at daybreak
luxuria, -ae, *f.,* unruly or willful behavior; indulgence, extravagance
luxus, -us, *m.,* luxury, opulence
Lyaeus, -a, -um, *adj.* (*m. subst.*), "the one who sets free," a cult title of Dionysius; (*poetic*) wine
Lycaonius, -a, -um, *adj.,* of or descended from Lycaon (either king of Arcadia or son of Priam)

Lycius, -a, -um, *adj.,* of Lycia, Lycian
Lydus, -a, -um, *adj. (m. subst.),* a native of Lydia, an Etruscan
lympha, -ae, *f.,* water

M

M. = **Marcus, -i,** *m.,* a Roman *praenomen*
M' = **Manius, -i,** *m.,* a Roman *praenomen*
macer, -cra, -crum, *adj.,* thin, lean, poor in quality
madeo, -ere, to drip, be wet
madidus, -a, -um, *adj.,* wet, sodden, softened by boiling
Maecenas, -atis, *m.,* C. Cilinius Maecenas, wealthy Roman *eques* and patron of Horace and Vergil
maestitia, -ae, *f.,* sadness, sorrow, grief
maestus, -a, -um, *adj.,* unhappy, sad, mournful
magis, *adv.,* more, rather
magister, -tri, *m.,* commander, master, chief officer, expert, teacher
magistratus, -us, *m.,* magistracy; magistrate
magnificentia, -ae, *f.,* majesty, splendor, grandeur
magnificus, -a, -um, *adj.,* splendid, magnificent
magnus, -a, -um, *adj.,* great in size or extent; big
Maia, -ae, *f.,* Maia, the mother of Mercury by Jupiter
maiestas, -atis, *f.,* dignity, majesty, sovereignty

maior, *gen.* **-oris,** *n.* **maius,** *comp. adj.,* greater; *m. pl. as subst.,* ancestors, forebears
malevolentia, -ae, *f.,* ill will, spitefulness
malo, -lle, -lui, to wish rather, prefer
malum, -i, *n.,* trouble, distress, pain, misfortune
malus, -a, -um, *adj.,* bad, not good, wicked, depraved, unwholesome
manicipium, -(i)i, *n.,* ownership; slave
mando (1), to hand over, consign, commit, entrust
mane, *adv.,* early in the day
maneo, -ere, mansi, mansum, to remain, stay, endure, last, await
mano, -are, -avi, to flow, trickle, drip; to extend, be diffused, spread
mantica, -ae, *f.,* traveling bag, knapsack
manus, -us, *f.,* hand; armed force (of any size); the power of a husband or *paterfamilias* over his wife or other female relative
mare, -is, *n.,* sea
maritus, -i, *m.,* husband
Marsi, -orum, *m. pl.,* the Marsi, a people of central Italy
Marsyas, -ae, *m.,* Marsyas, a satyr flayed by Apollo after losing a music contest
mater, -tris, *f.,* mother
materia, -ae, *f.,* wood, material, fuel; theme, occasion

maternus, -a, -um, *adj.,* of a mother, maternal; (*of relationships*) on the mother's side

Matinus, -a, -um, *adj.,* of or belonging to Mt. Matinus

matrona, -ae, *f.,* married woman, matron

mature, *adv.,* in good time, quickly; at an early age

maturo (1), to bring to ripeness; to hasten, hurry

maturus, -a, -um, *adj.,* ripe, full-grown, ready

Maurus, -i, *m.,* Moorish, Moroccan

Mavors, -tis, *m.,* the god Mars; battle

maxime, *adv.,* to the greatest extent, most, especially, for the most part

maximus, -a, -um, *adj.* also *archaic* **maxumus,** greatest in size, largest; greatest in number; greatest in age; most important; leading, mightiest

maxumus. *See* **maximus**

mediocris, -e, *adj.,* moderate in degree, middling

medium, -ii, *n.,* the middle part; the intervening space; the midst

medius, -a, -um, *adj.,* in the middle, mid, middle

Medus, -i, *m.,* a Mede

mel, mellis, *n.,* honey

melior, -us, *compar. adj.,* better

memorabilis, -e, *adj.,* worthy of being recorded, remarkable, memorable

memoria, -ae, *f.,* the faculty of remembering; memory, memorial

memoro (1), to utter, speak, say, narrate, relate, call to mind, remind

mendosus, -a, -um, *adj.,* full of faults or blemishes, faulty

mens, -tis, *f.,* mind, intention, will

mensis, -is, *m.,* month

mentio, -onis, *f.,* reference to a subject, mention

mentior, -iri, -itus, to lie

mentula, -ae, *f.,* penis

mentum, -i, *n.,* chin

merces, -edis, *f.,* payment, wage

mereo, -ere, -ui, -itum/mereor, -eri, -itus, to earn (*stipendium merere,* to draw pay as a soldier); merit; deserve, *abs.* with *adv.,* **bene, male,** *etc., and* **de** + *abl.,* to deserve well, ill, etc.; (*of a person*) behave well, badly, etc.

meretrix, -icis, *f.,* prostitute

merito, *adv.,* deservedly, justly

meritum, -i, *n.,* service; something that entitles one to a reward

Messalla, -ae, *m.,* Messalla, a Roman cognomen of the *gens Valeria*

Messapus, -i, *m.,* Messapus, a Latin in *Aeneid* 10

-met, *enclitic particle that adds emphasis*

metuo, -ere, -i, metutum, to fear, be afraid of

metus, -us, *m.,* fear

meus, -a, -um, *poss. adj.,* my, mine

Mezentius, -i, *m.,* Mezentius, an Etruscan chieftain in *Aeneid* 10
miles, -itis, *m.,* soldier
militaris, -e, *adj.,* of, or connected with, the army
militia, -ae, *f.,* military service, war
mille, *indecl. n. and adj.* (*pl.,* **milia**), one thousand, any large number
miluus, -i, *m.,* bird of prey, kite
Mimas, -antis, *m.,* Mimas, a Trojan in *Aeneid* 10
minae, -arum, *f. pl.,* threats, menaces
minax, -acis, *adj.,* threatening
Minerva, -ae, *f.,* Minerva, the Italian goddess of handicraft, identified with the Greek Athena
minime, *adv. also archaic* **minume,** in the least degree, by no means, not at all
minister, -tri, *m.,* servant, assistant; subordinate
ministerium, -(i)i, *n.,* service, attendance, duty, employment
ministro (1), to act as servant, attend; to wait on table
minor, -us, *compar. adj.,* smaller, inferior
minume. *See* **minime**
minus, *compar. adv.,* to a smaller degree, less
miraculum, -i, *n.,* an amazing object or sight; wonder, amazement
miror, -ari, -atus, to be surprised, amazed, bewildered; to look with wonder or awe at
mirus, -a, -um, *adj.,* remarkable, astonishing
misceo, -ere, miscui, mixtum, to mix
miser, -era, -erum, *adj.,* to be pitied, wretched, unfortunate; pitiful, contemptible
miserabilis, -e, *adj.,* pitiable, wretched
misereo, -ere, -ui, *also* **misereor, -eri, -itus,** to feel or show compassion, pity, feel sorry; (*impers.*) **me miseret** + *gen.,* I am moved to pity
miseria, -ae, *f.,* a wretched or pitiable condition; (*pl.*) a trouble or woe
miseror, -ari, -atus, *also* **misero** (1), to view with compassion, feel sorry for
missile, -is, *n.,* missile, projectile
mitto, -ere, misi, missum, to release, let go; to discharge; to send
modo, *adv.,* only, just
modus, -i, *m.,* way, manner
moenia, -ium, *n. pl.,* city walls, defensive walls
molestus, -a, -um, *adj.,* troublesome, annoying, tiresome
mollis, -e, *adj.,* pliant, flexible, soft, tender, gentle
moneo, -ere, -ui, -itum, to remind; to warn, advise
monitus, -us, *m.,* warning, omen

mons, -tis, *m.,* mountain, hill
monstrum, -i, *n.,* unnatural thing or event regarded as an omen; awful or monstrous thing or event; monstrous or horrible creature; horror, atrocity
monumentum, -i, *n.,* monument, reminder, memorial, document, record
morbus, -i, *m.,* disease, sickness
moribundus, -a, -um, *adj.,* dying
morior, -i, mortuus, to die
moror, -ari, -atus, to delay, wait, remain
morosus, -a, -um, *adj.,* hard to please, difficult, exacting
mors, -tis, *f.,* death
morsus, -us, *m.,* the act of biting; bite; bite wound
mortalis, -e, *adj.,* subject to death, mortal; *as subst. m. and f.,* a human, as opposed to a god
mortuus, -a, -um, *adj.,* dead
mos, moris, *m.,* custom, way, manner; *pl.,* morals, character
motus, -us, *m.,* motion, disturbance
moveo, -ere, movi, motum, to stir up, move; to dislodge, degrade, remove
mox, *adv.,* in the (near) future, (a little) later, next
mulctrum, -i, *n.,* milking pail
muliebris, -e, *adj.,* womanly, of a woman
mulier, -eris, *f.,* woman, wife; mistress
multitudo, -inis, *f.,* abundance, multitude, population, crowd
multo, *adv.,* much, by far
multus, -a, -um, *adj.,* much, many
mulus, -i, *m.,* mule
munitio, -onis, *f.,* protective wall, embankment; (*pl.*) defensive works, fortification
munitus, -a, -um, *adj.,* well fortified or defended
murus, -i, *m.* (*often pl.*), a wall built for defense, city walls
muto (1), to exchange, change, replace; to make different; to undergo a change, to change (for the worse)
mutuus, -a, -um, *adj.,* mutual, reciprocal

N

naevus, -i, *m.,* discolored mark, birthmark
nam, *conj.,* for, because
namque, *conj.,* certainly, to be sure, for, because
narro (1), to relate, tell, describe
nascor, -i, natus, to be born
nasus, -i, *m.,* nose
natio, -onis, *f.,* people, race, nation; nationality; place of origin
nato (1), to swim
Natta, -ae, *m.,* the name Natta, possibly Pinarius Natta; possibly also a variant of **nacca, -ae,** *m.,* fuller
natura, -ae, *f.,* the conditions of birth; the power that governs the physical universe; the power that governs the course of events; the physical world, creation

nauta, -ae, *m.,* sailor
navigo (1), to go by ship, sail
ne, *negative adv. and conj.,* so that not, lest
    ne ... quidem, not even
-ne, *encl. particle, added to a direct question as an interrogation mark*
nec. *See* **neque**
necessitas, -atis, *f.,* need, necessity, constraint, difficulty
neco (1), to put to death, kill
necopinatus, -a, -um, *adj.,* unexpected, unforeseen
nefandus, -a, -um, *adj.,* wicked, abominable
nefas, *n. indecl.,* an impious act, sacrilege
neglego, -gere, -xi, -ctum, to disregard, ignore, overlook, neglect
nego (1), to say (that ... not), deny (that)
negotium, -(i)i, *n.,* work, business, job
negotiosus, -a, -um, *adj.,* having much business, active, occupied
nemo, -inis, *m. or f.,* no one
nepos, -otis, *m.,* grandson, descendant
Neptunus, -i, *m.,* Neptune, god of the sea, the sea
nequaquam, *adv.,* by no means
neque *or* **nec,** *conj., adv.,* and not, nor; **neque ... neque,** *or* **nec ... nec,** *or* **neque ... nec,** neither ... nor
nequiquam, *adv.,* in vain

Nereus, -i *or* **-eos,** Nereus, a sea god; *meton.,* the sea
Nero, -onis, *m.,* Nero the emperor
nescio, -ire, -ivi/-ii, -itum, not to know, to be unaware of; **nescio an,** I am inclined to think
Nestor, -oris, *m.,* Nestor, an addressee of Martial's poems; also the aged Homeric hero from Pylos, famous for his long-winded speeches
neu. *See* **neve**
neve, *conj.,* and not, nor, and that not
nex, necis, *f.,* death, murder, slaughter
ni, *conj.,* = **si non, nisi,** if not, unless
niger, -gra, -grum, *adj.,* black, dark, gloomy
nihil, *n. indecl.,* nothing
nihilum, -i, *n.,* nothing
nil. *See* **nihil**
nimis, *n. indecl.,* an excessive amount; *adv.,* too much
nimium, -i, *n.,* an excessive amount or degree, too much, a great amount
nisi, *conj.,* except if, unless
nitor, -i, -xus/-sus, to lean upon, be supported by, rely upon; to struggle, strive; to direct one's efforts to (+ *inf.*)
nix, nivis, *f.,* snow
nobilis, -e, *adj.,* generally known, renowned, famous; aristocratic
nobilitas, -atis, *f.,* renown, celebrity; distinction, nobility
noceo, -ere, -ui, -itum, to do harm, injure, hurt

nocturnus, -a, -um, *adj.,* of or belonging to the night, nocturnal
nolo, nolle, nolui, to be unwilling; not to want
nomen, -inis, *n.,* name, renown
non, *adv.,* not
nonus, -a, -um, *adj.,* ninth
nos, *pron.,* we
nosco, -ere, novi, notum, to get knowledge of, come to know, learn; (*perf.*) to have learned, to know, understand
noster, -stra, -strum, *adj.,* our
noto (1), to mark, brand, stigmatize, distinguish, identify, single out, note
notus, -a, -um, *adj.,* known; (*of persons*) personally known to one; (*subst.*) an acquaintance
Notus, -i, *m.,* Notus, the south wind
novi, *perf. of* **nosco**
novitas, -atis, *f.,* newness, novelty
Novius, -i, *m.,* Novius, the name of a figure in Horace's *Satires*
novus, -a, -um, *adj.,* new, recent, strange, extreme; **novae res,** revolution
nox, noctis, *f.,* night
noxa, -ae, *f.,* injurious behavior, wrongdoing
nubes, -is, *f.,* cloud
nubilis, -e, *adj.,* suitable for marriage
nubilus, -a, -um, *adj.,* covered in cloud; *n. pl. as subst.,* the clouds
nubo, -bere, -psi, -ptum, (*of a woman*) to get married; to contract a marriage
nudus, -a, -um, *adj.,* naked, unclothed; bare, stripped
nugae, -arum, *f. pl.,* idle talk, nonsense, worthless stuff, trash, trifles, frivolities
nullus, -a, -um, *adj.,* not any, none, no; (*subst.*) *m.,* no one, nobody; *n.,* nothing
num, *adv. and interr. particle introducing a direct question expecting a negative answer; in an indirect question,* whether
Numa, -ae, *m.,* Numa Pompilius, the second king of Rome
numerus, -i, *m.,* number
Numitor, -oris, *m.,* Numitor, king of Alba; grandfather of Romulus and Remus
Numitorius, -i, *m.,* Numitorius, the name of Verginia's uncle, P. Numitorius
numquam/nunquam, *adv.,* never, at no time
nunc, *adv.,* now
nuntio (1), to announce, report
nuntius, -(i)i, *m.,* messenger, message
nupta, -ae, *f.,* married woman, wife
nuptiae, -arum, *f. pl.,* marriage, marriage ceremony, wedding
nuptialis, -e, *adj.,* of a wedding, nuptial
nurus, -us, *f.,* daughter-in-law
nusquam, *adv.,* nowhere; under no circumstances
nutrix, -icis, *f.,* a child's nurse

O

o, *interj.*, in addressing persons; in expressions of admiration, horror, etc., "o, what a …"; in expressing wishes, "o, would that …"

obeo, -ire, -ivi/-ii, -itum, to meet face to face, to meet up with; to attend, be present, keep a date

obicio, -ere, -ieci, -iectum, to throw or put before or in the way; to throw in one's teeth; *pass.*, to be in the way as a barrier

oboedio, -ire, -ivi/-ii, -itum, to listen to, obey, submit to

oborior, -iri, -tus, to spring up into view; to arise, occur

obscuro (1), to obscure, darken, conceal, hide

obsidio, -onis, *f.*, siege, blockade

obsoletus, -a, -um, *adj.*, worn out, shabby, dirty, dingy

obstinatus, -a, -um, *adj.*, stubborn, resolute

obtrunco (1), to cut to pieces; to kill

obviam, *adv.*, in the way; so as to meet

obvius, -a, -um, *adj.*, that is in the way, presenting itself, ready to hand

occubo, -are, to lie, lie dead

occupo (1), to seize, take possession of

occurro, -ere, -rri, -rsum, to run to meet, meet or confront (in a hostile manner), come upon

Oceanus, -i, *m.*, the great sea, outer sea, ocean

ocior, -ius, *compar. adj.*, swifter, quicker

octoni, -ae, -a, *pl. adj.*, eight each, eight apiece

oculus, -i, *m.*, eye

odium, -ii, *n.*, feeling of aversion, hatred, dislike

oenophorum, -i, *n.*, large wine vessel

offero, offerre, obtuli, oblatum, to put in one's way, show, present

officium, -i, *n.*, service, duty, task

olim, *adv.*, formerly, previously, once (upon a time)

oliva, -ae, *f.*, olive, olive tree

olivum, -i, *n.*, olive oil

olle, -us, -um, *pron. and adj.*, archaic equivalent of **ille**, that, that person or thing

olus, -eris, *n.* (*also* **holus, -eris,** *n.*), vegetables; a particular vegetable; green vegetables

omitto, -ittere, -isi, -issum, to release, discard, forsake, abandon

omnis, -e, *adj.*, all, each, every

onus, oneris, *n.*, burden, load; weight; care, task

opera, -ae, *f.*, task, effort

opifex, -icis, *m.*, craftsman, artificer

oportet, -ere, -uit, —, *impers.*, it is proper/right

opprimo, -imere, -essi, -essum, to press on; to smother, bury; to overpower

opprobrium, -(i)i, *n.*, reproach, shame, scandal

oppugno (1), to attack, assail
ops, opis, *f.,* power, ability, resources, wealth
optimus, -a, -um, *adj.* also archaic **optumus,** best
opto (1), to wish for, desire, choose
optumus. *See* **optimus**
opulentia, -ae, *f.,* riches, wealth, affluence
opus, -eris, *n.,* work, labor; the product of work; a literary work; **opus est** (+ *abl., gen.*), I have need of
oratio, -onis, *f.,* speaking, speech, a speech
orbis, -is, *m.,* disc, wheel, sphere; (*orbis terrarum*) the central land surface of the world
orbitas, -atis, *f.,* bereavement; loss of a relative, (*spec.*) of a child; orphanhood; childlessness
ordo, -inis, *m.,* row, line, rank
Orion, -onis, *m.,* the huntsman and constellation Orion
orior, -iri, -tus, to rise, emerge; to come into existence, be born; to arise
orno (1), to arrange, equip, prepare, adorn
ornus, -i, *f.,* ash tree
oro (1), to pray, beseech
Orodes, -is, *m.,* Orodes, a Trojan in *Aeneid* 10
Orpheus, -ei *or* **-eas,** *m.* (*acc.* usually **-ea**), Orpheus, the legendary Thracian singer
Orses, -ae, *m.,* Orses, a Trojan in *Aeneid* 10

os, oris, *n.,* mouth, face
os, ossis, *gen. pl.,* **ossium,** *n.,* bone
oscito, -are, -avi, *also* **-or, -ari,** to open the mouth, gape; to yawn
ostendo, -ere, -di, -tum, to show, display
ostento (1), to present to view, exhibit, display, show
ostrum, -i, *n.,* purple dye; material dyed purple
otior, -ari, -atus, to be at leisure, take one's ease
otiosus, -a, -um, *adj.,* not occupied by business, idle, at leisure; useless
otium, -(i)i, *n.,* unoccupied or spare time, freedom from business or work, leisure
ovile, -is, *n.,* sheepfold
ovo (1), to celebrate a minor triumph or ovatio; to exult, rejoice

P

P. = **Publius, -i,** *m.,* a Roman *praenomen*
Padus, -i, *m.,* the river Po
paean, -nis, *m.,* a hymn, usually of victory addressed to Apollo or another god
pallens, -ntis, *adj.,* pale, wan, pallid, dim
pallidus, -a, -um, *adj.,* pale, colorless, dim
pallor, -oris, *m.,* paleness, discoloration, dimness
Palmus, -i, *m.,* Palmus, a Trojan in *Aeneid* 10

palus, -udis, *f.,* swamp, marsh
panis, -is, *m.,* bread, loaf of bread
pantex, -icis, *m.* (*usually pl.*), the belly, the guts
papilio, -onis, *m.,* moth, butterfly
par, paris, *adj.,* equal
parco, -cere, peperci, to refrain from; to spare (+ *dat.*); to be merciful
parcus, -a, -um, *adj.,* thrifty, economical, restrained
parens, -entis, *m./f.,* parent
pareo, -ere, -ui, -itum, to submit to, obey
pario, -ere, peperi, partum, to bring forth, bear, produce; to procure
Paris, -idis, *m.,* Paris, a Trojan prince, son of Priam and Hecuba, brother of Hector
pariter, *adv.,* together, at the same time
paro (1), to furnish, supply, make ready, produce, acquire, prepare
pars, partis, *f.,* part, portion, section
parthenius, -a, -um, *adj.,* of Mt. Parthenius in Arcadia, Greece
Parthus, -a, -um, *adj.,* of Parthia; *subst. adj.,* a Parthian
parum, *n. indecl. and adv.,* too little, not enough, inadequate
parvus, -a, -um, *adj.,* small
pasco, -cere, pavi, pastum, to feed, pasture; to provide food for

passer, -eris, *m.,* a small bird, possibly a sparrow or thrush (also possibly a title given to the part of the Catullan corpus that includes Catullus's poems on Lesbia's pet bird)
passim, *adv.,* here and there, all over the place; at random
pater, -tris, *m.,* father, senator
patera, -ae, *f.,* broad, shallow bowl or dish
paternus, -a, -um, *adj.,* of a father, paternal; (*of relationships*) on the father's side
patiens, -entis, *adj.,* suffering, enduring, permitting
patior, -i, passus, to experience, suffer, undergo; to allow, permit
patria, -ae, *f.,* one's native land
patrius, -a, -um, *adj.,* of or belonging to a father, paternal
patruus, -i, *m.,* father's brother, paternal uncle
paucus, -a, -um, *adj.* (*usually pl.*), a small number, few, a little
paulatim, *adv.,* little by little, gradually
paulisper, *adv.,* for a short time
Paul(l)us, -i, *m.,* a surname, esp. of the *gens Aemilia*; the addressee of some of Martial's epigrams
pauper, -ris, *adj.,* poor, not wealthy; *as subst. m.,* poor man
paupertas, -atis, *f.,* poverty
pavidus, -a, -um, *adj.,* terror-struck, frightened; timorous
pavor, -oris, *m.,* sudden fear, terror, fright

pax, pacis, *f.,* peace
peccatum, -i, *n.,* error; moral failure, lapse
pecco (1), to blunder, commit a fault, do wrong
pectus, -oris, *n.,* chest; breast (*as seat of the emotions*)
pecunia, -ae, *f.,* property, wealth, money
pecus, -oris, *n.,* livestock, *esp.* sheep and cattle
pecus, -udis, *f.,* livestock, *esp.* sheep; an animal as opposed to a human being
pedes, -itis, *m.,* foot soldier, infantryman
Pedo, -onis, *m.,* Albinovanus Pedo, an Augustan poet
pellis, -is, *f.,* skin, hide, pelt
pello, -ere, pepuli, pulsum, to beat, strike, set in motion, impel, drive away
pendo, -dere, pependi, pensum, to weigh, consider, estimate; (*nihil pensi habere*) to regard as of no importance
penes, *prep. + acc.,* in control of
per, *prep. + acc.,* through; throughout a period; through the agency of
perago, -agere, -egi, -actum, to carry out, perform, complete; to get through, pass through
peragro (1), to travel over every part of, scour
percello, -ellere, -uli, -ulsum, to strike down; to strike hard, hit

percontor, -ari, -atus, to make inquiries about, investigate; to interrogate
perditus, -a, -um, *adj.,* broken, ruined, lost
perdo, -ere, -idi, -itum, to cause ruin; to destroy, ruin
peregre, *adv.,* to, in, or from foreign parts; abroad
peregrinor, -ari, -atus, to travel; to stay abroad; to feel oneself a foreigner
pereo, -ire, -ii/-ivi, -itum, to pass away, come to nothing, be destroyed, perish
pererro (1), to wander through; to wander about
perfero, -rre, pertuli, perlatum, to carry or convey to a person, deliver; to maintain; to endure
pergo, -gere, -rexi, -rectum, to make one's way; to proceed
periculum, -i, *n.,* test, trial, danger
perinde, *adv.,* just (as), according (as); in the same way (as); as much (as)
perlicio, -icere, -exi/-icui, -ectum *also* **pellicio,** to attract; to captivate, seduce
permitto, -ittere, -isi, -issum, to allow, grant, permit
permuto (1), to give and take; to swap
perpello, -ellere, -uli, -ulsum, to prevail on, constrain, force
perpetuus, -a, -um, *adj.,* continuous; permanent
perprimo, -imere, -essi, -essum, to press continuously

Persa, -ae, *m.,* a Persian
perscribo, -bere, -psi, -ptum, to write out in full; to write a detailed record of
persequor, -qui, -cutus, to follow persistently, pursue, dog
persona, -ae, *f.,* mask; character; (*in legal contexts*) person involved in a particular case
persuadeo, -dere, -si, -sum, to persuade
pertineo, -ere, -ui, to extend, reach, relate (to), be a concern (to)
pervenio, -ire, -veni, -ventum, to come, arrive (at)
pes, pedis, *m.,* foot
pessimus, -a, -um, *adj. also archaic* **pessumus,** worst, wickedest, most harmful, most painful
pessumus. *See* **pessimus**
pestifer, -era, -erum, *adj.,* deadly, noxious, disastrous, pestilential
petitor, -oris, *m.,* seeker, applicant, claimant, candidate
peto, -ere, -ivi/-ii, -itum, to reach out for; to make for, seek
petorritum, -i, *n.,* open four-wheeled carriage
petulantia, -ae, *f.,* impudence, rudeness, immodesty
pexus, -a, -um, *adj.,* neatly combed, brushed; (*of woolen cloth*) brushed to give it a silky nap; soft and silky
Phocaei, -orum, *m. pl.,* the Phocaeans, a people of Ionian Greece
Phrygius, -a, -um, *adj.,* Phrygian, Trojan
Phryx, -gis, *adj.,* Phrygian, (*subst.*) a Phrygian
piget, -ere, -guit *and* **pigitum est,** *impers.,* it pains, grieves, disgusts
pilleatus, -a, -um, *adj.,* wearing a pilleus, a felt cap as a sign of freedom (also worn at the Saturnalia)
pinguis, -e, *adj.,* fat, sleek, plump, greasy, rich; thick; slow-witted, dull
pinifer, -era, -erum, *adj.,* pine-bearing
pinna, -ae, *f.,* feather
pinus, -us, *f.,* pine tree, ship made of pine
piscis, -is, *m.,* fish
pius, -a, -um, *adj.,* dutiful, conscientious, devoted
placeo, -ere, -cui *or* **placitus sum,** to please, give pleasure
placidus, -a, -um, *adj.,* agreeable, tame, quiet, tranquil
plebeius, -a, -um, *adj.,* of or belonging to the plebeian class
plebs, -ebis, *f.,* the plebeian class, the commons
plenus, -a, -um, *adj.,* full
plerusque, -aque, -umque, *adj.,* the greater part or number of, most of
Plinius, -i, *m.,* Pliny, *esp.* Martial's friend, Pliny the Younger, a politician and writer of literary letters as well as verse, including a panegyric of the emperor Trajan

plostrum, -i, *n. also* **plaustrum,** vehicle for freight, wagon
plurimus, -a, -um, *adj. also archaic* **plurumus,** the greatest number, very many, the greatest, most
plurumus. *See* **plurimus**
plus, pluris, *n.,* more
poculum, -i, *n.,* cup
poeniteo (paeniteo), -ere, -ui, to cause dissatisfaction, give reason for regret; to affect with regret
poeta, -ae, *m.,* poet
pollens, -ntis, *adj.,* strong, potent
pondus, -eris, *n.,* weight, a weight, bulk, heavy object
pono, -ere, posui, positum, to put, place, set
pontus, -i, *m.,* the sea
popina, -ae, *f.,* cheap restaurant or shop selling cooked food
poples, -itis, *m.,* knee
popularis, -e, *adj.,* of or belonging to the people, popular
populus, -i, *m.,* a people, nation, the general public, crowd
porrigo, -igere, -exi, -ectum, to stretch out, lay prostrate, cause to spread out
porrum, -i, *n.* (*also* **porrus, -i,** *m.*), leek
Porsen(n)a, -ae, *m.,* Lars Porsenna, the Etruscan king who besieged Rome after the expulsion of the Tarquins
porta, -ae, *f.,* gate
porto (1), to transport, carry, bear, bring

possessio, -onis, *f.,* occupancy, seizure, control
possum, posse, potui, to be able, have power
post, *prep. + acc. also adv.,* behind, after
postea, *adv.,* subsequently, afterward
posterus, -a, -um, *adj.,* next, subsequent; *pl.,* coming generations, descendants
postquam, *conj.,* after; ever since
postulatio, -onis, *f.,* demand, request; application to a magistrate for redress of a wrong
postulo (1), to ask for; to make application to a magistrate for; to expect, require
potestas, -atis, *f.,* command, control, power, rule, reign
potior, -iri, -titus, to take possession, to obtain (+ *acc., gen., or abl.*)
potior, -ius, *adj., compar. of* **potis**
potis, *adj. indecl.,* able, capable
potius, *adv.,* rather, more than
poto (1), to drink; to drink convivially, tipple
prae, *prep. + abl. also adv.,* before, in comparison with
praebeo, -ere, -ui, -itum, to offer, make available, provide
praecipio, -ere, -cepi, -ceptum, to forestall, take first, anticipate; to advise, command
praeclarus, -a, -um, *adj.,* radiant, brilliant, outstanding, grand, glorious

praeco, -onis, *m.,* town crier; auctioneer
praeda, -ae, *f.,* booty, spoil, loot; reward, profit, prize
praedurus, -a, -um, *adj.,* very hard, very strong
praefectus, -i, *m.,* the officer in command (of)
praefor, -ari, -atus, to say beforehand or by way of preface, mention first
praegnas, -tis, *adj.,* pregnant
praelego, -egere, -legi, -lectum, to select; to read before a class, recite
praemium, -i, *n.,* payment, reward, prize
praepollens, -ntis, *adj.,* outstanding in power, dominant
praesens, -ntis, *adj.,* present, in person, face to face
praesertim, *adv.,* especially
praeses, -idis, *m.* (*f.*), guardian, custodian
praesidium, -i, *n.,* defense, protection; stronghold
praesto, *adv.,* ready, available, on the spot
praesto, -are, -iti, -atum, to be superior to others, excel, surpass; to furnish; (*with predicate adj.*) to keep (*safe, etc.*)
praetendo, -dere, -di, -tum, to hold out; to put forth as pretext
praeter, *prep. + acc., also adv. and conj.,* past, along, beyond; besides, other than
praeterea, *adv.,* as well, besides, furthermore
praetor, -oris, *m.,* praetor; a Roman magistrate concerned chiefly with judicial functions
prandeo, -dere, -di, -sum, to eat one's morning meal, lunch
prandium, -(i)i, *n.,* lunch
pravus, -a, -um, *adj.,* crooked, corrupt, perverse
precarius, -a, -um, *adj.,* that is given as a favor, that depends on the mercy of others
precor, -ari, -atus, to ask or pray; to beg, implore
pre(he)ndo, -dere, -di, -sum, to grasp, seize, take hold of; to take into custody, arrest
premo, -mere, -ssi, -ssum, to apply a steady force upon, press, press hard upon, attack
prenso (1), to grasp at, clutch at; to accost, buttonhole, canvass
pretium, -i, *n.,* reward, prize
prex, -ecis, *f.,* entreaty, prayer, supplication
Priapus, -i, *m.,* Priapus, a god of procreation
pridie, *adv.,* on the day before
primo, *adv.,* at first, to begin with
primoris, -e, *adj.,* first in position, the front; (*m. pl. as noun*) the leading men
primum, *adv.,* first, in the first place; *with* **ubi,** as soon as
primus, -a, -um, *adj.,* first, foremost, uttermost, earliest
princeps, -cipis, *adj.,* first, foremost

princeps, -cipis, *m.,* a person who is first, founder; a leading member, chief citizen (title adopted by Augustus to emphasize the nonmilitary nature of his rule)
prior, -ius, *compar. adj.,* ahead, earlier, first
priusquam, *conj., also* **prius ... quam,** before
privatus, -a, -um, *adj.,* private, particular to a person; *subst. m.,* private citizen
pro, *prep. + abl.,* in front of, in place of, on behalf of
probo (1), to approve of; to certify, authorize, sanction; to put to the proof, prove
probus, -a, -um, *adj.,* excellent, of upright character, virtuous
procacitas, -atis, *f.,* forwardness, license, wantonness
procedo, -ere, -ssi, -sum, to move forward, advance
proceres, -um, *m. pl.,* leading men of a city
procreo (1), to engender, beget; to bring forth, bear
procul, *adv.,* far, at a distance, far away, far
procurro, -ere, -curri *and* **-cucurri, -cursum,** to run forth, rush forward, charge
prodeo, -ire, -ii, -itum, to come forward, come forth, appear
proelium, -(i)i, *n.,* battle
profecto, *adv.,* without question, undoubtedly, assuredly

proficiscor, -icisci, -ectus, to start on a journey, set out, depart; to begin a series; to originate from
profor, -ari, -atus, to speak out, give utterance; to tell; to give warning
profugio, -ere, -fugi, to flee, run away, escape
profugus, -i, *m.,* exile, fugitive, refugee
profundo, -dere, -fudi, -fusum, to pour out, shed, cause to flow
profusus, -a, -um, *adj.,* immoderate in expenditure, extravagant, prodigal
prognatus, -a, -um, *adj.,* born, descended from
progredior, -di, -ssus, to go forward, advance, proceed
prohibeo, -ere, -ui, -itum, to keep off, exclude, prevent, forbid
proinde, *adv.,* accordingly
prolabor, -bi, -psus, to slide or slip forth, drop, collapse
proles, -is, *f.,* offspring, progeny
promiscue, *adv.,* without distinction, indiscriminately
promiscuus, -a, -um, *adj.,* possessed by each equally
promitto, -ere, -misi, -missum, to put forth, promise, hold out
promptus, -us, *m.,* (*in promptu*) within easy reach; in full view
pronus, -a, -um, *adj.,* bending forward; facing or directed toward the ground
prope, *adv.,* near; *prep. + acc.,* near, by

propello, -ellere, -uli, -ulsum, to push or thrust forward; to push away, repel
propero (1), to act with haste, hurry
propinquus, -a, -um, *adj.,* close, neighboring; (*as subst.*) kinsman
propior, -ius, *compar. adj.,* nearer, closer, earlier, more recent
propono, -onere, -osui, -ositum, to expose to view, exhibit; to set up, place before; to offer
proprius, -a, -um, *adj.,* own, personal, individual, particular
prosequor, -qui, -cutus, to accompany, to pursue
prospecto (1), to look at, look out for
prospectus, -us, *m.,* prospect, view, outlook
prosperus, -a, -um, *adj.,* successful, favorable
prosum, -desse, -fui, to be of use, do good
protervus, -a, -um, *adj.,* violent, vehement
Proteus, -eos/-ei, *m.,* a Greek sea god, herdsman of Poseidon's seals
protinus, *adv.,* straight on, directly on
provenio, -enire, -eni, -entum, to come forth, come forward; to be produced
provocatio, -onis, *f.,* the act of challenging to a fight; an appeal to the people; the right of such an appeal

prudens, -ntis, *adj.,* discreet, having good sense, sagacious, clever
prurio, -ire, to itch, have a sexual craving
pubes, -is, *f.,* the youth, young men
publicus, -a, -um, *adj.,* of the people, common to all, communal
pudicitia, -ae, *f.,* sexual purity, chastity, virtue
pudicus, -a, -um, *adj.,* sexually pure, chaste
pudor, -oris, *m.,* shame, sense of decency, modesty
puella, -ae, *f.,* girl
puer, -i, *m.,* nonadult male, boy; favorite, young male slave
pugna, -ae, *f.,* fight, battle
pugno (1), to fight, do battle, contend
pulcher, -chra, -chrum, *adj.,* beautiful, handsome; splendid, glorious
pullus, -a, -um, *adj.,* dark colored, dusky
pulmo, -onis, *m.,* the lungs
pulsus. *See* **pello**
purpura, -ae, *f.,* shellfish yielding a purple dye; purple dye, purple color
purpureus, -a, -um, *adj.,* purple
purus, -a, -um, *adj.,* clean, genuine, blameless
pustula, -ae, *f.,* inflamed sore, pustule; pimple
puto (1), to ponder, think, consider

putris, -e, *adj.,* decomposed, foul; crumbling
Pyrrha, -ae, *f.,* Pyrrha, with her husband Deucalion, one of two humans left alive after the flood
Pythagoras, -ae, *m.,* Pythagoras, a slave of Nero

Q

qua, *interr., indef., and rel. adv.,* by which route, where
quacumque (*also* **quacunque**), *adv.,* by whatever way, wherever; by whatever means
quadraginta, *indecl. adj.,* forty
quaero, -rere, -sivi, -situm, to search for, make inquiries, ask
quaestor, -oris, *m.,* annually elected magistrate who performed mainly financial duties
qualis, -e, *interr. and rel. adj.,* of which sort or quality, such as
qualiscumque, qualecumque, *rel. adj.,* of whatever sort or quality, whatever
quam, *adv.,* how; than
quando, *adv.,* at which time; when; seeing that
quantum, *interr. and rel. adv.,* how greatly? to what extent, degree
quantus, -a, -um, *rel. adj.,* how much, as much as
quare, *interr. and rel. adv.,* for what reason? wherefore, for which reason
quartus, -a, -um, *adj.,* fourth
quatio, -tere, —, -ssum, to shake; to brandish

quattuor, *indecl. adj.,* four
-que, *encl. conj.,* and
querella, -ae, *f.,* complaint, protest; grievance
queror, queri, questus, to express discontent, complain
qui, quae, quod, *rel. pron. and adj.; interr. pron.,* who, which, what; *indef. adj.,* any
quia, *conj.,* since, because
quicumque, quaecumque, quodcumque (*also* **quicunque,** etc.), *rel. and indef. pron. and adj.,* whoever, whatever
quidam, quaedam, quoddam, *indef. pron.,* a certain; a certain one, somebody
quidem, *adv.,* indeed, certainly
quies, -etis, *f.,* rest, relaxation
quiesco, -ere, -evi, -etum, to rest, repose, be quiet, be still, be composed
quietus, -a, -um, *adj.,* in a state of repose, at rest, asleep, doing nothing
quin, *adv.,* indeed, in fact; *conj.,* that not, (but) that
quindecim, *indecl. adj.,* fifteen
quinque, *indecl. adj.,* five
quippe, *partic.,* the reason is that, for; seeing that
Quirinus, -i, *m.,* Quirinius, the deified Romulus
Quirites, -itium, *m. pl.,* Quirites, *a name given to the citizens of Rome, esp. in solemn addresses*
quirito, -are, to cry in protest

quis, quid, *interr. pron. m. sg. and n. sg.,* who? what?
quisquam, quicquam, *indef. pron.,* anyone, anything
quisque, quaeque, quidque, *indef. adj. and pron.,* each, each one
quisquis, quidquid, *pron. and adj.,* whoever, whatever
quivis, quaevis, quidvis, *pron.,* whatever person/thing you please
quo, *adv.,* where, *interr. adv.,* to what place? to what end? of what use? why?
quocunque *also* **quocumque,** *rel. adv.,* to any place, wherever
quod, *rel. adv.,* as to which, inasmuch as, as to the fact that, because
quodsi = quod si, but if
quoniam, *conj.,* seeing that; since
quoque, *adv.,* besides, as well
quot, *indecl. interr. and rel. adj.,* how many? as many as
quotannis, *adv.,* every year, yearly

R
rabidus, -a, -um, *adj.,* raging, mad, frenzied
rado, -dere, -si, -sum, to scrape, scratch, shave
rapax, -acis, *adj.,* tearing, violent, grasping, insatiable
rapina, -ae, *f.,* the forceful carrying off of plunder; the carrying off of a woman
rapio, -ere, -ui, -tum, to seize and carry off; to snatch away

Rapo, -onis, *m.,* Rapo, an Etruscan in *Aeneid* 10
rarus, -a, -um, *adj.,* uncommon, rare, scarce; scattered
ratio, -onis, *f.,* reckoning, calculation; the act of reasoning
ratis, -is, *f.,* raft, float
raucus, -a, -um, *adj.* harsh-sounding, noisy
ravus, -a, -um, *adj.,* tawny
recipio, -ipere, -epi, -eptum, to admit, receive, allow to enter; (*with reflex.*) to withdraw, retire
recito (1), to read aloud, recite
recta, *adv.,* directly, straight
rectus, -a, -um, *adj.,* straight, direct; erect, upright
recuso (1), to object, protest, decline, reject
reddo, -ere, -idi, -itum, to give back, render; **rationem reddere,** to render an account
redeo, -ire, -ii, -itum, to go back, return
reditus, -us, *m.,* a going back, a return
refero, -rre, rettuli, relatum, to bring back; to report, record; to pay as due, render; to relate
refert, referre, retulit (*impers. or with n. pron. as subject*), it makes a difference, matters, is of importance
regina, -ae, *f.,* queen
regio, -onis, *f.,* direction, line; district, region, locality
regius, -a, -um, *adj.,* royal, kingly, regal

regnator, -oris, *m.,* one who rules as king, a lord
regno (1), to rule as king, reign
regnum, -i, *n.,* kingship, dominion, rule
rego, -ere, rexi, rectum, to direct, guide, control, command
regredior, -di, -ssus, to go back, return, retreat
Regulus, -i, *m.,* M. Aquilius Regulus, a famous advocate and example of eloquence
relatu. *See* **refero**
relinquo, -ere, -liqui, -lictum, to depart from; to leave behind
reliquus, -a, -um, *adj.,* left, remaining
remedium, -i, *n.,* remedy, care
remeo (1), to go or come back, return; to come around again
remex, -igis, *m.,* oarsman; *collective sg.,* bench of rowers
remotus, -a, -um, *adj.,* distant, remote, removed
Remus, -i, *m.,* Remus, brother of Romulus
reno, -are, -avi, to swim back
reor, -eri, ratus, to think, suppose
repello, -ere, reppuli, -pulsum, to push or thrust away; to drive back, repel
repeto, -ere, -ivi/-ii, -itum, to return to, seek again, attack again, go back for, recall, claim back
reprehendo, -ere, -endi, -ensum, to hold back; to censure, rebuke

requiesco, -escere, -evi, -etum, to rest, desist (from), stand idle, relax
res, rei, *f.,* property, thing, affair, deed; *pl.,* exploits
res publica, rei publicae, *f.,* republic
reservo (1), to keep for future use, withhold, reserve
resisto, -istere, -titi, to come to a standstill, plant oneself; to resist, withstand
respicio, -icere, -exi, -ectum, to look around, look back; turn one's thoughts to, take heed, have regard for
respondeo, -ere, -di, -sum, to answer, reply
responsum, -i, *n.,* answer, reply, answer given by an oracle or soothsayer
rete, -is, *n.,* net
retineo, -ere, -ui, retentum, to hold fast, retain, restrain
retorqueo, -quere, -si, -tum, to twist round, wrench back; to reverse the course of
revoco (1), to call back, call off
revolvo, -vere, -vi, -utum, to roll back (a scroll in order to read it), to go back over (past events) in thought or speech; to revert
rex, regis, *m.,* king
rideo, -ere, -si, -sum, to laugh
rigidus, -a, -um, *adj.,* stiff, unbending; primitive, rugged, stern, upright
rima, -ae, *f.,* narrow cleft, crack, fissure

ripa, -ae, *f.,* bank (of a river)
ritus, -us, *m.,* religious rites, ceremonies; *abl. sg. with adj.,* according to a given rite
rodo, -dere, -si, -sum, to gnaw, nibble; to slander, carp at
rogo (1), to ask, request
Roma, -ae, *f.,* Rome
Romanus, -a, -um, *adj.,* Roman, of Rome; *subst. adj.,* a Roman
rosa, -ae, *f.,* rose, rosebush
roseus, -a, -um, *adj.,* made of roses; rose-colored
rubens, -ntis, *adj.,* colored or tinged with red
ruber, -bra, -brum, *adj.,* red
rudis, -e, *adj.,* crude, rough, unpolished
ruo, -ere, -i, to move swiftly, rush headlong; to fall with violence, collapse
rupes, -is, *f.,* steep rocky cliff, crag
rursus, *adv.,* backward, in turn, back again, once more
rus, ruris, *n.,* country, land, country estate
rusticulus, -a, -um, *adj.,* somewhat uncouth or provincial
Rutuli, -orum, *m. pl.,* the Rutulians, a people of Latium

S

sacer, -cra, -crum, *adj.,* dedicated, consecrated, sacred; accursed, infamous
Sacrator, -oris, *m.,* Sacrator, an Etruscan in *Aeneid* 10

saeculum, -i, *n.,* generation, age, (the people of) a generation; lifetime
saepe, *adv.* (*compar.* **saepius**), often, frequently
saepio, -ire, -psi, -ptum, to surround
saevio, -ire, -ii, -itum, to behave savagely, rage, be violent
sagitta, -ae, *f.,* arrow
sal, salis, *m.,* salt; *pl.,* examples of wit, jokes
salarius, -(i)i, *m.,* dealer in salted fish
Salius, -i, *m.,* Salius, a Rutulian in *Aeneid* 10
salsus, -a, -um, *adj.,* salted, salty
saltem, *adv.,* at least, at all events
salutator, -oris, *m.,* one who greets; one who pays a morning call, a client
salus, -utis, *f.,* personal safety; physical well-being; security
saluto (1), to greet, salute; to make a morning call on a patron or other social superior
salve, *as a greeting,* hello, good morning; *as adv.,* with everything in order; *with* **satin,** is all well?
salvus, -a, -um, *adj.,* safe, secure, unharmed
sanctus, -a, -um, *adj.,* sacrosanct, inviolate, holy
sane, *adv.,* certainly, truly
sanguis, -inis, *m.,* blood
sanus, -a, -um, *adj.,* sound, healthy, sane, sensible

sapientia, -ae, *f.,* reason, soundness of judgment, wisdom
sapio, -ere, -ivi/-ii, to taste of (a quality); to have discernment
sarcio, -ire, sarsi, sartum, to patch, mend, repair
satin. *See* **satis** *and* **-ne**
satio (1), to satisfy the hunger of; to satisfy, content
satis, *n. indecl. subst.,* enough; *adv.,* enough, sufficiently; *compar.* **satius,** better
Satureianus, -a, -um, *adj.,* from Satureia, a town in Apulia
Saturnius, -a, -um, *adj.,* of Saturn; child of Saturn (usually of Juno or Jupiter)
saxum, -i, *n.,* stone, rock
sceleratus, -a, -um, *adj.,* accursed, heinously criminal
scelestus, -a, -um, *adj.,* impious, wicked, infamous, accursed
scelus, -eris, *n.,* crime, villainy, affliction
schola, -ae, *f.,* school
scindo, -ere, scicidi/scidi, -issus, to cut, tear, rend, divide
scio, -ire, -ii/-ivi, -itum, to know, understand
scortum, -i, *n.,* prostitute
scribo, -bere, -psi, -ptum, to inscribe, write, make a record of, compose
scrinium, -i, *n.,* writing case, case for papyrus rolls, bookcase
scriptor, -oris, *m.,* one who writes; writer of literary works (*with gen. of subject matter*)

scutum, -i, *n.,* shield
se, sese, *reflex. pron.,* himself, herself, itself, themselves
secedo, -dere, -ssi, -ssum, to draw aside, withdraw
secerno, -cernere, -crevi, -cretum, to separate off, isolate, set aside
secretus, -a, -um, *adj.,* secret, hidden
seculum, -i, *n.. See* **saeculum**
secum. *See* **se** *and* **cum**
secundum, *prep. + acc.,* behind, after, along, in accordance with
secundus, -a, -um, *adj.,* following, second, secondary, favorable, propitious
securis, -is, *f.,* ax, *esp. one carried on the fasces of a Roman magistrate*
sed, *conj.,* but
sedeo, -ere, sedi, sessum, to sit; (*of an army*) to remain encamped
sedes, -is, *f.,* seat, throne
seditio, -onis, *f.,* violent political discord; internal strife
seduco, -cere, -xi, -ctum, to draw aside; to lead astray, entice
sedulo, *adv.,* diligently, zealously
segnis, -e, *adj.,* sluggish, inactive, slow-moving
sella, -ae, *f.,* chair, sedan chair
semet, *a strengthened form of* **se**
semper, *adv.,* always
semen, -inis, *n.,* seed
senator, -oris, *m.,* member of the Senate, senator
senatus, -us, *m.,* the Senate

senex, -is, *adj.,* old, advanced in years; *as subst. m.,* old man
senior, -oris, *compar. of* **senex**
sententia, -ae, *f.,* opinion, judgment, thought, purpose, decision
sentio, -ire, sensi, sensum, to perceive, understand
sequor, -i, secutus, to follow, attend upon
Ser. = Servius, -(i)i, *m.,* a Roman *praenomen,* esp. Servius Tullius
sera, -ae, *f.,* a crossbar, bolt
sermo, -onis, *m.,* speech, talk, conversation
serus, -a, -um, *adj.,* slow, tardy, late
serva, -ae, *f.,* female slave
servilis, -e, *adj.,* of or belonging to a slave, servile, ignoble
servio, -ire, -ivi/-ii, -itum (*with dat.*), to be enslaved, serve
servitium, -i, *n.,* slavery, servitude; *pl.,* slaves
servitus, -utis, *f.,* the status of a slave, bondage, servitude
servo (1), to watch over, observe, preserve, reserve
servus, -i, *m.,* slave
sese. *See* **se**
seu. *See* **sive**
severitas, -atis, *f.,* strictness, austerity, sternness, severity
severus, -a, -um, *adj.,* stern, strict, serious, severe
Sex. = Sextus, -i, *m.,* a Roman *praenomen*
si, *conj.,* if
sic, *adv.,* thus, in this way; so

siccus, -a, -um, *adj.,* dry, desiccated
sicut/sicuti, *conj.,* in the same way as, just as
Sidonius, -a, -um, *adj.,* of Sidon, Phoenician
signum, -i, *n.,* mark, sign, military standard
silentium, -i, *n.,* silence
sileo, -ere, -ui, —, to be silent; to say nothing
Silius, -i, *m.,* Silius, the name of the writer of an epic on the Punic Wars
silva, -ae, *f.,* forest, wood
similis, -e, *adj.,* + *gen., dat.,* like
similitudo, -inis, *f.,* similarity, resemblance
simul, *adv.,* at the same time, together
simulator, -oris, *m.,* one who imitates, puts on a pretense, feigner
simulo (1), to pretend, simulate, make a pretense of
simultas, -atis, *f.,* quarrel, feud
sine, *prep.* + *abl.,* without
singuli, -ae, -a, *pl. adj.,* each one; every single; single, individual
singultim, *adv.,* gulpingly, in gulps
sinister, -tra, -trum, *adj.,* on the left, left; adverse or harmful
sino, sinere, sivi/sii, situm, to leave alone, let pass, allow, permit
sisto, -ere, steti/stiti, statum, to cause to stand, set up; to cause to appear in court at a certain time; to present

situs, -a, -um, *adj.,* stored, deposited; placed, centered, situated
sive *or* **seu,** *conj.,* or if; **sive ... sive** *or* **seu ... seu** (*poet. also,* **sive ... seu** *or* **seu ... sive**), whether ... or
sobrius, -a, -um, *adj.,* sober
socius, -(i)i, *m.,* companion, comrade, partner, ally
socordia, -ae, *f.,* sluggishness, torpor
sol, solis, *m.,* sun, sunlight, light of day, day
soleo, -ere, -itus, to be accustomed
sollicitus, -a, -um, *adj.,* troubled, anxious, uneasy in mind
solum, *adv.,* only, just, merely
solum, -i, *n.,* ground, earth, soil, land
solus, -a, -um, *adj.,* alone
solutus, -a, -um, *adj.,* free, unfettered, loose, detached
somnus, -i, *m.,* sleep
sono (1), to make a noise, resound, sound
sopio, -ire, -ivi/-ii, -itum, to cause to sleep; to render insensible
sordes, -is, *f.,* dirt or filth of any kind
sordidus, -a, -um, *adj.,* foul with dirt, grimy; squalid, dingy; poor in quality, shabby
sortior, -iri, -itus, to draw lots; to obtain by lot; to receive as one's portion, acquire
Sp. = Spurius, -i, *m.,* a Roman *praenomen*

Spartacus, -i, *m.,* Spartacus, leader of a slave revolt in 73–71 BCE
spectatus, -a, -um, *adj.,* known by observation, conspicuous, established
specto (1), to look at, watch, observe; to regard; to regard with approval, respect
speculum, -i, *n.,* mirror
spero (1), to look forward to; to hope; to anticipate
spes, spei, *f.,* hope, expectation
spiro (1), to breathe, be alive; to express the spirit of, emanate
sponda, -ae, *f.,* the frame of a bed or couch
spondeo, -dere, spopondi, sponsum, to give a pledge; to contract in marriage; to pledge oneself to pay, guarantee
(spons), -ntis, *f.,* will, volition; *usually in ablative expressions:* **sponte,** deliberately; **sponte sua,** *etc.,* of one's own accord
sponsa, -ae, *f.,* woman promised in marriage, fiancée
sponsor, -oris, *m.,* one who guarantees the good faith of another; a surety
sponsus, -i, *m.,* man promised in marriage, fiancé
stabulum, -i, *n.,* building for housing animals, stable
stagnum, -i, *n.,* pool, pond, lake
stativus, -a, -um, stationary, standing; (*pl. n. as subst.*) stationary camp
statuo, -uere, -ui, -utum, to set, erect, decree, appoint, decide

sterno, -ere, stravi, stratum, to lay out, spread out; to bring to the ground; to strike lifeless
stigma, -atis, *n.,* a mark tattooed or branded on runaway slaves or criminals
stipula, -ae, *f., coll. sg.,* stubble, straw
stirps, -pis, *f.,* stem, stalk; family or ancestral race; a person's offspring
sto, -are, steti, statum, to stand, remain; *with pron.,* to take sides with; to be fixed, established
Stoice, *adv.,* in the manner of a Stoic
stolatus, -a, -um, *adj.,* wearing a *stola* (the modest dress of Roman matrons)
stolidus, -a, -um, *adj.,* dull, brutish, stupid
strenue, *adv.,* with energy or vigor; briskly
stringo, -ngere, -nxi, -ctum, to bind fast, draw tight; to bare, unsheathe
studeo, -ere, -ui, to devote oneself to, concentrate on, support, favor, study
studium, -i, *n.,* zeal; devotion to a person, party, cause, etc.
stultus, -a, -um, *adj.,* stupid, foolish, silly, inept
stupeo, stupere, stupui, to be struck senseless, stunned, astounded, amazed
stupor, -oris, *m.,* torpor, bewilderment, dullness of apprehension
stupro (1), to violate the chastity of, defile by licentious conduct
stuprum, -i, *n.,* dishonor, shame, illicit sexual intercourse
suadeo, -dere, -si, -sum, to advise, urge, advocate
suaviter, *compar.* **-ius,** *adv.,* so as to please the senses, sweetly
sub, *prep. + abl.,* under, beneath; *+ acc.,* directly after, in response to
subdolus, -a, -um, *adj.,* sly, deceitful, treacherous
subicio, -icere, -ieci, -iectum, to place under; to lay before, furnish (to the mind)
subiectus, -a, -um, *adj.,* situated under; situated close at hand, adjacent
subigo, -igere, -egi, -actum, to drive under; to bring under authority, subjugate, subdue
subinde, *adv.,* immediately or shortly thereafter
sublatus, -a, -um. *See* **tollo**
submoveo, -overe, -ovi, -otum, to remove; to clear from the path (of)
subrideo, -ere, -si, -sum, to smile
subsido, -ere, -edi/-idi, to crouch down, adopt a position under
subsisto, -istere, -titi, to stand firm, come to a stop
Subura, -ae, *f.,* Subura, the valley between the Esquiline and Viminal Hills (a center of Roman nightlife)

succedo, -dere, -ssi, -ssum, to move to a position below; to approach, move into position (of); to relieve, take over (from)

succido, -dere, -di, -sum, to cut from below; (*with a part of the body, esp. the knee*) to hamstring

succurro, -rrere, -rri, -rsum, to run to the rescue of; to come to mind

Sulla, -ae, *m.,* Sulla, a cognomen of the *gens Cornelia,* esp. L. Cornelius Sulla Felix

sulpurata, -orum, *n. pl.,* wood treated with sulphur (to make it more combustible)

sum, esse, fui, futurum, to be

summa, -ae, *f.* the whole of a thing as distinct from its parts; the totality

summum, *adv.,* at most

summus, -a, -um, *adj.,* highest, topmost, uppermost

sumo, -ere, -mpsi, -mptum, to take up; to take on

sumptus, -us, *m.,* expenditure of money, outlay, expense

supellex, -ectilis, *f.,* furnishings, paraphernalia

super, *prep. + acc.,* over, above, beyond

superbia, -ae, *f.,* pride, arrogance

superbus, -a, -um, *adj.,* haughty, proud, arrogant

superemineo, -ere, to stand out above

superiacio, -acere, -eci, -ectum, to throw or scatter on top

supplicium, -(i)i, *n.,* punishment, reparation

suppono, -onere, -osui, -ositum, to place under; to substitute

supra, *prep. + acc.,* above, superior to

sura, -ae, *f.,* the calf of the leg

Sura, -ae, *m.,* Sura, a cognomen used by several *gentes*

surgo, -rgere, -rrexi, -rrectum, to get up, rise up; to rouse oneself to action

suspectus, -a, -um, *adj.,* viewed with mistrust

suspendo, -ere, -di, -sum, to hang, suspend; **suspendere naso,** to hang on one's nose (an expression of contempt)

suspicio, -icere, -exi, -ectum, to look upward to; to look up to, admire

sustineo, -ere, -tinui, -tentum, to keep erect; to support, hold up, sustain

suus, -a, -um, *poss. adj.,* his, her, its, their (own)

Syrus, -i, *m.,* a Syrian (especially used of a slave); a slave name

T

T. = Titus, -i, *m.,* a Roman *praenomen*

taberna, -ae, *f.,* hut, inn, shop, market stall

tabernaculum, -i, *n.,* tent

tabula, -ae, *f.,* flat piece of wood; board; writing tablet

taceo, -ere, -ui, -itum, to be silent, say nothing

tacitus, -a, -um, *adj.,* silent
taeter, -tra, -trum, *adj.,* foul, horrible, vile
talis, -e, *adj.,* such, of such a kind
tam, *adv.,* so; so much as
tamen, *adv.,* nevertheless
tametsi, *conj.,* even though, all the same
tamquam, *conj.,* as if, just as
tandem, *adv.,* at last
tantum, *adv.,* to such a degree; only
tantum, -i, *n. pron.,* such a quantity; (*with partitive gen.*) so much (of)
tantus, -a, -um, *adj.,* so much, so great, of such a size
tarde, *adv.,* slowly, with difficulty, with delay
Tarentum, -i, *n.,* Tarentum, a south Italian town (modern Taranto)
Tarquinius, -(i)i, *m.,* the name of an Etrusan family, especially Tarquinius Priscus, fifth king of Rome, and Tarquinius Superbus, the last king
taurus, -i, *m.,* bull
tectum, -i, *n.,* roof; roofed building, house, shelter
teges, -etis, *f.,* rush matting
tego, -gere, -xi, -ctum, to cover, roof, clothe, shield, conceal
tellus, -uris, *f.,* the earth, globe, land
telum, -i, *n.,* weapon, spear
temere, *adv.,* blindly, heedlessly, recklessly

temno, -ere, to scorn, despise
tempero (1), to exercise restraint; to restrain, moderate
tempestas, -atis, *f.,* a portion of time, period, season; weather, bad weather, storm
templum, -i, *n.,* area of sky or land marked out for taking of the auspices; temple
tempto (1), to test, try, make an attempt on
tempus, -oris, *n.,* time, period of time, period of history
tendo, -dere, tetendi, -tum/-sum, to extend outward or upward, hold out, offer, stretch from within, distend
tenebrae, -arum, *f. pl.,* darkness, obscurity, concealment
teneo, -ere, -ui, -tum, to hold, keep, occupy
tenuis, -e, *adj.,* slender, thin, fine, refined, subtle, simple
tepeo, -ere, to be warm, lukewarm, tepid
tepidus, -a, -um, *adj.,* lukewarm, tepid
ter, *adv.,* three times, thrice
tergum, -i, *n.,* the back
termes, -itis, *m.,* bough of a tree
tero, -ere, trivi, tritum, to rub, wear away; (*of time*) to use up, spend waste, kill
terra, -ae, *f.,* land, earth, ground
terreo, -ere, -ui, -itum, to frighten, terrify
terror, -oris, *m.,* fear, terror
testis, -is, *m. (f.),* witness
tetricus, -a, -um, *adj.,* stern, severe

Tettius, -i, *m.,* Tettius, one of Martial's addressees
Teucri, -orum, *m. pl.,* the descendants of Teucer, the Trojans
thalassio, -onis, *m.,* ritual cry used at a Roman wedding
Thalia, -ae, *f.,* Thalia, a muse associated especially with light verse
Theano, -onis, *f.,* Theano, mother of Mimas in *Aeneid* 10
theatrum, -tri, *m.,* theater
Thronius, -i, *m.,* Thronius, a Trojan in *Aeneid* 10
Tiberis, -is, *m.,* the river Tiber
Tiburs, -rtis, *adj.,* of or having to do with Tibur (modern Tivoli), about eighteen miles ENE of Rome, a fashionable resort spot
tigris, -is, *f. (m.),* tiger
Tillius, -i, *m.,* Tillius, the name of a character in Horace, *Satire* 1.6, possibly L. Tillius Cimber, one of Caesar's assassins
timeo, -ere, -ui, to fear, be afraid
Tisiphone, -es, *f.,* Tisiphone, one of the Furies
titulus, -i, *m.,* commemorative tablet, inscription; title of honor
toga, -ae, *f.,* toga
togatus, -a, -um, *adj.,* wearing a toga
tollo, -ere, sustuli, sublatum, to pick up, lift, raise; to get rid of, remove
tomaclum, -i, *n.,* a kind of sausage

Tonans, -ntis, *adj.,* making thunder; (*subst. m.*) the god of thunder (Jupiter)
tondeo, -ere, -sum, to cut or clip hair, shear
torqueo, -ere, torsi, tortum, to twist, bend, wrench, direct
torreo, -rrere, -rrui, tostum, to roast, scorch, burn
torridus, -a, -um, *adj.,* dried up, shriveled (by cold, etc.)
torus, -i, *m.,* strand, raised band, muscle; bolster, bed
tot, *indecl. adj.,* so many, that many
totiens, *adv.,* so many times, so often
totus, -a, -um, *adj.,* the whole of, all, entire
trado, -ere, -didi, -ditum, to hand over/down, pass on, bequeath
traho, -ere, traxi, tractum, to drag, pull, draw
trames, -itis, *m.,* footpath, track
transeo, -ire, -ivi/-ii, -itum, to come over; to go across, pass through
transfero, -ferre, -tuli, -latum, to transport, transfer, shift, bring over
transfigo, -gere, -xi, -xum, to pierce through; to drive or thrust (a weapon) through
Transtiberinus, -a, -um, *adj.,* situated or living across the Tiber
trepidus, -a, -um, *adj.,* alarmed, fearful, anxious
tres, tria, *adj. num.,* three

tribunal, -alis, *n.,* dais, platform, tribunal
tribunatus, -us, *m.,* the office of tribune
tribunicius, -a, -um, *adj.,* of or belonging to a tribune
tribunus, -i, *m.,* tribune
Tricipitinus, -i, *m.,* Tricipitinus, cognomen of Lucretius
triens, -ntis, *m.,* a third part (of a given quantity); a drinking vessel holding the contents of four *cyathi* (ladles)
trigon, -onis, *m.,* a ball game played by three players in a triangular arrangement
tristis, -e, *adj.,* gloomy, unhappy; bitter, ill-humored; stern, solemn; grim
tritus. *See* **tero**
triumphus, -i, *m.,* triumphal procession; victory, triumph
Troianus, -a, -um, *adj.,* of Troy, Trojan
tu, tui, *pron. sg.,* you
tuba, -ae, *f.,* trumpet
tueor, -eri, tuitus (tutus), to look at, view; to keep safe, preserve, maintain
Tullia, -ae, *f.,* Tullia, daughter of Servius Tullius
Tullius, -a, -um, *adj.,* the name of the Roman *gens Tullia,* especially of Servius Tullius, sixth king of Rome, or M. Tullius Cicero, orator, philosopher, and statesman
tum, *adv.,* then, at that moment; see also **cum . . . tum**
tumeo, -ere, -ui, to be distended, swell
tumultuosus, -a, -um, *adj.,* uproarious, tumultuous
tumultus, -us, *m.,* commotion, uproar; hostile incursion
tunc, *adv.,* then
tundo, -ere, tutudi, tunsum, to strike, beat, buffet
turba, -ae, *f.,* commotion; crowd
turbidus, -a, -um, *adj.,* violently agitated; turbid; agitated, wild, frantic
turbo (1), to riot, agitate, stir up, disturb
turpis, -e, *adj.,* foul, unsightly, shameful
tutus, -a, -um, *adj.,* safe
tuus, -a, -um, *sg. poss. adj.,* your, yours; (*emphatic*) your own
Tyrrhenus, -a, -um, *adj.,* Etruscan

U

uber, -ris, *n.,* teat, udder
ubi, *interr., rel., and indef. adv.,* in which place; where; when
udus, -a, -um, *adj.,* wet
ulcero (1), to cause to fester, make ulcerous
ulcus, -eris, *n.,* sore, ulcer
Ulixes, -ei, *m.,* Ulysses, the Latinized name of Odysseus
ullus, -a, -um, *adj.,* any, any at all
ulmus, -i, *f.,* elm tree
ultimus, -a, -um, *adj.,* most distant, farthest away, end of, remotest
ultor, -oris, *m.,* avenger

ultra, *prep. + acc. also adv.,* on the further side of, beyond
ultro, *adv.,* into the bargain; of one's own accord; spontaneously
ululatus, -us, *m.,* yelling, howling
umbra, -ae, *f.,* shadow, shade
umerus. *See* **humerus**
umquam, *adv., also* **unqu-,** at any time, ever
unctus, -a, -um, *adj.,* oily, greasy, enriched
unda, -ae, *f.,* wave, billow
unde, *rel. and interr. adv.,* whence, from which place
undique, *adv.,* from all sides; from every side
ung(u)o, -g(u)ere, -xi, -ctum, to smear with oil or grease, anoint
ungula, -ae, *f.,* hoof, claw, talon
unicus, -a, -um, *adj.,* one and only, sole; unique
unquam, *adv., also* **umqu-,** at any time, ever
unus, -a, -um, *adj.,* one
urbanus, -a, -um, *adj.,* of the city (particularly Rome), elegant, sophisticated
urbs, urbis, *f.,* city; *spec.,* The City, Rome
urbicus, -a, -um, *adj.,* of or belonging to the city
urceus, -i, *m.,* pitcher, jug
urgeo, -ere, ursi, to press upon, squeeze, thrust, weigh down, bear hard on; encroach on
uro, -ere, ussi, ustum, to burn, destroy by fire
ursus, -i, *m.,* bear

usquam, *adv.,* in any place; anywhere
usque, *adv.,* right on, without interruption, continuously
usquequaque, *adv.,* as far as one can go in any direction; in any respect whatsoever
usus, -us, *m.,* use, actual performance, practical experience
ut, *adv.,* how, just as; *conj. + indic.,* as, when, since; *conj. + subj.,* so that; with the result that
uti = **ut,** *conj.*
uterque, utraque, utrumque, *pron.,* each, each of two
utique, *adv.,* absolutely, without doubt, for certain
utor, -i, usus, to use, make use of; to employ
uxor, -oris, *f.,* wife
uxorius, -a, -um, *adj.,* belonging to a wife; fond or excessively attached to one's wife

V

vacuus, -a, -um, *adj.,* empty, clear, vacant
vado, -ere, to advance, proceed, rush; to go rapidly or purposefully
vadum, -i, *n.,* shallow place; *poet.,* the depths, bottom
vafer, vafra, vafrum, *adj.,* clever, cunning, ingenious
vagor, -ari, -atus, to wander, roam
vagus, -a, -um, *adj.,* roaming, wandering

valeo, -ere, valui, valitum, to be strong, be vigorous, have strength, be able
Valerius, -i, *m.,* a member of the *gens Valeria,* which was prominent in early Rome
Valerus, -i, *m.,* Valerus, an Etruscan in *Aeneid* 10
validus, -a, -um, *adj.,* powerful, robust, strong
vanus, -a, -um, *adj.,* insubstantial, empty, useless
vario (1), to diversify, make different, give divergent accounts (of); to behave in different ways
Varius, -i, *m.,* Varius, the name of L. Varius Rufus, an Augustan poet and acquaintance of Horace
varius, -a, -um, *adj.,* changeable, fluctuating, inconsistent
vastus, -a, -um, *adj.,* desolate, deserted
vates, -is, *m.,* prophet, seer
-ve, *encl. conj.,* or
vecto (1), to carry; (*pass.*) to ride
vehiculum, -i, *n.,* wheeled vehicle
vel, *adv.,* or even, even, assuredly; for instance, for example, especially
velum, -i, *n.,* sail, curtain, woven cloth
velut/veluti, *adv.,* as, just as, as if
veneror, -ari, -atus, to worship, pay homage to, revere
venia, -ae, *f.,* indulgence, kindness

venio, -ire, veni, ventum, to approach; to come
venor, -ari, -atus, to go hunting, hunt
venter, -tris, *m.,* belly, abdomen, stomach
ventus, -i, *m.,* wind
Venus, -eris, *f.,* Venus, the Roman goddess of sexual love, identified with the Greek Aphrodite; mother of Aeneas
verbero (1), to beat, strike, lash
verbum, -i, *n.,* word
vere, *adv.,* truly
vereor, -eri, -itus, to fear, be afraid, show respect for
Verginia, -ae, *f.,* Verginia, daughter of Verginius
Verginius, -i, *m.,* Verginius, a member of the *gens Verginia*
verna, -ae, *m.* (*f.*), slave born in the household; common, town-bred person
vero, *adv.,* certainly, indeed; however, yet
versiculus, -i, *m.,* short line of writing; brief line of verse
verso (1), to keep turning around; to turn over, stir; to turn (the eyes or the mind) this way and that; to turn over in the mind
versus, -us, *m.,* row, line of writing, verse
vertex, -icis, *m.,* whirlpool; the crown of the head; summit, peak; topmost part
verto, -ere, -ti, -sum, to turn
verum, *conj.,* but at the same time; yes, but

verus, -a, -um, *adj.,* real, true
vesanus, -a, -um, *adj.,* frenzied, mad
vespertinus, -a, -um, *adj.,* of or belonging to the evening
Vesta, -ae, *f.,* Vesta, the Roman goddess of the hearth
vester, vestra, vestrum, *pl. adj.,* your
vestibulum, -i, *n.,* forecourt
vestigium, -(i)i, *n.,* footprint, track, trace
vestio, -ire, -ivi/-ii, -itum, to clothe, dress, cover
vestis, -is, *f.,* clothing
Vesulus, -i, *m.,* Vesulus, a mountain in Liguria
veto, -are, -ui, -itum, to forbid, prohibit
vetulus, -a, -um, *adj.,* somewhat advanced in years, elderly, aging
vetus, -eris, *adj.,* old, veteran
vexo (1), to damage, harry, afflict, trouble, upset
via, -ae, *f.,* way, path
vicinus, -a, -um, *adj.,* neighboring, situated close by; *subst. m. or f.,* neighbor
victor, -oris, *m.,* victor
victrix, -icis, *f.; n. adj.,* prevailing, victorious, triumphant
video, -ere, vidi, visum, to see; *pass.,* to appear, seem
vigeo, -ere, -ui, to be active or lively, flourish, thrive
vigilia, -ae, *f.,* the act of keeping watch; vigilance, wakefulness
viginti, *indecl. adj.,* twenty

vigor, -oris, *m.,* physical or mental energy, vigor
vilis, -e, *adj.,* cheap
vinco, -ere, vici, victum, to conquer, prevail, overcome, defeat
vinculum, -i, *n.,* bond, fetter
vindex, -icis, *m.,* a champion of a person or their rights; defender; avenger
vindiciae, -arum, *f. pl.,* interim ownership of disputed property
vindico (1), to claim; to rescue; to avenge
vinea, -ae, *f.,* vineyard, vines in a vineyard
vinum, -i, *n.,* wine
violenter, *adv.,* with excessive force, violently
violentia, -ae, *f.,* violence, aggressiveness
violo (1), to violate, profane; to subject to outrage
vipera, -ae, *f.,* viper or similar poisonous snake
vir, viri, *m.,* man (*as opposed to a woman, child*); one possessing manly virtues; husband
virga, -ae, *f.,* twig, spray, branch; rod, stick
Virgilius, -i, *m.* (*also* **Vergilius**), the name of the poet Vergil (P. Vergilius Maro)
virginitas, -atis, *f.,* maidenhood
virgo, -inis, *f.,* girl of marriageable age; virgin
virtus, -utis, *f.,* manliness, valor, moral excellence

vis, vis, *f.,* physical strength, force, violence
viscera, -um, *n. pl.,* innards, internal organs
viso, -ere, -i, visum, to go see, visit; to go view
vita, -ae, *f.,* life, manner of life
vitium, -i, *n.,* moral failing, fault
vito (1), to steer clear of, shun, avoid
vitreus, -a, -um, *adj.,* made of glass; *subst. n.,* glassware
vividus, -a, -um, *adj.,* full of vital force, lively
vivo, -vere, -xi, -ctum, to be alive, live, be animated, survive
vivus, -a, -um, *adj.,* alive, fresh
vociferor, -ari, -atus; *also* **vocifero** (1), to shout, yell; to announce loudly
voco (1), to call, invoke; to summon
Volesus, -i, *m.,* Volesus, a Roman cognomen, esp. of the father of P. Valerius Publicola

volg-. *See* **vulg-**
volnus. *See* **vulnus**
volo (1), to fly
volo, velle, volui, to wish, want
voltus. *See* **vultus**
voluntarius, -a, -um, *adj.,* acting of one's free will, voluntary; voluntarily undertaken
voluntas, -atis, *f.,* will, wish, intention
voluptas, -atis, *f.,* pleasure, delight
volvo, -vere, -ui, -utum, to cause to travel in a circular motion; to travel in a circular motion; to roll; to cause to fall over
vos, *pl. pron.,* you
votum, -i, *n.,* vow, pledge
vox, vocis, *f.,* voice; spoken utterance, words
vulgus, -i, *n.,* the common people, crowd
vulnus, -eris, *n.,* wound, injury
vultus, -us, *m.,* facial expression, countenance; look; face

BC LATIN Readers
Series Editor: Ronnie Ancona,
Hunter College and CUNY Graduate Center

These readers, written by experts in the field, provide well-annotated Latin selections to be used as authoritative introductions to Latin authors, genres, or topics. Designed for intermediate/advanced college Latin students, they each contain approximately 600 lines of Latin, making them ideal to use in combination or as a "shake-it-up" addition to a time-tested syllabus.

See reviews of BC Latin Readers from *Bryn Mawr Classical Review, Classical Outlook,* and more at http://www.bolchazy.com/readers/

An Apuleius Reader
Selections from the METAMORPHOSES
Ellen D. Finkelpearl
xxxviii + 160 pp., 4 illustrations & 1 map (2012)
5" x 7 ¾" Paperback, ISBN 978-0-86516-714-8

A Caesar Reader
Selections from BELLUM GALLICUM *and* BELLUM CIVILE, *and from Caesar's Letters, Speeches, and Poetry*
W. Jeffrey Tatum
xl + 206 pp., 3 illustrations & 3 maps (2012)
5" x 7 ¾" Paperback, ISBN 978-0-86516-696-7

A Cicero Reader
Selections from Five Essays and Four Speeches, with Five Letters
James M. May
xxxviii + 136 pp., 1 illustration & 2 maps (2012)
5" x 7 ¾" Paperback, ISBN 978-0-86516-713-1

A Latin Epic Reader
Selections from Ten Epics
Alison Keith
xxvii + 187 pp., 3 maps (2012)
5" x 7 ¾" Paperback, ISBN 978-0-86516-686-8

A Livy Reader
Selections from AB URBE CONDITA
Mary Jaeger
xxiii + 127 pp., 1 photo & 2 maps (2010)
5" x 7 ¾" Paperback, ISBN 978-0-86516-680-6

A Lucan Reader
Selections from CIVIL WAR
Susanna Braund
xxxiv + 134 pp., 1 map (2009)
5" x 7 ¾" Paperback, ISBN 978-0-86516-661-5

A Martial Reader
Selections from the Epigrams
Craig Williams
xxx + 185 pp., 5 illustrations & 2 maps (2011)
5" x 7 ¾" Paperback, ISBN 978-0-86516-704-9

An Ovid Reader
Selections from Seven Works
Carole E. Newlands
xxvi + 196 pp., 5 illustrations (2014)
5" x 7 ¾" Paperback, ISBN 978-0-86516-722-3

A Plautus Reader
Selections from Eleven Plays
John Henderson
xviii + 182 pp., 1 map & 5 illustrations (2009)
5" x 7 ¾" Paperback, ISBN 978-0-86516-694-3

A Propertius Reader
Eleven Selected Elegies
P. Lowell Bowditch
xliv + 186 pp., 5 illustrations & 2 maps (2014)
5" x 7 ¾" Paperback, ISBN 978-0-86516-723-0

A Roman Army Reader
Twenty-One Selections from Literary, Epigraphic, and Other Documents
Dexter Hoyos
xlviii + 214 pp., 7 illustrations & 2 maps (2013)
5" x 7 ¾" Paperback, ISBN 978-0-86516-715-5

A Roman Verse Satire Reader
Selections from Lucilius, Horace, Persius, and Juvenal
Catherine C. Keane
xxvi + 142 pp., 1 map & 4 illustrations (2010)
5" x 7 ¾" Paperback, ISBN 978-0-86516-685-1

A Roman Women Reader
Selections from the Second Century BCE to the Second Century CE
Sheila K. Dickison and Judith P. Hallett
xxii + 225 pp., 3 illustrations (2015)
5" x 7 ¾" Paperback, ISBN 978-0-86516-662-2

A Sallust Reader
Selections from BELLUM CATILINAE, BELLUM IUGURTHINUM, and HISTORIAE
Victoria E. Pagán
xlv + 159 pp., 2 maps & 4 illustrations (2009)
5" x 7 ¾" Paperback, ISBN 978-0-86516-687-5

A Seneca Reader
Selections from Prose and Tragedy
James Ker
lvi + 166 pp., 6 illustrations & 1 map (2011)
5" x 7 ¾" Paperback, ISBN 978-0-86516-758-2

A Suetonius Reader
Selections from the LIVES OF THE CAESARS and the LIFE OF HORACE
Josiah Osgood
xxxix + 159 pp., 1 map & 7 illustrations (2010)
5" x 7 ¾" Paperback, ISBN 978-0-86516-716-2

A Tacitus Reader
Selections from ANNALES, HISTORIAE, GERMANIA, AGRICOLA, and DIALOGUS
Steven H. Rutledge
xlvii + 198 pp., 5 illustrations, 2 maps, & 3 charts (2014)
5" x 7 ¾" Paperback, ISBN 978-0-86516-697-4

A Terence Reader
Selections from Six Plays
William S. Anderson
xvii + 110 pp. (2009)
5" x 7 ¾" Paperback, ISBN 978-0-86516-678-3

A Tibullus Reader
Seven Selected Elegies
Paul Allen Miller
xx + 132 pp., 2 illustrations (2013)
5" x 7 ¾" Paperback, ISBN 978-0-86516-724-7

WWW.BOLCHAZY.COM

Other Volumes in the Series

These student-friendly annotated Latin texts offer selections from Latin prose and poetry. Same- and facing-page notes aid students in understanding the text and context of a diverse body of Latin literature. Introductions to each author and to each selection offer additional support.

Lectiones Memorabiles, Volume I
Selections from Catullus, Cicero, Livy, Ovid, Propertius, Tibullus, and Vergil
Marianthe Colakis

xii + 341 pp. (2015) 6" x 9" Paperback, ISBN 978-0-86516-829-9

Selections include Vergil, *Aeneid* 1.1–49, 223–493; 11.648–724; *Georgics* 4.315–529 • Catullus, *Carmina* 3, 5, 7, 8, 9, 45, 50, 64.48–158, 65, 72, 76, 85, 86, 92, 107, 109 • Propertius, *Elegies* 1.1, 2.12, 2.17, 2.19, 3.11, 3.23 • Tibullus, *Elegies* 1.1, 3.2, 3.3, 3.13, 3.14, 3.15, 3.16, 3.17, 3.18 • Ovid, *Heroides* 1 • Livy, *Ab Urbe Condita* 2.13 • Cicero, *Pro Caelio* 35–40 • Horace, *Carmina* 1.37.

Lectiones Memorabiles, Volume II
Selections from Horace, Lucretius, Seneca, Suetonius, and Tacitus
Yasuko Taoka

xi + 159 pp. (2015) 6" x 9" Paperback, ISBN 978-0-86516-830-5

Selections include Tacitus, *Annales* 2.70–76, 82–83; 3.1–6, 10–18 • Suetonius, *Tiberius* 22–26, 33–36, 39–42, 52–53 • Lucretius, *De Rerum Natura* 1.54–135; 2.1–61 • Horace, *Carmina* 1.9; 2.16; 3.26; 4.7 • Seneca, *Epistulae Morales* 1, 16; *De Tranquillitate Animi* 2–3.

Lectiones Memorabiles, Volume III
Selections from Caesar, Catullus, Horace, Livy, Ovid, and Vergil
Marianthe Colakis and Yasuko Taoka

(forthcoming, 2018) 6" x 9" Paperback, ISBN 978-0-86516-858-9

Selections include Vergil, *Aeneid* 12.614–952 • Vergil, *Eclogues* 1, 6 • Caesar, *De Bello Gallico* 7.68–74, 76–90 • Livy, *Ab Urbe Condita* 22.3–7 • Catullus, *Carmina* 2A, 13, 35, 40, 51, 62, 67, 70, 75, 87, 96, 99, 110 • Horace, *Carmina* 1.5, 13, 22; 3.26; 4.1 • Ovid, *Amores* 1.1, 3, 4, 6.

This work has been developed independently from and is not endorsed by the International Baccalaureate (IB).